TO THE MEMORY OF
MARC BLOCH

PREFACE

VOLTAIRE to the contrary, history is a bag of tricks which the dead have played upon historians. The most remarkable of these illusions is the belief that the surviving written records provide us with a reasonably accurate facsimile of past human activity. 'Prehistory' is defined as the period for which such records are not available. But until very recently the vast majority of mankind was living in a subhistory which was a continuation of prehistory. Nor was this condition characteristic simply of the lower strata of society. In medieval Europe until the end of the eleventh century we learn of the feudal aristocracy largely from clerical sources which naturally reflect ecclesiastical attitudes: the knights do not speak for themselves. Only later do merchants, manufacturers, and technicians begin to share their thoughts with us. The peasant was the last to find his voice.

If historians are to attempt to write the history of mankind, and not simply the history of mankind as it was viewed by the small and specialized segments of our race which have had the habit of scribbling, they must take a fresh view of the records, ask new questions of them, and use all the resources of archaeology, iconography, and etymology to find answers when no answers can be discovered in contemporary writings.

Since, until recent centuries, technology was chiefly the concern of groups which wrote little, the role which technological development plays in human affairs has been neglected. This book has a triple intention. First, it presents three studies of technology and social change in the European Middle Ages: one on the origins of the secular aristocracy; one dealing with the dynamism of the early medieval peasantry; one with the technological context of early capitalism. Second, it shows the kinds of sources and the means which must be used if the unlettered portions of the past (which involve far more than technological history) are to be explored. Third, it demonstrates that, long before Vasco da Gama, the cultures of the eastern hemisphere were far more osmotic than most of us have believed. To understand the sources and ramifications of developments in medieval Europe one must search Benin, Ethiopia and Timor, Japan and the Altai.

Since lately many people have become interested in the relation between technology and the alteration of social forms, I have tried to keep the text of this book fairly brief and fluid, hoping thus to make it useful to the general student. As a result, the notes are not only a documentation but often an orchestration, developing arguments for the specialist which would have slowed the pace of the text, or exploring bypaths into obscure regions which eventually must be mapped monographically. I hope most ardently that readers may be both provoked to correct errors and stimulated to amplify inadequacies, and that they will do me the favour of sharing their learning with me.

Longum erat to attempt to acknowledge all of the gracious assistance which has been given me by so many scholars and libraries. Often the passing mention of a book, or a casual remark, has sent me off on a new scent. Once, for example, over a dish of sweet-and-sour pork in a Chinese restaurant near Columbia University, the anthropologist Ralph Linton spoke of his theory that the introduction of the bean to Arizona and New Mexico had provided the nutritional basis for the development of the culture of the Cliff Dwellers. It was long after his lamented death that I realized that an enlarged supply of proteins might have something to do with the abounding vitality of Europe in the later tenth century. And my chief debts are to scholars whom I have not known save through their writings. Above all others Marc Bloch, the most original mind among medievalists in our century, envisaged medieval technology and social change as a unified area of study. He greeted with critical enthusiasm Lefebvre des Noëttes's pioneer researches on the utilization of animal power; he wrote the classic works both on medieval agrarian technology and on the diffusion of the water-mill. It is for these reasons that the book is dedicated to his memory.

I am particularly grateful to the authorities of the University of Virginia for inviting me to give the James W. Richard Lectures in History, of which this book is an elaboration. I thank the trustees of Mills College for permitting me a certain freedom from administrative duties for several months at the end of my fifteen years in the presidency of that institution, the regents of the University of California for granting me a leave of absence for research at the beginning of my appointment to their faculty, and the John Simon Guggenheim Memorial Foundation for enabling me to accept that leave. I am likewise much in debt to the museums and libraries which have provided photographs for this volume, and to Dr. Rosalie Green who presides so amiably over the incomparable Princeton Index of Christian Art.

LYNN WHITE, JR

Department of History
University of California, Los Angeles

*Non contemnenda quasi parva sine quibus
magna constare non possunt*

ST. JEROME

TABLE OF CONTENTS

LIST OF PLATES

(at end)

CHAPTER I

Stirrup, Mounted Shock Combat,
Feudalism, and Chivalry

THE history of the use of the horse in battle is divided into three periods: first, that of the charioteer; second, that of the mounted warrior who clings to his steed by pressure of the knees; and third, that of the rider equipped with stirrups.[1] The horse has always given its master an advantage over the footman in battle, and each improvement in its military use has been related to far-reaching social and cultural changes.[2]

Before the introduction of the stirrup, the seat of the rider was precarious.[3] Bit[4] and spur[5] might help him to control his mount; the simple saddle[6] might confirm his seat; nevertheless, he was still much restricted in his methods of fighting. He was primarily a rapidly mobile bowman and hurler of javelins. Swordplay was limited because 'without stirrups your slashing horseman, taking a good broadhanded swipe at his foe, had only to miss to find himself on the ground'.[7] As for the spear, before the invention of the stirrup it was wielded at the end of the arm and the blow was delivered with

[1] See p. 135.
[2] See p. 135.
[3] Cf. H. Müller-Hickler, 'Sitz und Sattel im Laufe der Jahrhunderte', *Zeitschrift für historische Waffen- und Kostümkunde*, x (1923), 9.
[4] R. Zschille and R. Forrer, *Die Pferdetrense in ihrer Formentwicklung* (Berlin, 1893); H. A. Potratz, 'Die Pferdegebisse des zwischenstromländischen Raumes', *Archiv für Orientforschung*, xiv (1941), 1–39; A. Mozsolics, 'Mors en bois de cerf sur le territoire du bassin des Carpathes', *Acta archaeologica* (Budapest), iii (1953), 69–109; M. Schiller, 'Trense und Kandare', *Wissenschaftliche Zeitschrift der Humboldt-Universität zu Berlin, Math.-naturwiss. Reihe*, vii (1957–8), 465–95.
[5] C. de L. Lacy, *History of the Spur* (London, 1911); J. Martin, *Der Reitersporn: seine Entstehung und früheste Entwicklung* (Leipzig, 1921); K. Friis-Johansen, 'Et bidrag til ryttarsporen aeldste historie', *Corolla archaeologica in honorem C. A. Nordman* (Helsinki, 1952), 41–57.
[6] A. Schlieben, 'Reit- und Packsättel der Alten', *Annalen des Vereins für Nassauische Altertumskunde*, xxi (1889), 14–27; R. Norberg, 'Om förhistoriska sadlar i Sverige', *Rig*, xii (1929), 97–113; J. Werner, 'Beiträge zur Archäologie des Attila-Reiches', *Bayerische Akademie der Wissenschaften, Phil.-hist. Klasse, Abhandlungen*, Heft 38A (1956), 50–53; infra, p. 7, n. 1.
[7] D. H. Gordon, 'Swords, rapiers and horseriders', *Antiquity*, xxvii (1953), 75.

the strength of shoulder and biceps.[1] The stirrup made possible—although it did not demand—a vastly more effective mode of attack: now the rider could lay his lance at rest, held between the upper arm and the body, and make at his foe, delivering the blow not with his muscles but with the combined weight of himself and his charging stallion.

The stirrup, by giving lateral support in addition to the front and back support offered by pommel and cantle, effectively welded horse and rider into a single fighting unit capable of a violence without precedent. The fighter's hand no longer delivered the blow: it merely guided it.[2] The stirrup thus replaced human energy with animal power, and immensely increased the warrior's ability to damage his enemy. Immediately, without preparatory steps, it made possible mounted shock combat, a revolutionary new way of doing battle.

What was the effect of the introduction of the stirrup in Europe?

I

The Classic Theory of the Origins of Feudalism, and its Critics

The historian of Frankish institutions too often recalls to the wearied mind Eliza on the ice: hypothesis clutched to bosom, he leaps from suspect charter to ambiguous capitulary, the critics baying at his heels. So thin and so slippery of interpretation are the written remains from the Germanic kingdoms that one might expect that scholars exploring the sources of feudalism would have made every effort to supplement the extant documents with the archaeological material which, in recent years, has begun so greatly to modify our view of the early Middle Ages. But this is not the case: the vast literature of ingenious controversy about feudal origins has been

---

[1] As noted first, among scholars, by H. Delbrück, *Geschichte der Kriegskunst* (Berlin, 1900), i. 141.

[2] In the twelfth century Usāmah clearly defined the greater efficiency of shock combat and the new relation between man and horse: 'He who is on the point of striking with his lance should hold his lance as tightly as possible with his hand and under his arm, close to his side, and should let his horse run and effect the required thrust; for if he should move his hand while holding the lance or stretch out his arm with the lance, then his thrust would have no effect whatever, and would result in no harm' (*An Arab–Syrian Gentleman and Warrior in the Period of the Crusades: Memoirs of Usāmah ibn Munqidh*, ed. and tr. P. K. Hitti [New York, 1929], 69–70; cf. also 173 and 175 for relation of stirrup to the lance at rest).

produced chiefly by legal and constitutional historians, and therefore is almost entirely a matter of textual exegesis.

The first stage in the discussion culminated in 1887 with the publication of Heinrich Brunner's 'Der Reiterdienst und die Anfänge des Lehnwesens'.[1] Brunner codified, synthesized, and extended the findings of his predecessors so brilliantly that his has become the classic theory of the inception of feudal society.

According to Brunner, feudalism was essentially military,[2] a type of social organization designed to produce and support cavalry. The early Germans, including the Franks, had fought to some extent on horseback, but in proportion as agriculture displaced herding as the basis of their economy, the use of cavalry declined. The Franks in particular came to fight almost entirely on foot: indeed, their typical weapon, the *francisca*, was efficient only in the hands of infantry. Brunner believed that as late as 732[3] Charles Martel's army which met the Saracens near Poitiers was composed primarily of footmen who, in the famous words of the so-called Isidorus Pacensis, 'stand rigid as a wall and, like a belt of ice frozen solidly together, slay the Arabs with the sword'.[4] Yet in an account of the battle of the Dyle in 891, we are told that 'the Franks are unused to fighting on foot'.[5] When did this change from infantry to cavalry take place among the Franks?

Brunner worked back through the available evidence and concluded that the armies of Charlemagne and his successors were primarily mounted. In 758 Pipin changed the Saxon tribute from cattle to horses.[6] In 755 the Marchfield, the traditional muster of the Frankish army, was transferred to May, presumably because the

---

[1] *Zeitschrift der Savigny-Stiftung für Rechtsgeschichte, Germanistische Abteilung*, viii (1887), 1–38; reprinted in Brunner's *Forschungen zur Geschichte des deutschen und französischen Rechts* (Stuttgart, 1894), 39–74. For the earlier discussion, see C. Stephenson, 'The origin and significance of feudalism', *American Historical Review*, xlvi (1941) 788–94.   [2] See p. 135.

[3] The date was an error. M. Baudot, 'Localisation et datation de la première victoire remportée par Charles Martel contre les Musulmans', *Mémoires et documents publiés par la Société de l'École des Chartes*, XII. i (1955), 93–105, shows that this battle occurred not in 732 but on 17 Oct. 733, a few kilometres north-east of the confluence of the Vienne and the Creuse.   [4] See p. 136.

[5] 'Francis pedetemptim certare inusitatum est' (*MGH, Scriptores*, i. 407). The importance of this passage is not diminished by E. von Frauenholz, *Das Heerwesen der germanischen Frühzeit, des Frankenreiches und des ritterlichen Zeitalters* (Munich, 1935), 65. See also the remark of Einhard, writing before 836, regarding Charlemagne's love of riding and hunting: 'Vix ulla in terris natio invenitur quae in hac arte Francis possit aequari' [*Vita Caroli magni*, c. 22, ed. L. Halphen (Paris 1923), 68].

[6] *MGH, Scriptores*, i. 140.

number of cavalry had become so large that more forage was needed than was available in March.[1] The military reform must therefore have occurred between the battle of Poitiers, dated by him in 732, and the year 755.

Brunner then turned his attention to the vast and ruthless confiscations of Church lands effected by Charles Martel. There is ample evidence that the great Mayor of the Palace seized these lands and distributed them to retainers in order to strengthen his armed forces. In 743 his son Carloman excused his own retention of these secularized estates 'propter imminentia bella et persecutiones ceterarum gentium quae in circuitu nostro sunt . . . in adiutorium exercitus nostri',[2] while Pope Zacharias accepted the deplorable situation 'pro eo quod nunc tribulatio accidit Saracinorum, Saxonum vel Fresonum'.[3] Martel's diversion of a considerable part of the Church's vast riches to military purposes therefore was contemporary with the shift of the focus of the Frankish army from infantry to cavalry.

No surviving document explicitly connects the two developments,[4] but in view of the great expense of maintaining war-horses, Brunner concluded that they were in fact related. Martel had felt some urgent compulsion suddenly to increase the cavalry at his disposal. In the agricultural economy of eighth-century Gaul, in which soil was the most important form of income-bearing wealth and in which the tax-collecting system was rudimentary, mounted warriors could only be maintained in large numbers by landed endowment. The estates of the Church were available for his purpose;[5] these he seized and handed over to an enlarged body of followers on condition that they serve him on horseback. Failure to fulfil this military duty involved forfeiture of the endowment held under such obligation.

---

[1] See p. 136.   [2] MGH, Capitularia, i. 28, c. 2.

[3] MGH, Epistolae, iii, no. 324; E. Lesne, Histoire de la propriété ecclésiastique en France, II. i: Les Étaps de la sécularisation des biens d'église du VIIIe au Xe siècle (Lille, 1922), 7–9, lends support to Brunner's thesis.

[4] Brunner might have adduced a passage in the Capitulare missorum, probably of 792 or 786 (MGH, Cap. i. 67), of which the text is very corrupt. Charlemagne commands an oath of loyalty to him by many minor personages: 'qui honorati beneficia et ministeria tenent vel in bassalatico honorati sunt cum domini sui et caballos, arma et scuto et lancea, spata et senespasio habere possunt.' This appears to mean that these men had been honoured with fiefs in order that they might equip themselves for cavalry service; cf. Stephenson, op. cit. 804; C. E. Odegaard, 'Carolingian oaths of fidelity', Speculum, xvi (1941), 284.

[5] E. Lesne, La Propriété ecclésiastique en France aux époques romaine et mérovingienne (Paris, 1910), 224, estimates that the Church held one-third of the cultivable land of Gaul.

The ancient custom of swearing allegiance to a leader (vassalage) was fused with the granting of an estate (benefice), and the result was feudalism. Protofeudal and seigniorial elements had, of course, saturated the very fluid Celtic, Germanic, late Roman, and Merovingian societies; but it was the need for cavalry felt by the early Carolingians which precipitated and crystallized these anticipations to form medieval feudalism.

Finally, Brunner tried to discover what military necessity led to such sudden and drastic measures on Charles Martel's part. The northern enemies of the Frankish kingdom did not use cavalry extensively; the campaigns against the Avars were either too early or too late to account for the reform. But the Muslim invasion seemed to fit the evidence.[1] Brunner believed that the Saracenic horde was mounted. While their charges had broken against the glacial line of the shield-wall of the Frankish footmen at Poitiers, Martel had been unable quickly to follow up his victory by means of his slow-moving infantry. Therefore he determined to create an adequate mounted force to be financed by confiscation of ecclesiastical property. Thus, Brunner concluded, the crisis which generated feudalism, the event which explains its almost explosive[2] development towards the middle of the eighth century, was the Arab incursion.

Brunner's synthesis has been the focal point of all subsequent discussion of European feudal origins. It has stood up remarkably well against assaults from all directions.

The chief attack has come from military historians who deny that the second quarter of the eighth century witnessed any decisive change in methods of fighting. However, as a British scholar has remarked, their arguments 'are not a little bewildering, and seem to some extent mutually destructive'.[3] One party holds that the transition from infantry to cavalry began with the disintegration of the Roman legion and was a centuries-long process which merely reached completion under Charlemagne.[4] The opposite sect insists that the armies of Charlemagne were made up far less of cavalry than of infantry levies of Frankish freemen.[5]

This latter view may be correct as regards numbers: indeed, footmen were never eliminated from medieval armies. On the contrary, as mounted shock combat developed, they continued to be essential,

[1] This weakest link in Brunner's chain of hypotheses was suggested by M. Jähns, *Roß und Reiter* (Leipzig, 1872), ii. 40. [2] See p. 137.
[3] H. A. Cronne, 'The origins of feudalism', *History*, xxiv (1939), 257.
[4] See p. 137. [5] See p. 138.

particularly as archers.[1] But no evidence has been produced to under-
mine Brunner's conclusion that under the early Carolingians the
striking force of the Frankish army came rapidly and increasingly to
consist of mounted feudal knights. As the Aachen regulations of 807
show,[2] in theory Charlemagne's army was composed of two parts:
first, the holders of benefices and their retinues; second, those who
served as freemen, and not by reason of tenure. Charlemagne's
edicts often mention the military service owed by all freemen, most
of whom, for economic reasons, must have fought on foot. But we
do not know to what extent such levies were actually called up for
personal service in the army, whereas it is clear that Charlemagne
did his best to extract some cavalry even from this class of poorer
landowners by organizing them into groups according to the size of
their holdings, each group to share the expenses of one fighter sent
mounted to the muster.[3] Since *jus* normally lags behind *factum*, one
would not expect a shift of emphasis from infantry to cavalry under
Martel to be reflected in any formal renunciation by his grandson of
a right to service which rested on centuries of precedent and which
might conceivably be useful upon occasion. As regards Charlemagne's practice, however, it may be significant that the only extant
military summons sent by him to a magnate of his realm, that issued
to Abbot Fulrad of Vermandois and Lobbes between 804 and 811,
speaks in detail of horsemen but does not indicate that the abbot
was expected to produce any footmen for war.[4]

Far more dangerous to Brunner's theories is the insistence, mentioned above, that the age of cavalry begins not in the eighth but in
the fourth century, or even earlier. The battle of Adrianople (A.D.
378), in which the Germanic horse was decisive in defeating the
Roman legionaries, has often been considered the turning-point in
military history between ancient and medieval times. In the words
of Sir Charles Oman: 'The Goth found that his stout lance and his
good steed would carry him through the serried ranks of the Imperial
infantry. He had become the arbiter of war, the lineal ancestor of all
the knights of the Middle Ages, the inaugurator of that ascendancy
of the horseman which was to endure for a thousand years.'[5]

Careful examination of the events at Adrianople does not confirm
such generalization.[6] It appears that no great portion of the Visigothic

---

[1] *Infra*, p. 149, n. 6.   [2] *MGH, Cap.* i. 134.
[3] *Infra*, p. 30, n. 1.   [4] *MGH, Cap.* i. 168.   [5] *Op. cit.* i. 14.
[6] W. Judeich, 'Die Schlacht bei Adrianopel', *Deutsche Zeitschrift für Geschichtswissen-*

host was mounted: although the Roman army was known to be near, the barbarian horse was on a foraging expedition when the Imperial forces marched to attack the German wagon fortress; moreover, the Romans drew up their line of battle in complete disregard of the possibility that the enemy cavalry might return to take part in the fray. One can only conclude that neither the Emperor Valens nor Fritigern, the Gothic commander, considered the horsemen an important element in the barbarian army. Valens arranged his infantry in the centre with cavalry on each wing. The right wing was to have opened the attack, but the infantry, irritable because of an 8-mile march in the August heat, impetuously opened the combat, thus destroying Valens's tactical plans. At just that moment the Gothic horsemen, recalled by Fritigern, appeared without warning and rushed upon the Roman right flank from the side or perhaps even from the rear, rolling it up in confusion. Then a portion of the German cavalry swung around the Roman rear to attack the Imperial left wing, and the process was repeated, while a horde of barbarian footmen poured from the circle of wagons shooting arrows and hurling javelins, as did the horsemen, into the crush of legionaries. Clearly, the catastrophe at Adrianople did not prove the superiority of cavalry over infantry. The Gothic horsemen routed the Romans, already confused by their own indiscipline, not because of superior strength, but rather by effecting a surprise attack which amounted almost to ambush.

The use of cavalry in the early Christian centuries demands much more careful investigation than it has received. Two contemporary developments somewhat increased the effectiveness of the mounted warrior. The more important was the saddle, which arrived in the West as a barbarian innovation in the first century after Christ,[1] and which gradually replaced the older horse-blanket and riding cushions. The saddle, with its rigid frame, although it did not add to a rider's lateral stability (a presupposition of mounted shock combat), nevertheless helped to prevent him from falling over his horse's tail. Secondly, a new type of mount, the heavy horse, ancestor of the

---

schaft, vi (1891), 1–21; F. Runkel, *Die Schlacht bei Adrianopel* (Rostock, 1903); G. Gundel, *Untersuchungen zur Taktik und Strategie der Germanen nach den antiken Quellen* (Marburg, 1937), 89, corrects Runkel's conclusion (37, 41) that the Visigothic horse struck the Roman left flank rather than the right.

[1] *Supra*, p. 1, n. 1, and W. Günther, 'Sattel', *Reallexikon der Vorgeschichte*, xi (1928), 214 and pl. 56*c*; F. M. Feldhaus, *Die Technik der Vorzeit* (Leipzig, 1914), 897; C. Daremberg and E. Saglio, *Dictionnaire des antiquités* (Paris, 1908), s.v. *sella equestris*.

medieval destrier and of the draught horse, likewise appeared in the West during the first Christian century.[1] Such a beast could carry a heavily armed soldier and might even itself be armoured.

Probably it was the saddle and the heavy horse which had stimulated among Central Asian peoples earlier experiments in novel methods of cavalry warfare. Excavations near the Aral Sea have shown that in the sixth century before Christ the Massagets were developing a heavy cavalry, with fairly massive armour for both horses and riders, the latter being normally armed with bows, but sometimes with long lances.[2] From pictures[3] we know that these lances were held in both hands at the charge, and Valerius Flaccus[4] may indicate that the thrust was delivered by both man and mount. While no spear held at the end of the arms could have struck a blow comparable to that delivered by one held at rest under the upper arm, nevertheless for some circumstances the two-handed lance was an improvement over the one-handed spear: the evidence appears in pictures of two-handed lances equipped with pennons.[5] The one-handed spear could not often impale an enemy deeply enough to make extraction of the blade difficult; the two-handed spear may occasionally have gone so deep as to resist withdrawal, thus disarming the successful warrior, to his own peril. The pennon, like the Mongol horsetail attached behind the blade of spears,[6] was a device to prevent too deep penetration and ensure retraction.

But those who imagine that the Sarmatian *clibanarius* was the model for the medieval knight have overlooked two essential points, quite apart from the necessarily inferior impact of the two-handed lance as compared with the lance held at rest. In the first place the

[1] See p. 138.

[2] B. Rubin, 'Die Entstehung der Kataphraktenreiterei im Lichte der chorezmischen Ausgrabungen', *Historia*, iv (1955), 264–83. The conclusions of S. P. Tolstov are summarized by R. Girshman, 'La Chorasmie antique: essai de récherche historico-archéologique', *Artibus Asiae*, xvi (1953), 292–7.

[3] e.g. from a tomb at Kerch of the first to second century A.D., in M. Rostovtzeff, *Iranians and Greeks in South Russia* (Oxford, 1922), pl. XXIX; *The Excavations at Dura-Europos*, ed. P. V. C. Baur, &c., Fourth season (New Haven, 1933), pls. XVII; XX. 3; XXII. 2; cf. XXII. 1 and pp. 217–21; and for a Korean instance, A. D. H. Bivar, in *Oriental Art*, i (1955), 63, also fig. 2.

[4] *Argonautica*, vi. 236–7: 'fert abies obnixa genu vaditque virum vi, vadit equum'; ed. J. H. Mozley (Cambridge, Mass., 1934), 319; cf. R. Syme, 'The *Argonautica* of Valerius Flaccus', *Classical Quarterly*, xxiii (1929), 129–37 for further discussion of the Sarmatian long lance.

[5] H. Appelgren-Kivalo, *Alt-altaische Kunstdenkmäler* (Helsinki, 1931), fig. 93.

[6] W. Shelesnow, 'Roßschweife an Lanzen', *Zeitschrift für historische Waffenkunde*, ii (1900–2), 233–4; cf. *infra*, pp. 27–28.

two-handed lance compelled the warrior to lay the reins on his horse's neck and to guide him solely by voice and pressure of the knees at the most critical moments of battle. Particularly if the horse were wounded, this must have been extraordinarily dangerous. In contrast, the medieval knight, with lance at rest, held the reins in his left hand[1] at the charge, and by means of a powerful and cruel bit he exerted a maximum of control over his mount. In the second place, the two-handed lance could not be used in conjunction with a shield. This meant that while it was fairly effective against footmen, a battle between two groups of cavalry both armed with two-handed lances would amount to general suicide. To the knight of feudal Europe, the shield on his left arm was as important as the lance under his right arm. Between them they provided the balance between offence and defence which was essential to mounted shock combat and which is not found in the Central Asian experiments with the two-handed lance.[2]

What was going on in the heart of Asia doubtless stimulated the development, both in the Iranian and in the eastern Roman empires, of the heavy-armed cataphract, but as Procopius's famous description of these warriors shows, they were essentially armoured bowmen, equipped likewise with swords, small shields, and at times with light one-handed spears.[3] However, thus far none of Brunner's critics has produced adequate evidence of any comparable increase of mounted warfare in the Germanic kingdoms of the West before the middle of the eighth century. The retinues and bodyguards of kings and of great chieftains were habitually mounted, but even this *élite* appears to have used the horse primarily for mobility and to have dismounted for combat.[4]

So much emphasis has been placed by Brunner's opponents[5] on the importance of cavalry in the Visigothic kingdom, that we are

[1] The common derivation of *destrier* from the assumption that with this type of horse the reins were held in the right hand does not find support in any contemporary evidence.

[2] A sixth-seventh-century graffito from the lower Yenessei valley (*supra*, p. 8, n. 5) shows a *clibanarius*, without stirrups, equipped with a two-handed lance: from the stock of the lance a cord ending in a cross-piece runs through the rider's fingers to permit him to recover the lance when it falls. Such a device confirms the inadequacy of the two-handed lance for shock combat. In this graffito what appears to be a small circular shield is attached to the chest in lieu of a breastplate; it does not seem to hang from the neck.

[3] *De bello Persico*, I. i; ed. and tr. H. B. Dewing (London, 1914), i. 6–8.

[4] See p. 139.

[5] Delbrück, op. cit. ii. 423; F. Kauffmann, *Deutsche Altertumskunde* (Munich, 1923), ii. 336; Mangoldt-Gaudlitz, op. cit. 15–18; E. Mayer, op. cit. 46; Dopsch, op. cit. ii. 297.

particularly fortunate to possess, from the pen of the eminent Spanish historian Claudio Sánchez-Albornoz, a more detailed study of the question than is available for any other area in that age. He concludes that while there is ample evidence of a continuing tradition of military horsemanship in Spain from Celtiberian times onward, nevertheless there is no basis for believing that cavalry was the major arm of the Visigothic host.[1]

Brunner's hypothesis, then, has survived the attacks of military historians regarding the use of cavalry by the Franks. But students of the history of institutions likewise tried to refute him, particularly in the early 1930's, by insisting that the union of benefice and vassalage is far older than the eighth century, that the custom of requiring military service for the enjoyment of lands was not an innovation of the eighth century, and that, consequently, Charles Martel's secularization of Church lands played no decisive part in the development of feudalism.[2] However, the consensus in favour of Brunner eventually reached proportions rare in the world of scholars.[3] As Carl Stephenson remarked: 'Whether the military benefice was or was not an eighth-century invention is a matter of secondary importance. Our chief interest is rather the wide extension of feudal tenure which came in the ensuing period.'[4] Even Sánchez-Albornoz, who in his studies of Visigothic Spain has come closest to demonstrating an approximation of feudal relationships before the Carolingian era, is careful to call them 'proto-feudal' and to insist that the real development of such institutions came in the Frankish realm of the eighth century.[5]

[1] 'La caballeria visigoda', in *Wirtschaft und Kultur: Festschrift A. Dopsch* (Baden bei Wien, 1938), 106–8; *En torno a los orígenes del feudalismo* (Mendoza, 1942), iii. 100–1.

[2] Dopsch, *Grundlagen*, 2nd edn. ii. 293–343; 'Beneficialwesen und Feudalität', *Mitteilungen des Österreichischen Instituts für Geschichtsforschung*, xlvi (1932), 1–36; 'Wirtschaft und Gesellschaft im frühen Mittelalter', *Tijdschrift voor rechtsgeschiedenis*, xi (1932), 387–90; F. Lot, *Destinées de l'empire*, 665; 'Origine et nature du bénéfice', *Anuario de historia del derecho español*, x (1933), 175–85.

[3] The precursor of the present view was H. Voltelini, 'Prekarie und Beneficium', *Vierteljahrschrift für Sozial- und Wirtschaftsgeschichte*, xvi (1923), 293–305. For later developments see particularly F. L. Ganshof, 'Note sur les origines de l'union du bénéfice avec la vasalité', *Études d'histoire dediées à la mémoire de Henri Pirenne* (Brussels, 1937), 173–89; *Qu'est-ce que la féodalité?*, 2nd edn. (Neuchâtel, 1947), 30–34; 'L'Origine des rapports féodo-vassaliques', in *I problemi della civiltà carolingia: Settimane di studio del Centro Italiano di Studi sull'Alto Medioevo*, i (Spoleto, 1954), 27–53.

[4] Op. cit. 807; cf. Cronne, op. cit. 259.

[5] *En torno a los orígenes del feudalismo*, iii. 288–9; *El 'stipendium' hispano-godo y las orígenes del beneficio prefeudal* (Buenos Aires, 1947), 142–6; 'España y el feudalismo carolingio' in *I problemi della civiltà carolingia* (Spoleto, 1954), 110–45.

Nor has the effort been successful to show[1] that the quantity of clerical lands seized and distributed to vassals by the early Carolingians was comparatively small. Lesne[2] judges them to have been very large; and indeed, Brunner may have been too modest in asserting that the secularizations were less severe in Neustria than in Austria:[3] vassals are found throughout Charlemagne's empire in considerable numbers.[4] By about 745 both monasteries and bishoprics were receiving a *census* in partial compensation for lost estates.[5] To carry through their great military reform, the early Carolingians needed vast tracts of lands. Their confiscations were so drastic as to redistribute a considerable portion of the wealth of their realm.

Thus we arrive once more at the crucial problem in the study of feudal origins: why did Charles Martel and his immediate successors brave the wrath of the Church by seizing ecclesiastical properties to endow cavalry? What military circumstance impelled them to disregard the peril of clerical censure, the dictates of conventional morality?

Brunner found his answer in the Saracenic invasion. He claimed that Martel realized that, despite the victory of Poitiers, the Franks would need an adequate cavalry to repel the mounted Muslim armies permanently.

But was the battle of Poitiers in fact so great a crisis? Were the Muslims considered by contemporaries to be the chief danger to the Frankish kingdom? One suspects that our present common judgement has been based less upon the records than upon the rhetoric with which Gibbon proposed to the horrified imagination of eighteenth-century agnostics the spectacle of an Oxford engrossed in perusing the Koran, and of a Europe habituated to circumcision, had Charles's hammer struck less resoundingly.[6] Martel turned his attention to Islam only after he had consolidated his realm.[7] The

---

[1] Meyer, op. cit. 66.   [2] *Sécularisations*, 29, 32.

[3] *Deutsche Rechtsgeschichte*, 2nd edn. by Schwerin, 336, n. 29.

[4] F. L. Ganshof, 'Benefice and vassalage in the age of Charlemagne', *Cambridge Historical Journal*, vi (1938), 170.

[5] Mitteis, *Lehnrecht*, 117, n. 27; *MGH, Epp.* iii. 324; cf. *infra*, p. 29, n. 2.

[6] *The History of the Decline and Fall of the Roman Empire*, ch. 52 (London, 1788).

[7] C. H. Becker, *Islamstudien* (Leipzig, 1924), 123–6; cf. G. Lokys, *Die Kämpfe der Araber mit den Karolingern* (Heidelberg, 1906), 6. It has long been recognized that internal strife within Muslim Spain was more important than Martel's campaigns in forcing the Saracens to withdraw beyond the Pyrenees; cf. E. Mercier, 'La Bataille de Poitiers et les vraies causes du recul de l'invasion arabe', *Revue historique*, vii (1878), 1–13.

sole contemporary source connecting his military reforms with the Muslim incursions is Pope Zacharias's letter, already noted,[1] referring to the 'tribulatio Saracinorum, Saxonum vel Fresonum'. The opinions of immediate posterity as to the relative importance of these three foes is shown by the fact that when, under Louis the Pious, the walls of the palace at Ingelheim were decorated with murals of the deeds of great rulers, Charles Martel was depicted not at Poitiers but rather conquering the Frisians.[2] Indeed, having defeated the Muslims, Martel made little effort for several years to follow up his victory. This would indicate that the Islamic invasion was not an adequate motive for the reorganization of Frankish society to secure cavalry.

Moreover, Brunner believed that the battle of Poitiers was fought in 732: not until 1955 did we learn that the correct date is 733.[3] But the first seizures of Church properties for distribution to vassals occurred in fact in 732 when Charles Martel took lands of the Bishop of Orleans and others so that 'honores eorum quosdam propriis usibus annecteret, quosdam vero suis satellitibus cumularet'.[4] Poitiers, therefore, cannot have inspired Charles's policy of confiscations for the improvement of his cavalry. His military reforms had begun a year earlier, although doubtless they had not yet greatly modified the structure of the Frankish forces when he met the Muslim invaders.

And finally, was Brunner correct in assuming that the Spanish Saracens at Poitiers were fighting chiefly on horseback? Certainly by the early ninth century the Franks thought of them as 'Mauri celeres . . . gens equo fidens'.[5] But here again the exhaustive researches of Sánchez-Albornoz into the Arabic sources have clarified the matter. He has shown that even twenty years after Martel's death the Spanish Muslims used cavalry only in small numbers: it was not until the second half of the eighth century that they too shifted the weight of their armies from footmen to mounted fighters.[6] Can it

[1] *Supra*, p. 4, n. 3.
[2] Ermoldus Nigellus, *In honorem Hludovici*, iv, l. 275; *MGH, Scriptores*, ii. 506.
[3] *Supra*, p. 3, n. 3.
[4] *Vita S. Eucherii episcopi Aurelianensis* in *Acta sanctorum*, Feb. iii (Antwerp, 1658), 218.   [5] Ermoldus, op. cit. i, l. 147; *MGH, Scriptores*, ii, 469.
[6] 'Los arabes y los orígenes del feudalismo', *Anuario de historia del derecho español*, x (1933), 517–18; 'Les Arabes et les origines de la féodalité', *Revue historique de droit français et étranger*, xii (1933), 219–20; *En torno a los orígenes del feudalismo, III: La caballería musulmana y la caballería franca del siglo VIII* (Mendoza, 1942), 253 ff. According to the very late evidence of al-Makkarī (d. A.D. 1632), the first Umaiyad

have been the Sons of the Prophet who imitated the Franks rather than the reverse? In any case it is now clear that the Muslim peril did not provoke Charles Martel's military reform and thus establish feudalism in Europe.

Only one alternative explanation of the seizure and distribution of the Church lands has been widely discussed. Roloff[1] suggests that the great *Major palatii*, himself a bastard and usurper, was trying to strengthen his political situation by largesse which would attract to his retinue most of the magnates of the realm. But Mangoldt-Gaudlitz[2] cogently objects, first, that such drastic action, while undoubtedly it would build up Charles's secular following, would likewise risk the dangerous enmity of the Church, the one authority which might consent—and eventually did consent—to legitimatize the rule of his dynasty; second, that Martel, an experienced warrior —Isidorus Pacensis calls him 'ab ineunte aetate belligerum et rei militaris expertum'[3]—would more probably be moved by military than by political considerations; and third, that the political situation of Martel's sons Carloman and Pipin was so firm that their immense new confiscations of clerical estates can best be explained on military grounds. But if, unlike Mangoldt-Gaudlitz, we cannot accept Brunner's hypothesis of the Muslim invasion, what military development or crisis in the 730's is adequate to account for such momentous events?

The whole of Brunner's magnificent structure of hypotheses stands, save its keystone. We are faced, in the reigns of Martel, Carloman, and Pipin, with an extraordinary drama which lacks motivation. A sudden and urgent demand for cavalry led the early Carolingians to reorganize their realm along feudal lines to enable it to support mounted fighters in much greater numbers than ever before. Yet the nature of the military exigency which brought about this social revolution has eluded us.

The answer to the puzzle is to be found not in the documents but in archaeology. It was first offered in 1923, at the end of a rambling footnote, by a master of Germanic antiquities. Speaking of the social cleavages which resulted when the new and expensive method of fighting on horseback led to the growth of a specialized aristocracy of mounted warriors, Friedrich Kaufmann remarked, almost as an

Caliph of Spain (d. A.D. 788) was served by a chief groom entitled Master of the Stirrup, *sāhib al-rikāb*; cf. *Encycl. Islam*, iii. 1160.

[1] Op. cit. 398.   [2] Op. cit. 29.   [3] *Infra*, p. 136.

afterthought: 'The new age is heralded in the eighth century by excavations of stirrups.'[1]

II

The Origin and Diffusion of the Stirrup

A priori speculation about the origin of the stirrup is reduced to absurdity by von Le Coq[2] who proposes that it may have been invented either by a race of habitual horsemen (e.g. the Turkomens) or else by a sedentary agricultural people (e.g. the Chinese) suddenly forced to learn to ride in order to protect itself against nomadic raids. Clearly, nothing is to be gained by imaginative excursions.

The Assyrian bronze doors, now in the British Museum, which illustrate an expedition of Shalmanaser III in 853 B.C., show the king on horseback with his feet resting on what appear to be long flat foot-boards suspended from the saddle-pad.[3] These are entirely isolated specimens which do not mark the beginnings of the stirrup.

Indeed, stirrups were unknown not only to the ancient Near East but to the Greeks and Romans as well. Literature is silent about them; the innumerable antique representations of riders lack them;[4] and the objects presented by archaeologists as classical stirrups are either of doubtful identification or of questionable provenance.[5] Towards the end of the fourth century Vegetius, the last classical author to leave us a discussion of mounting horses, says nothing of them.[6]

The rudimentary idea of the stirrup appeared in India in the late second century before Christ, as shown in sculpture at Sanchi, Pathaora, Bhaja, and Mathura: a loose surcingle behind which the rider's feet were tucked, and later a tiny stirrup for the big toe alone.[7]

[1] See p. 139.

[2] A. von Le Coq, *Bilderatlas zur Kunst- und Kulturgeschichte Mittelasiens* (Berlin, 1925), 22.

[3] L. W. King, *Bronze Reliefs from the Gates of Shalamanaser, King of Assyria* (London, 1915), pl. LVIII; A. D. H. Bivar, 'The stirrup and its origins', *Oriental Art*, new series, i (1955), 63, fig. 3; for the date, A. T. Olmstead, *History of Assyria* (New York, 1923), 116; cf. E. Unger, 'Steigbügel (Vorderasien)' in *Reallexikon der Vorgeschichte*, ed. M. Ebert, xii (1928), 392.   [4] See p. 139.

[5] E. Espérandieu, 'Note sur un étrier gallo-romain', *Pro Alesia*, i (1906), 17–18; H. Jacobi, 'Hatten die Römer Steigbügel?' *Germania*, vi (1922), 88–93. E. E. Viollet-le-Duc, *Dictionnaire du mobilier français*, v. 413, reports two Roman stirrups as being preserved in the Museum at Naples; but A. Schlieben, 'Geschichte der Steigbügel', *Annalen des Vereins für Nassauische Altertumskunde und Geschichtsforschung*, xxiv (1892), 187, ascertained that the Naples Museum contains no such objects.

[6] *De re militari*, i, c. 18.   [7] See p. 140.

Since the big-toe stirrup could not be used by shod riders, its diffusion was blocked towards the colder climates of the north. A Kushan engraved gem, now in the British Museum and datable c. A.D. 100, shows a booted rider with feet supported by what appear to be rigid hooks suspended from the saddle (Fig. 1).[1] Since such hooks might easily drag a fallen rider, the experiment can scarcely have proved satisfactory, but it demonstrates the efforts of the peoples of northern Pakistan and Afghanistan to adapt the big-toe stirrup to their needs.

The foot-stirrup presumably is a Chinese invention. It appears in China as a result of the great wave of Buddhist missionary activity which swept through Afghanistan and Turkestan to the Middle Kingdom, carrying so many elements of Indic culture.[2] It was known in Hunan by the first decades of the fifth century at latest, and the earliest mention of the stirrup in Chinese literature, in A.D. 477, indicates that it was then in common use.[3] Chinese representations of stirrups are extant from A.D. 523,[4] 529,[5] 551,[6] 554,[7] 636,[8] and 683,[9]

---

[1] British Museum, no. 1919, 7–9, 02. I am grateful to Mrs. James Caldwell of Mills College and to Dr. Douglas Barrett, Assistant Keeper of Oriental Antiquities of the British Museum, for securing the photograph, and to Dr. John Rosenfield of Harvard University for confirming Dr. Barrett's dating. Lefebvre des Noëttes, op. cit., fig. 263, and A. L. Basham, *The Wonder that was India* (London, 1954), 374, fig. XXIII, show a copper vase from Kulū, on the borders of Kashmir, supposedly of the first–second century after Christ, depicting a loose surcingle supporting the rider's feet. Dr. Barrett informs me by letter that he is not entirely convinced of the authenticity of this vase, which is in the British Museum.

[2] Cf. Hu Shih, 'The Indianization of China: a case study in cultural borrowing', *Independence, Convergence and Borrowing* (Cambridge, Mass., 1937), 219–47.

[3] See p. 140.   [4] Stele in Royal Ontario Museum, Toronto.

[5] Stele in Boston Museum of Fine Arts; cf. O. Sirén, *Chinese Sculpture from the Fifth to the Fourteenth Centuries* (New York, 1925), pls. 109–11. In 1939 I examined stirrups on a companion stele of the same date from the collection of C. T. Loo, then exhibited in San Francisco.

[6] Stele in Chicago Art Institute; cf. C. F. Kelley, *A Chinese Buddhist Stele of the Wei Dynasty* (Chicago, 1927), pl. 6.

[7] Boston Museum; cf. Sirén, op. cit., pl. 172; E. Chavannes, *Six monuments de la sculpture chinoise* (Brussels, 1914), pl. XL; L. Ashton, *Introduction to the Study of Chinese Sculpture* (London, 1924), pl. 56.

[8] University of Pennsylvania Museum; cf. E. Chavannes, *Mission archéologique dans la Chine septentrionale* (Paris, 1913), pls. 288–9; Sirén, op. cit., pls. 426–7b, and *History of Early Chinese Art: Sculpture* (London, 1930), pl. 93; Ashton, op. cit., pl. 47; H. E. Fernald, 'The horses of T'ang T'ai Tsung and the stele of Yu', *Journal of the American Oriental Society*, lv (1935), 420–8. O. Maenchen-Helfen, 'Crenelated mane and scabbard slide', *Central Asiatic Journal*, iii (1957), 120, believes that these trappings are Turkish in form.

[9] Chavannes, *Mission*, pl. 294; Sirén, *Chinese Sculpture*, pl. 430, and *Early Chinese Art*, pl. 94b.

while others which cannot be so exactly dated may be ascribed to the same period.[1] From China the stirrup spread to Korea by the fifth century,[2] and to Japan where it was known by the middle of the sixth century at latest.[3]

The efforts of Rostovtzeff[4] and Arendt[5] to endow the ancient Sarmatians or Scythians with stirrups are groundless. Yet since we know that by the fifth century of our era the idea of the stirrup had spread from India through the Khyber Pass to China along the ancient road of the silk trade, we might assume that some of the Central Asian peoples would have begun to use it. The Russian archaeologist S. V. Kiselev has recently placed in the sixth century certain stirrups from Turkish tombs of the Altai.[6]

However, the dating of nomadic tumuli is a marvellously delicate business. Graves lying side by side may have been dug centuries apart, and evidence from one cannot be used to date its neighbour. In times of crisis an old tomb occasionally received a second occu-

---

[1] Cf. *Pantheon*, iii (1929), 85; Laufer, *Chinese Clay Figures* (Chicago, 1914), pls. 71–72; C. Hentze, *Chinese Tomb Figures* (London, 1928), pls. 78–80, 84–85; London *Times*, 27 Mar. 1947, p. 6.

[2] S. Umehara, 'Deux grandes découvertes archéologiques en Corée', *Revue des arts asiatiques*, iii (1926), 33 and pl. XVII; A. Eckhardt, *History of Korean Art* (London, 1929), figs. 253, 361; H. Ikéuchi and S. Umehara in *T'ung-kou*, ii (1940), pls. IX, X, XIII, and p. 9; J. Werner, 'Beiträge zur Archäologie des Attila-Reiches', *Abhandlungen der Bayerischen Akademie der Wissenschaften, Phil.-hist. Kl.*, xxxviii (1956), pl. 67. 1.

[3] W. G. Ashton, 'Nihongi: Chronicles of Japan from the earliest times to A.D. 697', *Transactions and Proceedings of the Japan Society, London*, supplement i (1896), 357; E. Baelz, 'Zur Vor- und Urgeschichte Japans', *Zeitschrift für Ethnologie*, xxxix (1907), 308, fig. 15; N. Tsuda, *Handbook of Japanese Art*, 2nd edn. (Tokyo, 1936), 15, 17, fig. 12; A. Münsterberg, *Japanische Kunstgeschichte* (Brunswick, 1904), ii, fig. 118, no. 1. The oldest extant stirrups to which an exact date can be given (A.D. 752) are preserved in the Shōsōin at Nara; cf. J. Harada, *English Catalogue of Treasures in the Imperial Repository Shōsōin* (Tokyo, 1932), nos. 349–52, and pl. XLV.

[4] N. Vesselovsky orally assured Rostovtzeff that he had excavated stirrups from Sarmatian graves in the Kuban region, but Rostovtzeff did not see these discoveries, nor were they ever published, despite their obvious interest; cf. M. Rostovtzeff, *Iranians and Greeks in South Russia* (Oxford, 1922), 130; *The Animal Style in South Russia and China* (Princeton, 1929), 107, n. 2; *Skythien und der Bosphorus* (Berlin, 1931), i. 558, n. 1; cf. M. Ebert in *Reallexikon der Vorgeschichte*, xiii (1928), 110, and P. Pelliot in *T'oung pao*, xxiv (1926), 262, n. 2.   [5] See p. 141.

[6] His conclusions are summarized by R. Ghirshman in *Artibus Asiae*, xiv (1951), 184 and A. D. H. Bivar, op. cit. 65. As this book goes to press, Dr. O. Maenchen-Helfen of the University of California at Berkeley informs me that L. R. Kyzlasov, *Tashtykskaya epokha* (Moscow, 1960), 140, fig. 51. 9–10, announces the discovery in Siberia of miniature iron stirrups which can scarcely be later than the third century after Christ and some of which appear to go back to the first or second century. Since other miniature objects are found in the same cultures, these are probably not big-toe stirrups, which in any case would be useless in such a climate.

pant, to the archaeologist's confusion. And burial, with the dead, of heirlooms which may have been treasured for generations, complicates the effort to date all but rich graves by means of coins or objects of art. The cautious Teploukhov, after ten years of labour on the stratification of culture in the Minusinsk basin, in contrast to Kiselev, could not find the stirrup there earlier than the seventh century.[1] The numerous stirrups at Saltovo, in the Ukraine, are not earlier than the eighth century,[2] while those found at Laida, near Tambov,[3] and at Pereslav,[4] are of about the same age. The earliest Central Asian picture of a stirrup, in a rock-scratching from the Altai, is indecisive since it is probably not earlier than A.D. 400 and not later than A.D. 700.[5]

Our opinion about the dating of the use of stirrups by the nomadic horsemen may be influenced by the fact that Iran, with all of its Central Asian connexions, was not familiar with the stirrup until the end of the seventh century. This lack is the more curious because in the third and fourth centuries the Sassanids conquered and ruled considerable areas of the present Afghanistan and Pakistan[6] which presumably then had some form of hook-stirrup. But the many and detailed Sassanian representations of horse-trappings show not a single pair of stirrups: the famous bestirrupped silver plate in the Hermitage is now judged to be post-Sassanian, probably from the regions north of Iran, and to date from about A.D. 700 or even later.[7] Unfortunately, the Muslim aversion towards depicting men and animals descended on Iran in A.D. 641 and deprived us of visual

[1] S. A. Teploukhov, 'Essai de classification des anciennes civilisations métalliques de la región de Minoussinsk', *Materialy po etnografii Rossii*, iv (1929), 57, 62; cf. *American Anthropologist*, xxxv (1933), 321. A. Spitsyn, in establishing an archaeological stratification for the Kama region, produced no stirrup before the tenth century; *Materialy po archeologii Rossii*, xxvi (1902), pl. xxv. 20 and p. 63; cf. A. A. Zakharov, *Studia levedica* (Budapest, 1935), 39. However, this may be overly conservative; cf. A. Marosi and N. Fettich, *Trouvailles avares de Dunapentele* (Budapest, 1936), 87.

[2] Zakharov, op. cit. 40.

[3] *Materialy po archeologii Rossii*, x (1893), pl. x. 1; cf. Zakharov, op. cit. 30

[4] J. R. Aspelin, *Antiquités du nord finno-ougrien* (Helsinki, 1878), 210.

[5] H. Appelgren-Kivalo, *Alt-altaische Kunstdenkmäler* (Helsinki, 1931), fig. 80. I owe the dating to O. Maenchen-Helfen of the University of California at Berkeley. Pictures of stirrups from Chinese Turkestan of the eighth to tenth centuries are found in A. Grünwedel, *Altbuddhistische Kulturstätten in Chinesisch-Turkistan* (Berlin, 1912), fig. 513, and *Alt-Kutscha* (Berlin, 1920), i, fig. 54; A. von Le Coq, *Bilderatlas*, figs. 69, 70, 132, 134, and p. 22; A. Stein, *Preliminary Report of a Journey of Archaeological and Topographical Exploration in Chinese Turkestan* (London, 1901), pl. 2d, and *Ancient Khotan* (Oxford, 1907), ii, pl. 59.

[6] Cf. A. Banerji, 'Side-lights on the later Kuṣānas', *Indian Historical Quarterly*, xiii (1937), 105–16.   [7] See p. 141.

records for many generations thereafter. Philology and literature, however, offer pertinent evidence.

Pelliot has pointed out[1] that since the Persians use the Arabic word *rikāb* for stirrup, the stirrup probably reached Persia in the later seventh or early eighth centuries when the ruling and fighting class in Iran was Arabic-speaking.

Two ninth-century recorders of the *Ḥadith*, Abu-Dāwūd (d. A.D. 888) and al-Tirmidhi (d. A.D. 883–93) wrote down the following tradition which was circulating in Persia: 'I have seen 'Ali (d. A.D. 661) bring forth a mount in order to ride. When he placed his foot in the *rikāb* he said "In the name of God" three times.'[2] More than 200 years of oral transmissions had intervened, and that 'Ali ever used a *rikāb* is rendered doubtful by the fact that observant Muslim authors have left us an exact and consistent account of the stirrup's introduction, at least in metallic form, thirty-three years after 'Ali's assassination. Al-Jāḥiz (d. A.D. 868) describes the current contempt of the native Persian Shū'ūbīyah for the Arabs. The former said to the Arabs: 'You were accustomed to ride your horses in battle bare-back, and whenever a horse did have a saddle on its back it was made of leather but had no stirrups. But stirrups are among the best trappings of war for both the lancer who wields his spear and the swordsman who brandishes his sword, since they may stand in them or use them as support.' To which al-Jāḥiz replies: 'As to stirrups, it is agreed that they are very old, but iron stirrups were not used by the Arabs before the days of the Azraqites.'[3]

The reference to the sect of the Azraqites is clarified by a passage from the writings of another ninth-century author al-Mubarrad (d. A.D. 898) who tells us that 'stirrups were first made of wood and therefore broke very easily, with the result that whenever [the warrior] wished to brandish his sword, or the lancer to strike with his spear, he had no support. Consequently al-Muhallab ordered that they be made of iron. He thus became the first to have stirrups made of iron'.[4] In A.D. 694 the general al-Muhallab[5] was campaigning

---

[1] *T'oung pao*, xxiv (1926), 262, n. 1.

[2] Abu-Dāwūd, *Jihād*, 74; al-Tirmidhi, *Da'awat*, 46; cf. *Encycl. Islam*, i. 82; iv. 796. I am indebted to Dr. N. H. Faris of the University of Beirut for translation of these texts.

[3] Al-Jāḥiz, *al-Bayān w-al-Tabyīn* (Cairo, 1926–27), iii. 8, 12; cf. *Encycl. Islam*, i. 1000.

[4] See p. 142.

[5] S. M. Yūsuf, 'Al-Muhallab-Bin-Abī-Sufra: his strategy and qualities of general-ship', *Islamic Culture*, xvii (1943), 2, significantly credits al-Muhallab not only with introducing iron stirrups but also with copying the Turkish habit of cropping the tails of horses.

against the Azraqites in central Persia, and it would appear from our sources that he borrowed stirrups, or at least iron stirrups, from his adversaries at that time.

What shall we think of the insistence of both al-Jāḥiz and al-Mubarrad that wooden or leather stirrups considerably antedated iron stirrups? Such a view still pervades the literature on the history of horsemanship,[1] but it is merely logical or schematic, and has no adequate basis either in archaeology or in the extant representations of horse-trappings. Like hook-stirrups, rope and leather stirrups may drag a rider who has lost his seat. Unless they were stoutly reinforced, wooden stirrups made by techniques available to the ancients would have been insufficiently strong. It is as hard to believe that metalworking peoples would for long or generally use rope, leather, or wooden stirrups without making the substitution of bronze or iron as it would be to hold that non-metallic stirrups never existed merely because they have not survived to be excavated. The Persian opponents of al-Jāḥiz were probably quite correct in the essential fact: the Arabs entered Iran without the stirrup for their horses. We may conclude that the Muslims first appropriated it in A.D. 694 in Persia, whither it must recently have come from Turkestan, since it had been unknown in the Sassanian realm.

Incidentally, it is likely that the first Indian form of foot support for a rider, the loose surcingle (which could be used by a sandal-wearing aristocracy), reached Arabia earlier than the foot-stirrup, and was applied to camels under the name *gharz*.[2] After the *rikāb* or foot-stirrup was introduced, this latter was, at times, used with both the Bactrian camel and the dromedary,[3] and the *gharz* became obsolete. To judge by modern evidence, the second phase of the Hindu stirrup, the big-toe stirrup, spread wherever ancient India had contact with peoples whose ruling classes were habitually barefoot: on the east as far as Timor[4] and the Philippines,[5] and on the west to Ethiopia.[6] Since the region of the Upper Nile had close contact with India during Roman times,[7] we must ask whether the stirrup in any form may have reached Egypt from Ethiopia.

[1] See p. 142.   [2] See p. 143.

[3] M. A. Stein, *Ancient Khotan* (Oxford, 1907), ii, pl. II; E. Schroeder, *Persian Miniatures in the Fogg Museum of Art* (Cambridge, Mass., 1942), pl. VII and p. 49.

[4] Schlieben, op. cit. 198.

[5] J. Montano, 'Reise auf den Philippinen', *Globus*, xlvi (1884), 36.

[6] M. Parkyns, *Life in Abyssinia* (New York, 1856), ii. 30; S. W. Baker, *Exploration of the Nile Tributaries of Abyssinia* (Hartford, 1868), 263.

[7] Cf. J. Halévy, 'Traces d'influences indo-parsie en Abyssinie', *Revue sémitique*, iv

Negative evidence is, first, that no ancient Ethiopian word for stirrup is known, and that all modern words of the region derive from the Arabic *rikāb*;[1] second, that no trace of a stirrup has turned up among the numerous horse-trappings in the royal tombs of Lower Nubia from the third to the sixth centuries;[2] third, that no Coptic representations of stirrups can be dated with any assurance earlier than the ivories on the pulpit at Aachen, carvings which, after much dispute, are now firmly dated somewhat before 750.[3] One must conclude that the stirrup was diffused to the West through Central Asia.

In view of the constant contact of the Byzantines with the peoples of the steppes and the considerable influence of these latter upon Byzantine military methods,[4] it is probable that Constantinople received the stirrup shortly after it spread across the great plains of Asia to the region north of the Black Sea. The first Byzantine indication of it appears in a *Strategikon* traditionally ascribed to the Emperor Maurice (582–602), which twice speaks of 'iron stirrups'.[5] Even if the attribution of this military treatise had never been challenged on other grounds, the evidence of the introduction of the stirrup to Iran would make us suspicious of it. Considering the perpetual struggles of the Eastern Empire first with the Sassanians and then with the Caliphate, is it imaginable that these latter would have remained ignorant of the stirrup for a century if in fact it had been standard equipment for the Byzantine cataphract since about 600? In neglect of the archaeological and Islamic data relevant to the stirrup, the battle over the dating of this *Strategikon* has been waged almost entirely in the field of philology; nevertheless, a respectable body of scholarship places the Pseudo-Maurice not in the late sixth

(1896), 258–65; E. Littmann, 'Indien und Abessinien', *Beiträge zur Literaturwissenschaft und Geistesgeschichte Indiens: Festgabe H. Jacobi* (Bonn, 1926), 406–17; E. H. Warmington, *The Commerce between the Roman Empire and India* (Cambridge, 1928), 13; A. J. Arkell, 'Meroe and India', in *Aspects of Archaeology*, ed. W. F. Grimes (London, 1951), 32–38, and his *History of the Sudan* (London, 1955), 166, figs. 20, 21; for gymnosophists in Ethiopia, cf. J. Filliozat, 'Les Échanges de l'Inde et de l'empire romain aux premiers siècles de l'ère chrétienne', *Revue historique*, cci (1949), 1–29.

[1] According to Dr. Wolf Leslau of the University of California, Los Angeles.

[2] W. B. Emery, *The Royal Tombs of Ballana and Qustal* (Cairo, 1938), i. 251–71; ii, pls. 55–56. Sudanese frescoes shortly after A.D. 1000 show curious uncertainty about how foot-stirrups should be attached to the rest of a horse's harness; cf. L. Griffith, 'The church of Abd el-Gādir near the Second Cataract', *Annals of Archaeology and Anthropology*, xv (1928), pls. XXXV and XLIII.   [3] See p. 143.

[4] Cf. E. Darko, 'Influences touraniennes sur l'évolution de l'art militaire des Grecs, des Romains et des Byzantins', *Byzantion*, x (1935), 443–69, xii (1937), 119–47, and 'Le Rôle des peuples nomades cavaliers dans la transformation de l'Empire romain aux premiers siècles du moyen âge', ibid. xviii (1946–8), 85–97.   [5] See p. 144.

but rather in the early eighth century[1]—a period more consonant with all else that we know about the diffusion of the stirrup.

In the controversy over the *Strategikon*, whenever stirrups are mentioned it is assumed that the Byzantines had got them from the Avars who, in turn, are assumed to have brought them from Central Asia when they first invaded Pannonia in 568. Despite prodigious labours by Hungarian archaeologists,[2] the stratification of Avar materials is not yet clear. 'Avar' finds are scattered chronologically from the later sixth century to the Magyar invasion more than 300 years later. The Avars were constantly receiving and assimilating ethnic strains and cultural influences.[3] They, or the neighbouring Kuturgur Bulgars, may well have been the first people of Europe to use the stirrup, but the time of its arrival is still uncertain. The widespread belief that the Avars of the late sixth century had stirrups seems to rest on the great authority of Hampel, who insisted that they were 'well dated' in the excavations of Szent-Endre.[4] Yet the Szent-Endre grave which loomed largest in his thinking, because it contained both stirrups and coins, cannot be sixth-century: the coins are not only of Justin I (518–27) but also of Phocas (602–10),[5] and in any case they provide no more than a *terminus a quo*. Moreover, Werner has noticed[6] that this particular grave is singularly indecisive because it was either a double grave or else was later disturbed by a second burial. It cannot, therefore, even be used, as Csallány has attempted,[7] to prove that the Avars possessed the stirrup by the decade 620–30.

The difficulty which dating the arrival of the stirrup among the Avars has caused to archaeologists is illustrated by Kovrig's argument that the cemetery at Jutas developed in such a direction that two graves containing stirrups probably antedate a grave containing

[1] See p. 144.

[2] For systematization of bibliography and sites, but not of chronology, see D. Csallány, *Archäologische Denkmäler der Awarenzeit in Mitteleuropa: Schrifttum und Fundorte* (Budapest, 1956).

[3] Cf. J. Eisner, 'Pour dater la civilisation "avare" ', *Byzantino-slavica*, ix (1947), 45–54.

[4] J. Hampel, *Alterthümer des frühen Mittelalters in Ungarn* (Brunswick, 1905), i. 217, 223.

[5] L. Huszár, 'Das Münzmaterial in den Funden der Völkerwanderungszeit im mittleren Donaubecken', *Acta archaeologica* (Budapest), v (1954), 96; Csallány, *Denkmäler*, 240.

[6] J. Werner, *Münzdatierte austrasische Grabfunde* (Berlin, 1935), 73. G. László, 'Études archéologiques sur l'histoire de la sociéte des Avars', *Archaeologia hungarica*, xxxiv (1955), 270, is likewise puzzled because this grave contained *three* stirrups!

[7] D. Csallány, 'Grabfunde der Frühawarenzeit', *Folia archaeologica*, i (1939), 171.

a coin of Phocas (602–10).[1] But this coin may have been buried
either a few years or a few generations after it was struck. The belief,
fathered by Hampel, in sixth-century Avar stirrups seems to be dead
among Hungarian scholars, and the tendency is to push the arrival
of the stirrup in the Danubian basin later and later into the seventh
century.[2] In any case, Avar stirrups can no longer be used to buttress
a late sixth-century date for the Pseudo-Maurice's *Strategikon*.

A variety of stirrups has been found in East Prussia and Lithuania.
O. Kleemann has claimed as the earliest, perhaps as early as any in
Europe, those discovered in graves 8, 9, 12, and 6/38 at Elenskrug-
Forst. He places them in the first half of the seventh century on the
basis of related ceramics and especially of a late form of fibula.[3] For
the dating of a technological item which may have been introduced
as a novelty while the necropolis was still being used for burials,
one must consider the individual interments rather than the cemetery
as a whole. Graves 9 and 12 had insufficient material, in addition to
the stirrups, to permit close dating. Grave 8 contained a vase typical
not only of the seventh but also of the eighth century.[4] Grave 6/38
had a similar vase and a pair of fibulae of a fully evolved type which
Åberg ascribes not to the first half but rather to the middle of the
seventh century.[5] Moreover, at the time of burial these fibulae were
not new: one of them had been carefully mended after breakage.[6]
A late seventh- or early eighth-century date would therefore be
preferable for the stirrups of Elenskrug-Forst.

---

[1] J. Kovrig, 'Contribution au problème de l'occupation de la Hongrie par les Avars',
Acta archaeologica (Budapest), vi (1955), 175.

[2] In his incidental datings of 1090 Avar sites, Csallány, *Denkmäler*, 77–220, makes
no claim for sixth-century stirrups. He believes that seventh-century stirrups have been
found at Baja (no. 45), Bácsújfalu (no. 60), Komárom (no. 518), Linz-St. Peter (no. 566),
Pereg (no. 759), and Szegvár (no. 870a). To this may be added a grave containing a
stirrup which J. Kovrig, 'Deux tombes avares de Törökbálint', *Acta archaeologica*
(Budapest), ix (1957), 131–3, dates in the early seventh century. It should be noted that
Kovrig tends to date objects earlier than does Csallány; cf. Kovrig, 'Contribution', 184,
who objects to Csallány's placing the Bácsújfalu stirrups *c.* 640; cf. Csallány, 'Trouvaille
d'objets incinérés de l'époque avare à Bácsújfalu', *Archaeologiai értesítő*, lxxx (1953),
140–1.

[3] O. Kleemann, 'Samländische Funde und die Frage der ältesten Steigbügel in
Europa', *Rheinische Forschungen zur Vorgeschichte*, v (1956), 116. Kleemann, 117, rightly
regards as very doubtful the sixth-century dating of a stirrup found at Hofzumberge
near Mitau; cf. H. Moora, *Die Eisenzeit in Lettland*, i (Dorpat, 1929), 57; ii (1938), 529.

[4] Kleemann, op. cit., pl. xxxi, *g*; for date, cf. O. Tischler, *Ostpreussische Altertümer
aus der Zeit der großen Grabfelder* (Königsberg, 1902), pl. 30. 1.

[5] N. Åberg, *Ostpreußen in der Völkerwanderungzeit* (Uppsala, 1919), 126–7, fig. 182.

[6] Kleemann, op. cit., pl. xxxii, *b*.

If the Avars had brought the stirrup with them from Central Asia, one would have expected the Lombards to be the first Germanic people to receive it, since they were thrust from Pannonia into Italy by the impact of the Avar invasion of 568.[1] The Lombards had become sufficiently Christianized to omit horses from the burials of their warriors, but occasionally, perhaps touched by some pagan doubt, they included bridles and even saddles in the graves. None of these saddles was equipped with stirrups. Nor can the absence of stirrups be blamed on rusting: iron bits and weapons survive in the graves holding saddle ornaments. Grave 119 at Castel Trosino is particularly important, since it contained fragments of Avar armour, an iron bit, remains of a saddle, spurs, but no stirrups.[2] The only known Lombard stirrups, a very handsome bronze pair, emerged from Castel Trosino grave 41; they had been placed by sorrowing parents in the tomb of an infant girl who presumably had developed a childish liking for them. If we may judge by its location, grave 41 was one of the most recent in the cemetery, and therefore probably of the eighth century.[3]

For the Merovingian period, literary sources are silent about stirrups.[4] Nevertheless, Veeck in 1931,[5] followed by Müller-Karpe in 1949,[6] asserted on archaeological grounds that the Germans received the stirrup in the later seventh century, finds of this period being claimed from Andelfingen, Oetlingen, and Pfahlheim in Württemberg, and from Budenheim near Mainz.

Lindenschmidt, who published the Budenheim stirrup, was reluctant to date it more exactly than 'Frankish',[7] and there is no adequate reason for altering his judgement. Neither Veeck's inventory of the finds at Andelfingen, nor his source, mentions stirrups.[8] The cemetery at Oetlingen was in use during the period of the introduction of the stirrup: from one grave an iron spur and bit emerged, but

---

[1] Cf. I. Bóna, 'Die Langobarden in Ungarn', *Acta archaeologica* (Budapest), vii (1956), 183–242. [2] See p. 145.

[3] Mengarelli, op. cit. 239, fig. 100; for dates of the cemetery as a whole, cf. ibid. 186; for the probable dating of grave 41, ibid. 187 and its location next to the church of Santo Stefano on pl. II. [4] See p. 145.

[5] W. Veeck, *Die Alemannen in Württemberg* (Berlin, 1931), i. 75.

[6] H. Müller-Karpe, *Hessische Funde von der Altsteinzeit bis zum frühen Mittelalter* (Marburg, 1949), 62.

[7] *Westdeutsche Zeitschrift für Geschichte und Kunst*, xxi (1902), 433, pl. 11, n. 12.

[8] Veeck, op. cit. 335; Reuß, 'Bericht über die Funde aus einigen "celtischen" Grabhügeln bei Hailtingen und einem "romanischen" bei Andelfingen', *Verhandlungen des Vereins für Kunst und Alterthum in Ulm und Oberschwaben*, ix–x (1855 [not 1858]), 90.

no stirrups; in a neighbouring grave stirrups were found.[1] The Pfahlheim cemetery is richer, and covers the same period: of seven horse-burials, only one—doubtless the latest—included stirrups.[2] Evidence that the Germans of this region did not have stirrups in the second half of the seventh century is provided by their absence from the very complete horse equipment coming from the grave of an Alemanic chieftain of that period found in Alsace.[3] Presumably both at Oetlingen and at Pfahlheim horse-burials with warriors continued until the Alemans were effectively Christianized, that is, until the 730's.[4]

We must therefore return to the view of the older Germanic archaeologists that stirrups first appeared in the West some time in the early eighth century.[5] In addition to the Oetlingen and Pfahlheim stirrups, finds of this period have come from Wilflingen[6] and perhaps Gammartingen-Simaringen,[7] both in Württemberg, from Windecken in Hesse,[8] and perhaps from Bingen on the Rhine.[9] Thereafter the labours of St. Boniface and his tonsured evangelists to persuade the heathen Germans that the gates of heaven exclude imports[10] banished horse-burials to the still unregenerate Scandinavian north.[11]

Neither in Byzantium nor in the West does art provide us with significant material on the diffusion of the stirrup. Throughout the early Middle Ages the artists of all Christendom, with rare exceptions, were little concerned with depicting the observable objects of the world around them. Naturalism had small place in the conscious methods of the craftsmen of that day—they were dedicated to elaborating traditional, and often inherited classical, patterns having

---

[1] Veeck, op. cit. 329.   [2] Ibid. 165–8.

[3] J. Werner, *Der Fund von Ittenheim: ein alamannisches Fürstengrab des 7. Jahrhunderts im Elsaß* (Strassburg, 1943), 12, fig. 4; 29.

[4] Veeck, op. cit. 112.

[5] e.g. L. Lindenschmidt, *Handbuch der deutschen Alterthumskunde I: Die Alterthümer der merovingischen Zeit* (Brunswick, 1880), 288; J. Hampel, op. cit. i. 217; É. Salin and A. France-Lanord, *Rhin et Orient, II: Le Fer à l'époque mérovingienne* (Paris, 1943), 220. H. Stolpe and T. J. Arne, *La Nécropole de Vendel* (Stockholm, 1927), pl. XLII, fig. 13, show an object rather securely datable 650–700 which is interpreted as an iron reinforcement for a wooden stirrup, primarily because of its position in the horse-burial. But the U-shaped cross-section and lack of a ring at the top makes the identification improbable. Pl. XIV, fig. 1 shows stirrups from the same site datable *c.* 800; cf. 59. 21–22.

[6] L. Lindenschmidt (Sohn), *Die Alterthümer unserer heidnischen Vorzeit*, v (Mainz, 1911), 196, pl. 36, figs. 576–7.   [7] See p. 145.

[8] Müller-Karpe, op. cit. 61, fig. 28; 65 for date.

[9] Mangoldt-Gaudlitz, op. cit. 74.

[10] Cf. P. Reinecke, 'Reihengräber und Friedhöfe der Kirchen', *Germania*, ix (1925), 103–7.   [11] See p. 145.

symbolic value.[1] As a result, iconography lagged behind actuality, and innovations were seldom reflected in objects of art until their novelty had worn off and they were taken for granted.

One of the earliest representations of the stirrup in Christian art comes from a region where surely it had been known for a century previous. It is found in a miniature of the Magi riding to Bethlehem (Fig. 2), ornamenting a Jacobite Syriac homiliary thought to come from the region of Mardīn in northern Mesopotamia, inside the Caliphate, and to date from the late eighth or early ninth century.[2] Yet, as we have seen, the Muslim armies first acquired the stirrup in A.D. 694 only a few hundred miles from Mardīn.

An even more severe lag is found in the Byzantine representations.[3] Only in the later ninth century do stirrups appear in three Greek books: MS. grec 510 (datable 880–6)[4] and MS. grec 923,[5] both of the National Library in Paris, and the Chludoff Psalter in Moscow.[6]

[1] L. White, jr., 'Natural science and naturalistic art in the Middle Ages', *American Historical Review*, lii (1947), 421–35. J. Pijoan, *Summa artis* (Madrid, 1935), 420, points out that the most conspicuous reaction against this tradition was the iconoclastic effort to produce a profane figurative art in close imitation of the antique manner; but this, of course, would have omitted stirrups.

[2] Berlin State Library, MS. Syr. 28, fol. 8ᵛ; cf. A. Baumstark, 'Spätbyzantinische und frühchristlich-syrische Weinachtsbilder', *Oriens christianus*, new series, iii (1913), 118, 123; E. Sachau, *Verzeichnis der syrischen Handschriften der Königlichen Bibliothek zu Berlin* (Berlin, 1899), 121. This date is accepted by A. Heisenberg in *Byzantinische Zeitschrift*, xxii (1913), 617; G. Millet, *Recherches sur l'iconographie de l'Évangile* (Paris, 1916), 149; H. Buchthal and O. Kurz, *Handlist of Illuminated Oriental Christian Manuscripts* (London, 1942), 9, no. 3.

[3] The ivory in the Cluny Museum ascribed to the ninth century by R. Lefebvre des Noëttes, *L'Attelage*, fig. 344, is of the eleventh–twelfth centuries according to A. Goldschmidt and K. Weitzmann, *Byzantinische Elfenbeinskulpturen* (Berlin, 1930–4), no. 41. M. Bárány-Obershall, *The Crown of the Emperor Constantine Monomachos* (Budapest, 1937), 61, pl. XIII. 2, ascribes a Byzantine textile from the treasury at Mozac, and showing stirrups, to the eighth century on the basis of an unsupported legend that it was given to Mozac by Pipin the Short. H. d'Hennezel, *Decorations and Designs of Silken Masterpieces Ancient and Modern Belonging to the Textile Historical Museum at Lyon* (New York, 1930), pl. 9, places it in the ninth century.

[4] Fols. 409ᵛ, 440ʳ; cf. C. R. Morey, 'Notes on East Christian miniatures', *Art Bulletin*, xi (1929), 92; H. Omont, *Miniatures des plus anciens manuscrits grecs de la Bibliothèque Nationale* (Paris, 1929), 10, pls. LIV, LIX; J. Martin in *Late Classical and Mediaeval Studies in Honor of A. Friend* (Princeton, 1955), 191.

[5] Fols. 329ʳ and perhaps 31ʳ; photographs in Princeton Index of Christian Art; cf. H. Bordier, *Descriptions des peintures et autres ornements contenus dans les manuscrits grecs de la Bibliothèque Nationale* (Paris, 1883), 90; K. Weitzmann, 'Die Illustrationen der Septuaginta', *Münchener Jahrbuch der bildenden Kunst*, iii–iv (1952–3), 105, 111.

[6] Moscow Historical Museum, MS. Greek 129, 97ᵛ, 140ᵛ; photographs in Princeton Index. Fol. 97ᵛ is shown in O. Strunk, 'The Byzantine office at Hagia Sophia', *Dumbarton Oaks Papers*, ix–x (1956), 175–202, fig. 2. This Psalter may be of very early tenth century; cf. J. Martin, op. cit. 190. Indeed, L. H. Grondijs, 'La Datatien des psautiers byzantins,

But from the writings of the Emperor Leo VI (886–911)[1] we know that by that time stirrups were standard equipment in the Byzantine cavalry, as indeed they had been some five generations earlier if we accept the very probable ascription of the *Strategikon* of the Pseudo-Maurice to the early eighth century.[2]

In view of this, we should not be astonished by a similar lag in the West: on the contrary, we may be surprised that the artists of the Frankish realms began to show stirrups a few decades earlier than those of the Greek East. Lefebvre des Noëttes believed that stirrups first appeared in the West about 840 in the Apocalypse of Valenciennes, 'd'origine espagnole'.[3] The more recent opinion, however, credits this manuscript to the German Alps, and to somewhat after the middle of the ninth century[4] along with the closely related Apocalypse of Paris, which likewise shows stirrups.[5] However, two stirrupped horsemen appear in panels made about 840 for the famous altar of Sant' Ambrogio in Milan.[6] Moreover, in the Golden Psalter of St. Gall, dating from the second half of the ninth century, of the nine riders in its miniatures whose equipment can be judged, seven have stirrups:[7] clearly by that time stirrups were habitual so far as the artist was concerned.

et en particulier du psautier Chludof', *Byzantion*, xxv–xxvii (1955–7), 591–616, tries to place it in the eleventh century, with doubtful success.

[1] *Leonis imperatoris Tactica*, vi. 10, ed. R. Vári (Budapest, 1917), i. 105. The attempt of K. Zachariae von Lingenthal to ascribe this work to Leo III (717–40) has failed; cf. M. Mitard, 'Études sur le règne de Leon VI', *Byzantinische Zeitschrift*, xii (1903), 585–93, and E. Gerland in *Deutsche Literaturzeitung*, xli (1920), 469.

[2] *Infra*, p. 144.

[3] Op. cit. 237, fig. 294. Ibid., fig. 366, he suggests that an Indian chessman, supposedly given to Charlemagne by Hārūn ar-Rashīd, may have introduced the idea of the stirrup to the Franks; cf. A. Goldschmidt, *Die Elfenbeinskulpturen aus der romanischen Zeit* (Berlin, 1926), iv. 5, fig. 6. But this figure belongs to the time of the Crusades; cf. W. M. Conway, 'The abbey of Sant-Denis and its ancient treasures', *Archaeologia*, lxvi (1915), 152, pl. XII, fig. 5.

[4] Valenciennes Public Library, MS. 99, fols. 12ᵛ, 13ʳ, 19ʳ, 35ʳ; photographs in Princeton Index; Bibliothèque Nationale, *Les Manuscrits à peintures en France du VIIᵉ au XIIᵉ siècle*, 2nd edn. (Paris, 1954), 41 (97); cf. W. Neuß, *Die Apokalypse des Hl. Johannes in der altspanischen und altchristlichen Bibel-Illustrationen* (Münster i. W., 1931), i. 249, 265, 286; H. Omont, 'Manuscrits illustrés de l'Apocalypse aux IXᵉ et Xᵉ siècles', *Bulletin de la Société française de Reproductions de Manuscrits à Peintures*, vi (1922), pls. XVIII, XXVII; A. Boinet, *La Miniature carolingienne* (Paris, 1913), pls. CLVIII and CLIX; M. R. James, *The Apocalypse in Art* (London, 1931), 37.

[5] National Library, Paris, MS. nouv. acq. latin 1132, fols. 8ᵛ, 29ʳ; photographs in Princeton Index; cf. Omont, op. cit. 64; *Manuscrits à peintures*, 41 (98).

[6] G. B. Tatum, 'The Paliotto of Sant' Ambrogio at Milan', *Art Bulletin*, xxvi (1944), 45, fig. 20; for date cf. V. Elbern, *Der karolingische Goldaltar von Mailand* (Bonn, 1952).

[7] See p. 146.

It is archaeology, then, and not art history, which is decisive for the dating of the arrival of the stirrup in western Europe. And that date may be placed in the first part of the eighth century, that is, in the time of Charles Martel.

However, even if the Benedictine missionaries had worked a bit faster in extinguishing horse-burials, and had thus deprived us of the spade's testimony of the arrival of the stirrup in Germanic lands, we could have discovered by other means that it must have reached the Franks in the early eighth century. At that moment the verbs *insilire* and *desilire*, formerly used for getting on and off horses, began to be replaced by *scandere equos* and *descendere*,[1] showing that leaping was replaced by stepping when one mounted or dismounted. But a more explicit indication of the drastic shift from infantry to the new mode of mounted shock combat is the complete change in Frankish weapons which took place at that time.

The *francisca*, the distinctively Frankish battle-axe, and the *ango*, or barbed javelin, both infantry weapons, disappear in the eighth century, while the old *spatha* lengthens into a longsword for horsemen.[2] Moreover, from the ninth century onward these Germanic longswords were greatly prized by both Byzantines and Saracens.[3] But above all, in the early decades of the eighth century there comes into wide use a spear having a heavy stock and spurs below the blade[4] to prevent too deep penetration of the victim which might result in difficulty in withdrawing the weapon. This quickly developed into the typical Carolingian wing-spear, with a prominent cross-piece.[5] Such lances were used, if we may believe the miniatures, both by infantry and cavalry. But their novel design is intelligible in terms of the new style of mounted shock combat with lance at rest. As we have already noted,[6] a footman or an unstirrupped rider wielding the lance at the end of his arm could seldom have impaled an adversary so deeply that his weapon would get stuck. On the other hand, a stirrupped horseman with lance at rest delivering the stroke with the

[1] Schlieben, op. cit. 180.   [2] See p. 146.

[3] A. Zeki Validi, 'Die Schwerter der Germanen nach arabischen Berichten des 9–11. Jahrhunderts', *Zeitschrift der Deutschen Morgenländischen Gesellschaft*, xc (1936), 19–37. Salin, op. cit. iii. 97, 105–7, 112, 196, finds mass production of fine laminated swords for export in the Carolingian Rhineland; but, 107, believes that by the eleventh century the Germanic damascened sword passed out of use because of heavier defensive armour. However, such swords continued to be made into the twelfth century; cf. C. Panseri, 'Ricerche metallografiche sopra una spada da guerra del XII secolo', *Documenti e contributi per la storia della metallurgia*, i (1954), 5–33.

[4] See p. 147.   [5] See p. 147.   [6] *Supra*, p. 8.

full momentum of his own body and that of his horse must often have done so, unless his spear were fitted with some baffle behind the blade. The generalization of the wing-spear in itself is evidence that under Charles Martel and his sons the meaning of the stirrup for shock combat was being realized.[1]

The historical record is replete with inventions which have remained dormant in a society[2] until at last—usually for reasons which remain mysterious—they 'awaken' and become active elements in the shaping of a culture to which they are not entirely novel. It is conceivable that Charles Martel, or his military advisers, may have realized the potential of the stirrup after it had been known to the Franks for some decades. However, the present state of our information indicates that it was in fact a new arrival when he used it as the technological basis of his military reforms.

As our understanding of the history of technology increases, it becomes clear that a new device merely opens a door; it does not compel one to enter. The acceptance or rejection of an invention, or the extent to which its implications are realized if it is accepted, depends quite as much upon the condition of a society, and upon the imagination of its leaders, as upon the nature of the technological item itself. As we shall see, the Anglo-Saxons used the stirrup, but did not comprehend it; and for this they paid a fearful price. While semi-feudal relationships and institutions had long been scattered thickly over the civilized world, it was the Franks alone—presumably led by Charles Martel's genius—who fully grasped the possibilities inherent in the stirrup and created in terms of it a new type of warfare supported by a novel structure of society which we call feudalism.

III

Mounted Shock Combat and the Temper of Feudal Life

The feudal class of the European Middle Ages existed to be armed horsemen, cavaliers fighting in a particular manner which was made possible by the stirrup. This *élite* created a secular culture closely related to its style of fighting and vigorously paralleling the ecclesiastical culture of the Church.[3] Feudal institutions, the knightly class,

---

[1] See p. 147.   [2] e.g. the mechanical crank; cf. *infra*, pp. 110-15.

[3] In its relationships with the ecclesiastical culture, chivalric culture seems to have been highly selective; e.g. E. R. Labande, 'Le "Credo" épique: à propos des prières

and chivalric culture altered, waxed and waned; but for a thousand years they bore the marks of their birth from the new military technology of the eighth century.

While money had by no means gone out of circulation in the Frankish realm, the West of the eighth century was closer to a barter economy than was either contemporary Byzantium or Islam.[1] Moreover, the bureaucracy of the Carolingian kingdom was so slender that the collection of taxes by the central government was difficult. Land was the fundamental form of riches. When they decided that it was essential to secure cavalry to fight in the new and very expensive manner, Charles Martel and his heirs took the only possible action in seizing Church lands and distributing them to vassals on condition of knight's service in the Frankish host.[2]

Fighting in the new manner involved large expenditures. Horses were costly, and armour was growing heavier to meet the new violence of mounted shock combat. In 761 a certain Isanhard sold his ancestral lands and a slave for a horse and a sword.[3] In general, military equipment for one man seems to have cost about twenty oxen,[4] or the plough-teams of at least ten peasant families. But horses get killed: a knight needed remounts to be effective; and his squire should be adequately mounted. And horses eat large quantities of grain, an important matter in an age of more slender agricultural production than ours.

Although in the Frankish realm the right and duty to bear arms rested on all free men regardless of economic condition,[5] naturally the great majority could afford to come to muster only on foot, equipped with relatively inexpensive weapons and armour.[6] As has been mentioned, even from this group Charlemagne tried to raise horsemen[7] by commanding that the less prosperous freemen should

dans les chansons de geste', *Mémoires et documents publiés par la Société de l'École des Chartes*, xii. ii (1955), 62–80, shows that these knightly prayers contain chiefly Biblical materials, and far less apocryphal and legendary matter than is to be found in the iconography of contemporary churches.   [1] See p. 148.

[2] Prejudice against confiscation of Church lands was so strong that by 755 the Carolingians began to require the holders of such *precariae verbo regis* to pay to their former clerical owners one-fifth of the produce annually. Clarifying much earlier confusion, G. Constable, '*Nona et decima*: an aspect of Carolingian economy', *Speculum*, xxxv (1960), 224–50, shows that these payments were quite distinct from the regular tithe which was due from all lands.

[3] H. Wartmann, *Urkundenbuch S. Gallen* (Zürich, 1863), i. 34, no. 31.

[4] *Lex ribuaria*, xxvi. 11, *MGH, Leges*, v. 231; cf. Delbrück, op. cit. iii. 4; Kaufmann, op. cit. i. 339, n. 1.   [5] See p. 148.   [6] See p. 149.

[7] Fehr, op. cit. 118–19, shows that the effort of A. Dopsch, *Wirtschaftsentwicklung*

band together, according to the size of their lands, to equip one of their number and send him to the wars.[1] Such an arrangement would be hard to administer, and it did not survive the confusion of the later ninth century.[2] But inherent in this device was the recognition that if the new technology of warfare were to be developed consistently, military service must become a matter of class. Those economically unable to fight on horseback suffered from a social infirmity which shortly became a legal inferiority. In 808 the infelicitous wording of a capitulary *De exercitu promovendo* distinguishes 'liberi' from 'pauperes':[3] the expression is legally inexact, but it points to the time when freedom was to become largely a matter of property. Two capitularies of 825 show how rapidly concepts were moving. One separates 'liberi' from 'mediocres quippe liberi qui non possunt per se hostem facere'; while the other refers to those latter as 'liberi secundi ordinis'.[4] With the collapse of the Frankish empire, the feudality which the Carolingians had deliberately created, in terms of the new military method of mounted shock combat, to be the backbone of their army became the governing as well as the fighting *élite*. The old levy of freemen (although not all infantry) vanished, and a gulf appeared between a warrior aristocracy and the mass of peasants. By about the year 1000, *miles* had ceased to mean 'soldier' and had become 'knight'.[5]

The feudal aristocrat might, indeed, be a ruler, but this was incidental to his being a warrior. A student of medieval poetry has remarked that the 'essential note of true knighthood is to put down wrong-doers—not a magistracy but a substitute or supplement for magistracy'.[6] The image of the cavalier reflected in his literature

der *Karolingerzeit* (Weimar, 1913), ii. 18–19, to prove that this plan of sharing military burdens is older than Charlemagne rests upon a misinterpretation of a capitulary of 825 (*MGH, Cap.* i. 325, c. 3).

[1] *MGH, Cap.* i. 134, c. 2; cf. Brunner, *Deutsche Rechtsgeschichte*, 2nd edn. (Munich, 1928), ii. 273–5.

[2] It last appears in 864; cf. *MGH, Cap.* ii. 310.

[3] *MGH, Cap.* i. 137, c. 2.

[4] Ibid. 329, c. 1; 325, c. 3; cf. K. Bosl, 'Freiheit und Unfreiheit: zur Entwicklung der Unterschichten in Deutschland und Frankreich während des Mittelalters', *Vierteljahrschrift für Sozial- und Wirtschaftsgeschichte*, xliv (1957), 206–7.

[5] G. Duby, *La Société aux XIe et XIIe siècles dans la region mâconnaise* (Paris, 1953), 231; F. L. Ganshof, 'Les Relations féodo-vassaliques aux temps post-carolingiens', *Settimane di studio del Centro Italiano di Studi sull'Alto Medioevo*, ii (1955), 83–85; K. J. Hollyman, *Le Développement du vocabulaire féodal en France pendant le haut moyen âge* (Paris, 1957), 129–34.

[6] G. Mathew, 'Ideals of knighthood in late fourteenth-century England', *Studies in Medieval History presented to F. M. Powicke* (Oxford, 1948), 360.

shows that his self-respect was based primarily on two ideal virtues: loyalty to his liege (after the troubadours had done their work, to his lady as well), and prowess in combat. Both *loiautee* and *proesce* were integral to feudal origins.

The members of the feudal class held their lands and enjoyed their status by reason of loyalty in regard to their obligation of knight's service. Gradually the concept was broadened to include other 'aids', notably assisting at the court of one's liege lord. But the original and basic knight's service was mounted shock combat. When the central royal authority evaporated during the later ninth century, subinfeudation assured that the concept of feudal loyalty remained vigorous. Feudal tenures quickly became hereditary, but they could be inherited only by one able to fulfil the duty of knight's service. Elaborate rules for the wardship of minors, and regulations requiring widows and heiresses to marry, guarded this essential requirement for enfiefment.

The chivalric class never repudiated the original condition of its existence: that it was endowed to fight, and that anyone who could not or would not meet his military obligations forfeited his endowment. The duty of knight's service is the key to feudal institutions. It is 'the touchstone of feudalism, for through it all else was drawn into focus; and its acceptance as the determining principle of land-tenure involved a social revolution'.[1]

The feudal sense that the enjoyment of wealth is inseparable from public responsibility chiefly distinguishes medieval ideas of ownership from both classical and modern. The vassal class created by the military mutation of the eighth century became for generations the ruling element of European society, but through all subsequent chaos, and despite abuses, it never lost completely its sense of *noblesse oblige*, even when a new and rival class of burghers revived the Roman notion of the unconditional and socially irresponsible possession of property.

The second element in a knight's pride, prowess, was inherent in the adequate performance of his service. Quite apart from the cost of arms and horses, the new mode of fighting necessarily destroyed the old Germanic idea that every freeman was a soldier. Mounted shock combat was not a business for part-time warriors: one had to be a skilled professional, the product of a long technical training, and in excellent physical condition. Towards the middle of the ninth

[1] H. A. Cronne, 'The origins of feudalism', *History*, xxiv (1939), 253.

century Hrabanus Maurus quotes a Frankish proverb that to learn
to fight like a knight one must start at puberty. Even more significant
is Hrabanus's indication that in his time the households of great
lords had already become schools in which boys were trained in the
chivalric arts, probably including practice in the tilt-yard.[1]

Stenton has remarked that 'the apprenticeship which preceded
knighthood is the most significant fact in the organization of feudal
society'.[2] It welded together a self-conscious, cosmopolitan military
caste, aware of its solidarity and proud of its traditions, an essential
part of which was great rivalry among knights in feats of arms. When
a youth was at last admitted to the guild of knights,[3] he was profes-
sionally committed to slaying dragons. The new mode of combat,
with its high mobility and fearful impact, opened fresh fields for
deeds of individual prowess. The old days were gone of standing
in formation in the shield-wall and thrusting and hacking. While in
the feudal age major battles were often planned carefully, and
executed with admirable discipline by squadrons of knights,[4] the
emotional life of the chivalric warrior was highly individualized.
Long passages of the *chansons de geste* are devoted to blow-by-blow
accounts of mighty encounters which can be appreciated only if one
pictures the technical interests of the feudal audience. And at last,
in Froissart's *Chronicle*, the chivalric world produced a philosophy
of history which announced the recording of great feats of arms for
the edification of posterity to be the chief duty of Clio.[5]

Keeping physically fit and dexterous in the use of arms in shock
combat were the presuppositions of ability to display both loyalty to
the liege and prowess in battle. To that end the chivalric stratum

[1] See p. 149.
[2] F. M. Stenton, *First Century of English Feudalism, 1066-1166* (Oxford, 1932), 131.
[3] See p. 150.
[4] P. Pieri, 'Alcuni quistioni sopra la fanteria in Italia nel periodo comunale', *Rivista
storica italiana*, l (1933), 567-8; J. F. Verbruggen, 'La Tactique militaire des armées
de chevaliers', *Revue du nord* xxix (1947), 161-80, and his *De krijgskunst in West-Europa in
de middeleeuwen, IXe tot begin XIVe eeuw* (Brussels, 1954), esp. 52-58, 148-54, destroy
the conventional view that medieval battles were disorderly slaughter. On the contrary,
knights habitually fought, both in the field and at tournaments, in *conrois* of from twelve
to forty horsemen operating as a shock-combat group and placing great stress upon
maintaining a line formation at the charge.
[5] *Chroniques de J. Froissart*, ed. S. Luce (Paris, 1869), i. 1: 'Afin que les grans merveilles
et li biau fait d'armes, qui sont avenu par les grans guerres de France et d'Engleterre et
des royaumes voisins, dont li roy et leurs consaulz sont cause, soient notablement
registré et ou temps present et a venir veu et cogneu, je me voel ensonnüer de l'ordonner
et mettre en prose.'

developed and elaborated a deadly and completely realistic game of war—the tournament. In 842 there was a formidable passage at arms near Strassburg in the presence of Charles the Bald and Louis the German, and evidently at that time such events were not exceptional.[1] However, concrete evidence about such knightly free-for-alls is scanty until the twelfth century. Thereafter they 'formed the pastime of the higher class up to the Thirty Years War'.[2]

As the violence of shock combat increased, the armourer's skill tried to meet it by building heavier and heavier defences for the knight. Increasingly he became unrecognizable beneath his carapace, and means of identification had to be developed.[3] In the Bayeux Tapestry of the late eleventh century the pennons are more individualized than the shields.[4] By the early twelfth century, however, not only armorial devices but hereditary arms were coming into use in France, England, and Germany.[5] It is not playing tricks with semantics to insist that the feudal knight himself, and his society, knew who he was in terms of his arms. The exigencies of mounted shock combat, as invented by the Franks of the eighth century, had formed both his personality and his world.

Wherever the Carolingian realm extended its vast borders, it took its mode of fighting, its feudal institutions, and the seeds of chivalry. In Italy, for example, although anticipations of feudal relationships can be discovered in the Lombard kingdom, the feudal combination of vassalage and benefice was introduced by Charlemagne's conquest

[1] Nithard, iii. 6, *MGH, Scriptores*, ii. 667: 'Ludos etiam hoc ordine *saepe* causa exercitii frequentabant.' Cf. F. Niederer, *Das deutsche Turnier im XII. und XIII. Jahrhundert* (Berlin, 1881), 7.

[2] R. C. Clephan, *Defensive Armour* (London, 1900), 77. K. G. T. Webster, 'The twelfth-century tourney', in *Anniversary Papers by Colleagues of G. L. Kittredge* (Boston, 1913), 227–34, and N. Denholm-Young, 'The tournament in the thirteenth century', in *Studies in Medieval History presented to F. M. Powicke* (Oxford, 1948), 240–68, emphasize the brutal realism of the tourney as practice for war.

[3] That identification, not merely ornamentation, was the functional reason for the emergence of heraldry is indicated by the fact that the earliest term for arms is *cunuissances* or *conoissances*; cf. R. Chabanne, *Le Régime juridique des armoiries* (Lyons, 1954), 3–4. Since all warriors, until our age of camouflage, have decorated their arms, we should beware of discovering heraldry in the early tenth century when Abbo, *De bellis Parisiaci urbis*, i. 1. 256–7, in *MGH, Scriptores*, ii. 783, says that from the walls of besieged Paris 'nihil sub se nisi picta scuta videt'. [4] See p. 150.

[5] P. Gras, 'Aux origines de l'héraldique: La decoration des boucliers au début du XIIe siècle, d'après la Bible de Citeaux', *Bibliothèque de l'École des Chartes*, cix (1951), 198–208; A. R. Wagner, *Heralds and Heraldry in the Middle Ages* (Oxford, 1956), 13–17; C. U. Ulmenstein, *Über Ursprung und Entstehung des Wappenwesens* (Weimar, 1935), 15, 56–60.

of the late eighth century.[1] But even where Frankish institutions and attitudes did not penetrate, their mode of fighting could not be disregarded.

In Byzantium the new military technology of the Franks was making itself felt by the time of Nicephoras II Phocas (963–9) who, because of the great increase in the cost of arms, felt compelled to raise the value of the inalienable minimum of a military holding from four to twelve pounds of gold.[2] Here, as in the West, military change on such a scale involved profound social change. As Ostrogorsky remarks, it 'must certainly have meant that the Byzantine army would henceforth be composed of a different social class. The heavily armed soldiers of Nicephoras . . . could no longer be the old peasant militia'.[3] Like their Germanic neighbours, the Greeks increased their emphasis on cavalry to the point where, in the tenth century, the garrison of Constantinople consisted of four regiments of horse as compared with one of infantry.[4]

Even the forms and uses of Byzantine arms came to be copied from the West. The earliest Frankish pictures of the lance held at rest come from the end of the ninth century;[5] the first Byzantine representations are of the tenth to eleventh centuries.[6] By about the year 1000 the demands of mounted shock combat had led the Franks

[1] P. S. Leicht, 'Gasindi e vassali', *Rendiconti della Reale Accademia Nazionale dei Lincei, Classe di scienze morali, etc.*, ser. 6, iii (1927), 291–307, and 'Il feudo in Italia nell'età carolingia', *Settimane di studio del Centro Italiano di Studi sull'Alto Medioevo*, i (1954), 71–107.

[2] F. Dölger, *Regesten der Kaiserurkunden des oströmischen Reichs* (Munich, 1924), i. 93, no. 721; J. and P. Zepos, *Jus graecoromanorum* (Athens, 1931), i. 255–6. P. Lemerle, 'Esquisse pour une histoire agraire de Byzance: les sources et les problèmes', *Revue historique*, ccxx (1958), 53, rightly deplores the lack of special studies of Byzantine armament which would permit us to judge exactly the basis of Nicephoras Phocas's drastic action.

[3] In *Cambridge Economic History of Europe*, i (Cambridge, 1941), 208; cf. E. H. Kantorowicz, ' "Feudalism" in the Byzantine Empire', *Feudalism in History*, ed. R. Coulborn (Princeton, 1956), 161–2. Lemerle, loc. cit., n. 4, challenges Ostrogorski on this point; but whatever Nicephoras Phocas's intentions, would not the result of his decree be to raise the endowed soldier to a higher social class?

[4] C. Diehl and G. Marcais, *Le Monde oriental de 395 à 1081* (Paris, 1936), 464.

[5] *Infra*, p. 148.

[6] A. Goldschmidt and K. Weitzmann, *Die byzantinische Elfenbeinskulpturen des X.–XIII. Jahrhunderts* (Berlin, 1930), i, nos. 12, 20; also no. 98e, of the twelfth century, in which the authentic portion of a modern forgery shows two Byzantine riders charging each other with lances at rest. D. Koco, 'L'Ornamentation d'un vase à mesurer du Musée Cluny et les "Stecci" bosniaques', *Artibus Asiae*, xv (1952), 198, fig. 2, shows a Bosnian tombstone of the later Middle Ages with two knights wearing helmets of oriental design but equipped with Western shields, and jousting with the lance at rest.

to modify the older circular or oval shield by lengthening it to a pointed kite shape which gave greater protection to the knight's left leg.[1] A century later this is found in Constantinople.[2] Moreover, the cross-bow, which the West had invented, or revived, or borrowed from China in the later tenth century as an 'anti-tank gun' to penetrate the massive new armour,[3] was a complete novelty to Anna Comnena in Byzantium at the time of the First Crusade.[4]

Nor was Islam exempt, even before the First Crusade, from the contagion of Frankish military ideas. In 1087, when Armenian architects built the Bāb an-Naṣr, one of the three great gates of Cairo, it was decorated with a frieze of shields, some round, but some rounded above and pointed below such as we see the Normans carrying in the Bayeux Tapestry.[5] The Arabic word for such pointed shields, tārīqa, is derived from the French targe.[6] By Saladin's day, the Muslims were using several kinds of cross-bows;[7] they employed the new method of shock combat;[8] and their word for the heavy lance, qunṭariya, was either of Greek or Romanic derivation.[9] They much admired the brilliance of the Christian painted shields,[10] and there can be little doubt that the basic concept of Saracenic heraldry is a reflection of the Frankish. By the later thirteenth century the tournament on the Western pattern was practised by the Muslim chivalry of Syria and Egypt.[11] Perhaps most significant is the admiration with which al-Herewī (d. A.D. 1211) describes the carefully co-ordinated battle tactics of the Franks, and the way cavalry and infantry gave mutual support.[12]

---

[1] For a West German ivory of c. 1000, cf. H. Schnitzler, Der Dom zu Aachen (Düsseldorf, 1950), pl. 59; for the Catalan Farfa Bible, fols. 94ᵛ, 161ʳ, 342ʳ, 352ʳ, 366ᵛ, see infra, p. 150; for the Codex aureus Epternachensis, fol. 78, datable c. 1035–40, cf. A. Grabar and C. Nordenfalk, Early Medieval Painting (New York, 1957), 212.

[2] Octateuch of the Library of the Seraglio, MS. 8, fols. 134ʳ, 136ᵛ, 139ʳ, 368ʳ; photographs in Princeton Index. For date, cf. K. Weitzmann, The Joshua Roll (Princeton, 1948), 6. [3] See p. 151.

[4] Alexiad, tr. E. A. S. Dawes (London, 1928), 255.

[5] K. A. C. Cresswell, 'Fortification in Islam before A.D. 1250', Proceedings of the British Academy, xxxviii (1952), 114.

[6] C. Cahen, 'Un traité d'armurerie composé pour Saladin', Bulletin d'études orientales de l'Institut français de Damas, xii (1948), 137, 155, n. 2, 160.

[7] Ibid. 127–9, 150–1. [8] Supra, p. 2, n. 2. [9] Ibid. 134–6, 154–5.

[10] Ibid. 137, 155, n. 2; L. A. Mayer, Saracenic Heraldry, a Survey (Oxford, 1933), does not offer evidence of East–West influences.

[11] H. Ritter, 'La Parure des cavaliers [of ibn Hudail] und die Literatur über die ritterlichen Künste', Der Islam, xviii (1929), 122, 127. W. B. Ghali, La Tradition chevalresque des arabes (Paris, 1919), 28, 32–33, concludes that the idea of an 'order' of knighthood was likewise adopted from the West in the twelfth century. [12] Ritter, op. cit. 147.

If such was the situation in the Levant, we should expect even greater Frankish influence upon Spanish Islam. We have already noted[1] that the Moors developed their emphasis on cavalry a generation after Charles Martel's reform, and were possibly inspired by it. In any case by the thirteenth century the knights of the Reconquista were setting the styles for their Saracenic adversaries. Ibn Sa'īd tells us that 'Very often the Andalusian princes and warriors take the neighbouring Christians as models for their equipment. Their arms are identical, likewise their surcoats of scarlet or other stuff, their pennons, their saddles. Similar also is their mode of fighting with bucklers and long lances for the charge. They use neither the mace nor the bow of the Arabs, but they employ Frankish crossbows for sieges and arm infantry with them for their encounters with the enemy.'[2] Since the Berbers across the Strait of Gibraltar were not so often in contact with Christian arms, Ibn Sa'īd notes that they could use light equipment, whereas the Christian peril compelled the Spanish Muslim warriors to be 'weighed down by the burden of buckler, long thick lance and coat of mail, and they cannot move easily. Consequently their one aim is to stick solidly to the saddle and to form with the horse a veritable iron-clad whole.'[3]

The most spectacular extension, however, of the Frankish military technology, together with all its social and cultural concomitants, was the Norman conquest of England. The Anglo-Saxons were acquainted with the stirrup,[4] but did not sufficiently modify their methods of warfare in terms of it. In Anglo-Saxon England there were seigniorial elements, as there had been in Merovingian Gaul; but there was little tendency towards feudalism or the development of an *élite* of mounted warriors.[5] Harold, his thegns and housecarls, rode stirrupped horses: at the battle of Stamford Bridge King Harold Hardrada of Norway said of him 'That was a little man, but he sat firmly in his stirrups'.[6] However, when they reached Hastings

---

[1] *Supra*, pp. 12–13, n. 1.

[2] Quoted by E. Lévi-Provençal, *L'Espagne musulmane au Xème siècle* (Paris, 1932), 146.

[3] See p. 152.

[4] For the Anglo-Saxon word, see *infra*, pp. 142–3. A stirrup of the Viking age has been found in the Thames; cf. *London Museum Catalogues, No. 1: London and the Vikings* (London, 1927), 39, fig. 17. On the use of cavalry by the invading Norsemen, see J. H. Clephan, 'The horsing of the Danes', *English Historical Review*, xxv (1910), 287–93, rather than F. Pratt, 'The cavalry of the Vikings', *Cavalry Journal*, xlii (1933), 19–21.

[5] Stenton, op. cit. 125, 130–1.

[6] *Heimskringla*, iv. 44, tr. S. Laing (London, 1930), 230. R. Glover, 'English warfare

they dismounted to do battle on foot, in the old Germanic shield-wall[1] with which Charles Martel had defeated the Saracens at Poitiers.

At Hastings[2] the Anglo-Saxons had the advantage of position on the hill of Senlac; they probably outnumbered the Normans; they had the psychological strength of fighting to repel invaders of their homeland. Yet the outcome was certain: this was a conflict between the military methods of the seventh century and those of the eleventh century. Harold fought without cavalry and had few archers. Even the English shields were obsolete: the Bayeux Tapestry shows us that while the royal bodyguard fought with kite-shaped shields—probably a result of Edward the Confessor's continental education—most of the Anglo-Saxons were equipped with round or oval shields.[3] From the beginning William held the initiative with his bowmen and cavalry, and the English could do nothing but stand and resist a mobile striking power which at last proved irresistible.

When William had won his victory and the crown of England, he rapidly modernized, i.e. feudalized, his new kingdom. Naturally he preserved and incorporated into the Anglo-Norman order whatever institutions of the Anglo-Saxon régime suited his purpose; but innovation was more evident than continuity. Just as the Carolingians 300 years earlier had deliberately systematized and disciplined the long-established tendencies towards seigniority in Frankish society in order to strengthen their position, so William the Conqueror used the fully developed feudal organization of the eleventh century to establish the most powerful European state of his generation.[4]

Indeed, the England of the later eleventh century furnishes the

in 1066', *English Historical Review*, lxvii (1952), 5–9, defends the use of this late source for an understanding of the battle of Stamford Bridge.

[1] W. G. Collingwood, *Northumbrian Crosses of the Pre-Norman Age* (London, 1927), 172, fig. 211, shows an Anglo-Saxon relief of *c.* 1000 from Gosforth in Cumberland depicting an army with heavy swords and round shields overlapping to form a shieldwall.

[2] Cf. W. Spatz, *Die Schlacht von Hastings* (Berlin, 1896); A. H. Burne, *The Battlefields of England* (London, 1950), 19–45. In his brilliant reappraisal not only of Hastings but of the entire campaign of which it was the culmination, R. Glover, op. cit., 1–18, shows that Anglo-Saxons could fight effectively as cavalry, and explains some of the special circumstances which led to their reversion to infantry at Senlac. However (14, n. 3) he underestimates the iconographic conservatism of the Bayeux Tapestry in representing Norman methods of combat (cf. *infra*, p. 147), and his findings, as is remarked by G. W. S. Barrow, *Feudal Britain* (London, 1956), 34, do not alter the essential fact 'that Hastings was a decisive defeat of infantry by cavalry-with-archers'.

[3] K. Pfannkuche, *Der Schild bei den Angelsachsen* (Halle a. S., 1908), 52–53.

[4] See p. 153.

classic example in European history of the disruption of a social order by the sudden introduction of an alien military technology. The Norman Conquest is likewise the Norman Revolution. But it was merely the spread across the Channel of a revolution which had been accomplished by stages on the Continent during the preceding ten generations.

Few inventions have been so simple as the stirrup, but few have had so catalytic an influence on history. The requirements of the new mode of warfare which it made possible found expression in a new form of western European society dominated by an aristocracy of warriors endowed with land so that they might fight in a new and highly specialized way. Inevitably this nobility developed cultural forms and patterns of thought and emotion in harmony with its style of mounted shock combat and its social posture; as Denholm-Young has said: 'it is impossible to be chivalrous without a horse.'[1] The Man on Horseback, as we have known him during the past millennium, was made possible by the stirrup, which joined man and steed into a fighting organism. Antiquity imagined the Centaur; the early Middle Ages made him the master of Europe.

[1] Op. cit. 240.

CHAPTER II

The Agricultural Revolution of the Early Middle Ages

FROM the Neolithic Age until about two centuries ago, agriculture was fundamental to most other human concerns. Before the late 1700's there was probably no settled community in which at least nine-tenths of the population were not directly engaged in tillage. Rulers and priests, craftsmen and merchants, scholars and artists, were a tiny minority of mankind standing on the shoulders of the peasants. Under such circumstances any lasting change in climate, soil fertility, technology, or the other conditions affecting agriculture would necessarily modify the whole of society: population, wealth, political relationships, leisure, and cultural expression.

Yet this has not been obvious to the world of scholars: nowhere are the urban roots of the word 'civilization' more evident than in the neglect which historians have lavished upon the rustic and his works and days. While the peasant has normally been a lively and enterprising fellow, quite unlike the tragic caricature of combined brutishness and abused virtue presented in Millet's and Markham's 'Man with the Hoe',[1] he has seldom been literate. Not only histories but documents in general were produced by social groups which took the peasant and his labours largely for granted. Therefore while our libraries groan with data on the ownership of land, there is an astonishing dearth of information about the various, and often changing, methods of cultivation which made the land worth owning.[2]

[1] F. Martini, *Das Bauerntum im deutschen Schrifttum von den Anfängen bis zum 16. Jahrhundert* (Halle, 1944), esp. 390–3, analyses the very old elements entering into the modern stereotype of the peasant as they emerge in the works of medieval poets and preachers. On the one hand, the peasant is obtuse, grotesque, at times dangerous; on the other, he is hardworking, attached to the good old traditions, the supplier of food for all mankind, and loved of God for his humility. When the actualities rather than the fictions of rural life are examined, they appear as kaleidoscopic as those of any other form of human activity; cf. C. Parain, 'La Notion de régime agraire', *Mois d'ethnographie française*, iv (1950), 99, and 'Les Anciennes techniques agricoles', *Revue de synthèse*, lxxviii (1957), 326.

[2] For example, A. Dopsch, 'Die Herausgabe von Quellen zur Agrargeschichte des Mittelalters: ein Arbeitsprogram', in *Verfassungs- und Wirtschaftsgeschichte des Mittelalters* (Vienna, 1928), 516–42, is entirely legal and institutional in emphasis.

To be sure, we have heard that in the late seventeenth and eighteenth centuries 'Turnip' Townshend and a few other adventurous agronomists in Britain and on the continent developed root and fodder crops, reformed agriculture, and thus provided the surplus food which permitted labour to leave the fields and to man the factories of the so-called Industrial Revolution. Yet it is practically unknown that northern Europe from the sixth to the ninth century witnessed an earlier agricultural revolution which was equally decisive in its historical effects.

In the nature of things there is much which we do not know about these matters and perhaps can never know with certainty. For example, the habit among prehistorians of establishing an Iron Age in a region as soon as they turn up the earliest scrap of iron may distort our view of the actualities. Iron was long a rare and costly metal, used almost exclusively for arms and for cutting edges. While there was much iron in Pompeii, one's total impression of its remains is that in the later first century even so prosperous a Roman city was still living more in a Bronze than in an Iron Age. Northern Europe—Noricum especially—was far richer in iron resources than was the Mediterranean. It would seem, from the finds, that more iron was used in the Roman period for plough parts, spade-tips, sickles, and the like north of the Alps than to the south, despite the fact that we should expect the damper boreal climate to have destroyed the northern evidences of iron more often by corrosion.

One aspect of the rapid development of northern Europe in Carolingian times was the opening up of great new iron mines,[1] which presumably made that metal cheaper and therefore more available to common uses as well as to the military. Writing in the later ninth century, the Monk of St. Gall tells us how in 773 Charlemagne and his host mounted an assault against Pavia, the capital of the Lombard realm. Coming out upon his walls to view the enemy, King Desiderius was overwhelmed by the spectacle of the massed and glittering Frankish armour and weapons: 'Oh, the iron! Alas, the iron!' he cried, and the captain with him fell fainting.[2] While the Monk of St. Gall is notoriously a novelist rather than an historian, nevertheless in this episode he symbolizes, even if he does not record, Europe's effective transition, under Charlemagne, to the Iron Age.

---

[1] See p. 153.
[2] 'O ferrum! heu ferrum!', *Gesta Karoli*, ii. 17, ed. H. Pertz, in *MGH, Scriptores*, ii (1829), 760.

While no statistical proof is possible, it is the consensus among historians of agriculture that the medieval peasantry used an amount of iron which would have seemed inconceivable to any earlier rural population, and that the smithy became integral to every village.[1] What this meant for increased productivity cannot be demonstrated; it must be imagined.

In general the history of tools and implements is still rudimentary. For example, it is believed that a new type of felling axe, developed in the tenth century, does much to account for the great new extension of arable land beginning about that time [2] But so few archaeologists or historians can view an axe with the eye of a professional woodsman judging the balance of the blade and the length and angle of the haft in terms of the job to be done, that the matter remains uncertain. A few tools, however, notably the plough, have been studied in much detail.

I

The Plough and the Manorial System

In 1895 A. Meitzen realized that the form of plough chiefly used in Germany might explain many peculiarities in the arrangement of fields and in the co-operative agriculture often found in medieval villages.[3] A generation of scholarly activity not only in Germany but in France, Britain, Scandinavia, and the United States produced in 1931 a synthesis from the pen of Marc Bloch which was the more persuasive because his convictions were so gracefully garnished with his doubts, expressed not only at the time but during the following decade in a brilliant shower of essays and reviews of books.[4]

The plough was the first application of non-human power to agriculture. The earliest plough was essentially an enlarged digging-stick dragged by a pair of oxen. This primitive scratch-plough is still widely used around the Mediterranean and in the arid lands to the east where it is reasonably effective in terms of soil and climate. Its conical or triangular share does not normally turn over the soil,

[1] e.g. G. Duby, 'La Révolution agricole médiévale', *Revue de géographie de Lyon*, xxix (1954), 361, 364; H. Mottek, *Wirtschaftsgeschichte Deutschlands* (Berlin, 1957), 68.
[2] Duby, op. cit. 363.
[3] A. Meitzen, *Siedlung und Agrarwesen der Westgermanen und Ostgermanen, der Kelten, Römer, Finnen und Slaven* (Berlin, 1895), i. 272–84.
[4] M. Bloch, *Les Caractères originaux de l'histoire rurale française* (Oslo, 1931), reprinted (Paris, 1955) with a supplementary volume (1956) in which Bloch's later comments and modifications are compiled by R. Dauvergne.

and it leaves a wedge of undisturbed earth between each furrow. Thus cross-ploughing is necessary, with the result that, in regions where the scratch-plough is used, fields tend to be squarish in shape, roughly as wide as they are long. Cross-ploughing pulverizes the soil, and this both prevents undue evaporation of moisture in dry climates and helps to keep the fields fertile by bringing subsoil minerals to the surface by capillary attraction.

But this kind of plough and cultivation was not well suited to much of northern Europe, with its wet summers and generally heavier soils. As agriculture spread into the higher latitudes, inevitably it was largely confined to well-drained uplands with light soils, which were inherently less productive than the alluvial lowlands: the scratch-plough could not cope with these richer terrains. Northern Europe had to develop a new agricultural technique and above all a new plough.

One of the obstacles was that heavy, moist soils offer so much more resistance to a plough than does light, dry earth, that two oxen often are not able to provide enough pulling power to be effective. Our first secure evidence that a new kind of plough was being used comes in the middle of the first century after Christ when Pliny contrasts the light plough found in Syria with the fact that 'multifaram in Italia octoni boves ad singulos vomeres anhelent'.[1] We may safely assume that he was referring not to all of Italy but to the Po Valley, the only part of Italy where, for reasons of soil and climate, the heavy plough was much used in later times. In his next paragraph Pliny may be speaking of this same plough when he tells us that 'Non pridem inventum in Raetia Galliae [that is, the foothills of the Italian Alps] duas adderent tali rotulas, quod genus vocant plaumo-rati'.[2] Here we would seem to have the 'medieval' eight-ox, wheeled, heavy plough. And if we can accept the emendation[3] of the unintelligible 'plaumorati' to 'ploum Raeti', we have the first appearance of the non-classical word 'plough' (as distinct from 'aratrum' for scratch-plough), and an indication that Pliny's heavy plough in the Po Valley is a reflection of great innovations taking place among the barbarians north of the Alps.

The wheels on the typical heavy plough both make it more mobile

---

[1] Pliny, *Naturalis historia*, xviii. 18, ed. C. Mayhoff (Leipzig, 1882), iii. 189.

[2] Ed. cit. iii. 190.

[3] First proposed by G. Baist, 'Ploum-plaumorati', *Archiv für lateinische Lexikographie und Grammatik*, iii (1886), 285–6.

in going from field to field and assist the ploughman to regulate the depth of his furrow—a matter more difficult with several yokes than with a single team. But to understand why the heavy plough eventually affected the whole of northern European life, one must understand how it attacks the soil. Unlike the scratch-plough, the share of which simply burrows through the turf, flinging it to either side, the heavy plough has three functioning parts. The first is a coulter, or heavy knife set in the plough-pole and cutting vertically into the sod. The second is a flat ploughshare set at right angles to the coulter and cutting the earth horizontally at the grass-roots. The third is a mouldboard designed to turn the slice of turf either to the right or to the left, depending on how it is attached. Clearly, this is a far more formidable weapon against the soil than is the scratch-plough.

For purposes of northern European agriculture, its advantages were three.

First, the heavy plough handled the clods with such violence that there was no need for cross-ploughing. This saved the peasant's labour and thus increased the area of land which he might cultivate. The heavy plough was an agricultural engine which substituted animal-power for human energy and time.

Second, the new plough, by eliminating cross-ploughing, tended to change the shape of fields in northern Europe from squarish to long and narrow, with a slightly rounded vertical cross-section for each strip-field which had salutary effects on drainage in that moist climate. These strips were normally ploughed clockwise, with the sod turning over and inward to the right. As a result, with the passage of the years, each strip became a long low ridge, assuring a crop on the crest even in the wettest years, and in the intervening long depression, or furrow, in the driest seasons.

The third advantage of the heavy plough derived from the first two: without such a plough it was difficult to exploit the dense, rich, alluvial bottom lands which, if properly handled, would give the peasant far better crops than he could get from the light soils of the uplands. It was believed, for example, that the Anglo-Saxons had brought the heavy Germanic plough to Celtic Britain in the fifth century; thanks to it, the forests began to be cleared from the heavy soils, and the square, so-called 'Celtic' fields, which had long been cultivated on the uplands with the scratch-plough, were abandoned, and generally remain deserted today.

The saving of peasant labour, then, together with the improvement of field drainage and the opening up of the most fertile soils, all of which were made possible by the heavy plough, combined to expand production and make possible that accumulation of surplus food which is the presupposition of population growth, specialization of function, urbanization, and the growth of leisure.

But the heavy plough, according to Bloch, did more than stimulate northern Europe by raising the level of productivity: it played a decisive part in reshaping the peasant society of the north. The manor as a co-operative agricultural community was, in fact, typical not of the Mediterranean lands but only of areas which employed the heavy plough, and there appeared to be a causal connexion between plough and manor.

As we have seen, this plough, with its coulter, share, and mould-board, offered much greater resistance to the soil than had the scratch-plough, and thus, at least in its earlier forms, it needed not one yoke but four—that is, as Pliny pointed out, eight oxen. Few peasants owned eight oxen. If they wished to use the new and more profitable plough, they would therefore pool their teams. But such a pooling would involve a revolution in the pattern of a peasant group. The old square shape of fields was inappropriate to the new plough: to use it effectively all the lands of a village had to be reorganized into vast, fenceless 'open fields' ploughed in long narrow strips. Moreover, the only practical way to distribute these strips was to assign them in sequence to the various peasants who owned the plough and the oxen constituting the co-operative team. Thus a peasant might 'own' and harvest fifty or sixty small strips scattered over the entire arable of the village.

Obviously such tiny parcels could not be operated individually, each man planting what and when he would. The result was the growth of a powerful village council of peasants to settle disputes and to decide in detail how the total lands of the community should be managed. These arrangements were the essence of the manorial economy in northern Europe. They are intelligible only in terms of the heavy plough. South of the Loire and the Alps, where a drier climate encouraged the older method of scratch-ploughing, the social structure was very different, and much more individualistic. In 1931 Bloch still perceived the landscape of his native France divided into two regions in terms of these two traditions of agronomy.[1]

[1] E. Juillard and A. Meynier, *Die Agrarlandschaft in Frankreich: Forschungsergebnisse der letzten zwanzig Jahre* (Regensburg, 1955), 10-12.

No one was more aware than Bloch of the lacunae and confusions in the evidence supporting his grand hypothesis, or more conscious of the difficulty of dating precisely the stages of the development which he had described. In the decades since his book was published, serious doubt has been cast upon nearly every part of his interpretation; yet no alternate synthesis has been proposed.

The plough turns out to be an almost infinitely varied implement which refuses to fall neatly into the two species of scratch ('symmetrical') and heavy ('asymmetrical'), if only because modern observation shows that by tilting a scratch plough the ploughman can turn the sod,[1] and the greater wear on one side of certain archaeological specimens of symmetrical shares proves that this in fact was done in early times, at least occasionally.[2] Pliny's wheeled, eight-ox plough becomes a bit clearer: on the basis of archaeological data we now know that the Romans had a wheeled scratch-plough,[3] presumably designed to get deeper tillage and therefore needing more power. If its action were sufficiently violent, with adequate harrowing perhaps no cross-ploughing would be needed. Since, unlike the medieval wheeled plough, this Roman apparatus had a curved rather than a straight plough-pole, we can identify it with the *currus* mentioned by Virgil, a native of the Po Valley, in the first century B.C.[4] As for the eight oxen, it appears that at just this time the ability to harness animals in file was developing simultaneously all over Eurasia: a Gallo-Roman relief in the museum at Langres shows two teams of horses harnessed in sequence;[5] a single brick from Szechuan, dated not later than the second century, shows a four-wheeled cart—a

---

[1] F. G. Payne, 'The plough in ancient Britain', *Archaeological Journal*, civ (1947), 93, pl. VIIa.

[2] F. G. Payne, 'The British plough', *Agricultural History Review*, v (1957), 75–76; A. Steensberg, 'Northwest European plough-types of pre-historic times and the Middle Ages', *Acta archaeologica* (Copenhagen), vii (1936), 258; P. V. Glob, 'Plows of the Dørstrup type found in Denmark', ibid. xvi (1945), 97, 104; A. G. Haudricourt and M. J. B. Delamarre, *L'Homme et la charrue* (Paris, 1955), 98.

[3] B. Bratanič, 'On the antiquity of the one-sided plough in Europe, especially among the Slavic peoples', *Laos*, ii (1952), 52–53, fig. 4; Haudricourt and Delamarre, op. cit. 111–12.

[4] *Georgica*, i. 174. Lacking the more recent finds, A. S. F. Gow, 'The ancient plow', *Journal of Hellenic Studies*, xxxiv (1914), 274, denied that this could be a wheeled plough. It was, however, so identified by Servius, Virgil's great commentator, in the early fifth century as then being in use in the Po region; cf. *Servii grammatici qui feruntur in Vergilii Bucolica et Georgica commentarii*, ed. G. Thilo (Leipzig, 1887), III. i. 173: '*Currus* autem dixit propter morem provinciae suae, in qua aratra habent rotas, quibus iuvantur.'

[5] See p. 153.

great rarity for Han China—being drawn by two horses tandem;[1] while an ancient Indian document, difficult to date, states that 'this barley they did plough vigorously with yokes of eight and yokes of six'.[2]

Following the publication of Bloch's book there were a few years of scholarly euphoria in which it was widely believed that the interrelation of the parts of a plough was so necessary that from a fragment one could reconstruct the whole, as a palaeontologist rebuilds a mastodont from a single bone. A square-framed plough found in a Danish bog at Tømmerby was reconstructed with wheels[3] even though there was no evidence of them; the discovery of Belgic and Roman coulters in Britain immediately credited the Celtic Belgic invasion of c. 75 B.C. with having introduced the full wheeled plough, the strip system of ploughing, and perhaps even the open fields.[4] But while wheeled ploughs are certainly associated with moist climates, as their distribution in Iberia exclusively on the Portuguese, Galician, and Basque coasts illustrates,[5] some of the most effective heavy ploughs, particularly for very wet soils, do not have wheels.[6] Moreover, coulters have been used on scratch-ploughs, and in no way imply the heavy plough.[7] Indeed, the Romans may have mounted the coulter on a separate frame which went ahead of the scratch-plough.[8]

And while Bloch had elaborated the two basic equations of Meitzen, first, that scratch-plough = squarish fields, and second, that coulter+horizontal share+mouldboard+wheels = strips = open-fields = communal agriculture, it quickly became clear that there is no absolute correlation between field-shape and plough-form. Although from the earliest times scratch-ploughs cross-ploughed, sometimes in surprisingly sticky soil,[9] they also ploughed strips, one

[1] R. C. Rudolph, *Han Tomb Art in Western China* (Los Angeles, 1951), 33–34, pl. 84.

[2] See p. 154.

[3] See p. 154.

[4] J. B. P. Karslake, 'Plough coulters from Silchester', *Antiquaries Journal*, xiii (1933), 455–63; R. G. Collingwood, 'Roman Britain', in *An Economic Survey of Ancient Rome*, ed. T. Frank (Baltimore, 1937), 74, 77–78.

[5] J. Dias, 'Die portuguesischen und spanischen Pflüge', *Laos*, i (1951), 130, fig. 12; cf. 132–3.

[6] Payne, in *Archaeological Journal*, civ. 97.

[7] R. Lennard, 'From Roman Britain to Anglo-Saxon England', in *Wirtschaft und Kultur: Festschrift A. Dopsch* (Baden bei Wien, 1938), 69–70; Payne, op. cit. 92, 96.

[8] Haudricourt and Delamarre, op. cit. 108–10.

[9] P. Kjaerum, 'Criss-cross furrows: plough furrows under a Stone Age barrow in Jutland', *Kuml* (1954), 28.

surviving specimen being twenty-two times as long as it is wide.[1]
While such strips were usually simply adjacent to squarish fields, in
Finland scratch-ploughs long cultivated elaborate strip-systems,[2] as
they do today in Syria[3] and Sardinia,[4] in this latter case with a full
panoply of open fields and communal control. In pre-conquest
Mexico, the Nahua Indians, quite without any plough, produced
open fields of privately cultivated strips;[5] while in the Early Iron
Age certain long narrow fields in the Netherlands were turned not
with a plough but with a hoe.[6] For such reasons the scanty indications[7] of strip cultivation in Roman Britain cannot be used to prove
the presence of any particular form of plough.

Wherever the system of inheritance permits division of land
among heirs, there is a tendency towards strips. Indeed, in complete
reaction against the Meitzen thesis, it has now even been suggested
that this principle of inheritance may have produced a plough appropriate to the cultivation of strips.[8] It follows that there is no
absolute connexion between strip cultivation and open fields or communal agriculture. The strip has been much more widespread than
the open fields, and dominates areas which have never had communal
cultivation.[9]

[1] G. Hatt, *Oldtidsagre* (Copenhagen, 1949), 156–7; K. Wührer, 'Die agrargeschicht-
liche Forschung in Skandinavien zeit 1945', *Zeitschrift für Agrargeschichte und Agrarsoziologie*, v (1957), 77; D. Hannerberg, 'Die Parzellierung vorgeschichtlicher Kammer-
fluren und deren späterer Neuparzellierung durch "Bolskifte" und "Solskifte" ', ibid.
vi (1958), 26.

[2] E. Jutikkala, 'How the open fields came to be divided into numerous selions',
Sitzungsberichte der Finnischen Akademie der Wissenschaften (1952), 140.

[3] A. Latron, *La Vie rurale en Syrie et au Liban* (Beirut, 1936), 20.

[4] M. LeLannou, 'Sur les origines de l'openfield', *Livre jubilaire offert à Maurice
Zimmermann* (Lyons, 1949), 111–18.

[5] O. Schmieder, *The Settlements of the Zapotec and the Mije Indians, State of Oaxaca,
Mexico* (Berkeley, 1930), 27–29, fig. 3; 82, plan 2.

[6] Hatt, *Oldtidsagre*, 166.

[7] L. Aufrère, 'Les Systèmes agraires dans les Isles Britanniques', *Annales de géographie*, xliv (1935), 398, fig. 5; J. D. M. Stuart and J. M. Birkbeck, 'A Celtic village
on Twyford Down', *Proceedings of the Hampshire Field Club and Archaeological Society*,
xiii (1938), 188–200; O. G. S. Crawford, *Archaeology in the Field* (London, 1953),
206–7, fig. 37.

[8] H. Mortensen, 'Die mittelalterliche deutsche Kulturlandschaft und ihr Verhältnis
zur Gegenwart', *Vierteljahrschrift für Sozial- und Wirtschaftsgeschichte*, xlv (1958), 30.

[9] J. Tricart and M. Rochefort, 'Le Problème du champ allongé', *Comptes rendus du
Congrès International de Géographie, Lisbonne 1949*, iii (1951), 495–6; E. Otremba,
'Die Entwicklungsgeschichte der Fluren im oberdeutschen Altsiedelland', *Berichte zur
deutschen Landeskunde*, ix (1951), 371, 378; H. L. Gray, *English Field Systems* (Cambridge,
Mass., 1915), 272–304; D. C. Douglas, *Social Structure of East Anglia* (Oxford, 1927),
205–6.

Likewise the strip and the ridge-and-furrow should not be con-fused: in many regions of light soil strips have been cultivated flat.[1] The essential purpose of ridge-and-furrow was drainage,[2] and per-haps secondarily, in some soils, the ploughing up of subsoil minerals from the furrow.[3] The influence of terrain and of handling water seems usually to have been decisive. In the region of Osnabrück, for example, the oldest fields occupy relatively high and dry locations, and ridges tend to run with the slope to facilitate the removal of water.[4] In Lower Normandy there is a general, but not invariable, correlation between strip and open-field cultivation and the more level and heavy soils.[5] The same kind of plough may have been used differently in different contexts.

It appears, then, that in plough structure and field arrangement there are many elements, no two of which have any constant and necessary relationship. But while everything might vary according to local climate, soils, topography, rules of inheritance, tradition, taste, or personal whim, in practice one finds many normally constant relationships. Scholars like Meitzen and Bloch had a keen sense of fact, and they observed the averages. On the continent, north of the Loire and the Alps, heavy ploughs normally had the full equipment of coulter, horizontal share, mouldboard, and wheels. The regions which used such ploughs are almost always, or were until recently, cultivated in strips. A high proportion of the area arranged in strips was also organized in terms of open fields, which involved com-munal husbandry. This was the 'typical' manorial economy which, by the end of the Middle Ages, extended, with interruptions in particular areas because of special circumstances, from Ireland on the west to southern Sweden and the Slavic lands on the east.

The scholarly increment in agrarian history during recent decades has been not only new information but also an increased caution in weighing evidence. Is it possible as yet to trace the growth, coalescence into normal patterns of relationship, and spread of the various elements involved in ploughs and fields?

[1] E. Kerridge, 'Ridge and furrow and agrarian history', *Economic History Review*, 2nd series, iv (1951), 18–19.   [2] See p. 154.   [3] See p. 155.

[4] G. Wrede, 'Die Langstreifenfluren in Osnabrücker Lande: ein Beitrag zur ältesten Siedlungsgeschichte im frühen Mittelalter', *Osnabrücker Mitteilungen*, lxi (1954), 59–60.

[5] P. Brunet, 'Problèmes relatifs aux structures agraires dans la Basse-Normandie', *Annales de Normandie*, v (1955), 120–1. According to M. de Boüard, 'Paysage agraire et problèmes de vocabulaire: le bocage et la plaine dans la Normande médiévale', *Revue historique de droit français et étranger*, xxxi (1953), 327–8, the dispersal of separate holdings in the open fields did not occur in Normandy until the thirteenth century.

As we have seen, in the Po Valley at least, the Romans sometimes used large teams and wheeled scratch-ploughs. North of the Alps they sometimes used coulters, but we do not know to what sorts of ploughs they were attached, if indeed they were not separated from the plough. Occasionally the Romans used a plough with two symmetrical wings or flanges to open a furrow,[1] presumably when ploughing for drainage. It is inconceivable to the modern mind that they did not have a single-wing plough designed to push the sod simply to one side. Yet apparently Antiquity had nothing approaching a mouldboard.[2] The few traces of what may be long fields in Roman Britain are ambiguous: if they were experiments with a new agricultural method, their influence did not spread, even in Britain. In that island the Romans and Celts continued to farm the lighter soils, avoiding the more demanding but more rewarding areas.[3] Despite a certain ferment of new ideas, the Romans made little progress in solving the distinctive agricultural problems of the north.

Important new evidence on the origin of the heavy plough comes from philology. Plough terminology in the Teutonic, Celtic, and Romanic languages is singularly chaotic. But B. Bratanič of the University of Zagreb has shown that twenty-six technical terms connected with the heavy plough and methods of ploughing with it (including the words for ways of laying out ridge-and-furrow) are found in all three of the great Slavic linguistic groups, the eastern, western, and southern. This means that the heavy plough and its use for both strip cultivation and ridging were familiar to the unified Slavs before their separation in the later sixth century.[4] Moreover, this entire vocabulary is Slavic, except for the key-word *plug*, or 'plough'. This last belongs to a mysterious group of *p*-words (such as 'path' and 'penny') which are apparently neither Slavic, Teutonic, Celtic, nor Romanic in origin.[5] Bratanič does not claim the invention

---

[1] Payne, *Archaeological Journal*, civ, 97, pl. viii; *History of Technology*, ed. Singer, ii (1956), fig. 49.

[2] F. Harrison, 'The crooked plough', *Classical Journal*, xi (1915–16), 323–32.

[3] S. Applebaum, 'Agriculture in Roman Britain', *Agricultural History Review*, vi (1958), 69; Collingwood, op. cit. 75.

[4] B. Bratanič, 'On the antiquity of the one-sided plough in Europe, especially among the Slavic peoples', *Laos*, ii (1952), 56–58; cf. J. Janko, 'Über Berührung der alten Slaven mit Turko-tataren und Germanen, vom sprachwissenschaftlichen Standpunkt', *Wörter und Sachen*, i (1909), 105; M. Bloch, 'Champs et villages', *Annales d'histoire économique et sociale*, vi (1934), 475.

[5] *Oxford English Dictionary*, s.v. 'plough'; cf. H. Schneider, *Germanische Altertumskunde*, 2nd edn. (Munich, 1951), 92. The effort of E. Werth, *Grabstock, Hacke und Pflug*

of the heavy plough for the Slavs, but for 'some northern peasant culture' as yet unidentified. Since the Slavic vocabulary surrounding *plug* probably would have developed very rapidly, once the Slavs got the heavy plough, we have no reason to date its arrival among them very long before the Avar invasion of 568 severed the south Slavs from frequent contact with peoples speaking other varieties of that linguistic family.

In their tribal wandering the Goths had close contact with the Slavs, and when these latter had some superior object, the Goths tended to adopt both the thing and the word for it: e.g. the admirable Slavic laminated swords led them to take over the word *meki* for 'sword'.[1] In the fifth century the Goths in Transylvania had coulters[2] but evidently they were used either as a separate apparatus or with scratch-ploughs because the Gothic word for plough is *hôha*,[3] a cognate of 'hoe'. When the Angles and Saxons invaded Britain in waves between 449 and 584, they apparently took with them only some form of scratch-plough which they called *sulh*,[4] a cognate of the Latin *sulcus* or 'furrow'. In the Rhineland, in the *Lex salica* of *c.* 507–11, the word *carruca*, which later means 'wheeled plough' (French *charrue*), still means 'two-wheeled cart' rather than 'plough'.[5] If we reject the questionable emendation of the Pliny text's *plaumorati*,[6] the word 'plough' first appears in 643, in north Italy, as the latinized Lombard *plovum*.[7] In 724–30 the *Lex Alemannorum* shows that in south-west Germany *carruca* has come to mean a plough with two wheels in front,[8] while by the early ninth century the new

(Ludwigsburg, 1954), 193–4, to prove the origin of the wheeled plough in southern Germany by showing its modern occurrence east, west, and north, is indecisive.

[1] Cf. B. P. Lozinski in *Speculum*, xxxiii (1958), 420.

[2] Cf. A. Bashmakoff, 'L'Évolution de la charrue à travers les siècles au point de vue ethnographique', *L'Anthropologie*, xlii (1932), 86, for a find at Szilágy-Serulyo.

[3] *OED*, loc. cit.; W. Mitzka, 'Pflügen und seine Wortgeographie', *Zeitschrift für Agrargeschichte und Agrarsoziologie*, vi (1958), 113.   [4] *OED*, loc. cit.

[5] H. Geffcken, *Lex salica* (Leipzig, 1898), 139; on the date, cf. R. Buchner, *Die Rechtsquellen*, Beiheft of *Deutschlands Geschichtsquellen im Mittelalter*, ed. W. Wattenbach and W. Levison (Weimar, 1953), 17. T. Frings, 'Deutsch *Karch* "Wagen", französisch *charrue* "Pflug"', *Zeitschrift für Volkskunde*, xl (1930), 100–5, presents further philological evidence that the heavy plough was introduced into southern and western Germany in Frankish times.   [6] *Supra*, p. 42, n. 3.

[7] *Edictus Rotharii*, in *MGH, Leges*, iv, 69, 373; on date, cf. Buchner, op. cit. 34. In view of the Slavic evidence, one need not take seriously the contention of L. Franz, 'La Terra natale dell'aratro a carrello, l'Italia', *Rivista di scienze preistoriche*, v (1950), 95–96, that the Lombards learned this word in Italy.

[8] *Lex Alemannorum*, xcvi, § 2: 'si carrucam inviolat, aut rumpit rotas primerias'; another version reads: '. . . rotas de davante', in *MGH, Leges*, iii. 80, 116; on date, cf. Buchner, op. cit. 31.

meaning had generally overlaid, if not entirely displaced, the older one, at least in the northern parts of the Frankish realm.[1]

Across the Channel insufficient attention has been paid to the derivation of English 'plough' from Old Norse *plógr*.[2] Although the Anglo-Saxon form *ploh* has not been found earlier than *c.* 1100,[3] the Norse term was presumably introduced to Britain during the Danish invasion and settlement of north-eastern England from the middle ninth into the eleventh century. The significance of these linguistic facts has been obscured by the opinion[4] that the existence among the Anglo-Saxons of open fields composed of strips is documented by the laws of King Ine of Wessex datable 688–94, and that such an arrangement implied a heavy plough which had doubtless, therefore, been brought over by the first Germanic invaders, if not by the Celtic Belgae five centuries earlier.

But Kirbis has pointed out, first, that the extant text of the laws of Ine is a reissue by Alfred the Great (871–901), presumably updated in some respects; second, that the Alfredian version of Ine's laws does not mention open fields or co-operative village agriculture, but only strips and common pasture.[5] There is some evidence that the fields of the early Germanic settlers in England were arranged in strips,[6] but we have seen above that strips may be cultivated by a scratch-plough. Open fields are not securely documented among the Anglo-Saxons until the tenth century.[7] About 945 the Welsh laws of Hywel Dda[8] speak clearly of the heavy plough and of

---

[1] K. Verhein, 'Studien zu den Quellen zum Reichsgut der Karolingerzeit', *Deutsches Archiv für Erforschung des Mittelalters*, x (1953–4), 352–5, esp. n. 229.

[2] *OED*, loc. cit.

[3] *Leechdoms, Wortcunning, and Starcraft of Early England*, ed. O. Cockayne (London, 1866), iii. 286.

[4] F. Seebohm, *The English Village Community*, 4th edn. (London, 1890), 109; Gray, op. cit. 61–62; R. Trow-Smith, *English Husbandry* (London, 1951), 38, who, however, 34–35, emphasizes that we know almost nothing about the development of Anglo-Saxon agriculture. We can only judge its end result—that the England of *Domesday Book* of 1086 is vastly better cultivated than the Britain which Rome abandoned. We are as yet unable to judge exactly when, during the intervening period, the chief advance was made.

[5] W. Kirbis, 'Siedlungs- und Flurformen germanischer Länder, besonders Großbritanniens, im Lichte der deutschen Siedlungsforschung', *Göttinger geographisch Abhandlungen*, x (1952), 45–47.   [6] Ibid. 29–30.

[7] Gray, *English Field Systems*, 57, lists charters the language of which indicates open fields: the first dates from 904, the next from 953; thereafter they are frequent; cf. J. M. Kemble, *Codex diplomaticus aevi saxonici* (London, 1839–48), nos. 339, 1169.

[8] A. Owen, *Ancient Laws and Institutions of Wales* (London, 1841), i. 153; cf. F. G. Payne, 'The Plough in ancient Britain', *Archaeological Journal*, civ (1947), 84–85. While

ploughing in strips in open fields under community control: each plough-team is to plough at least twelve acre-strips before it breaks up, assigning one strip apiece to the ploughman, the driver, the owner of the plough-irons, the owner of the plough-frame, and to the owner of each of the eight oxen. When the invading Danes brought with them a plough so distinctive that the Anglo-Saxons felt impelled to take its name from the alien tongue, there is no reason to believe that either they or the Welsh would delay in adopting the thing itself in areas where it could be used profitably.

There is further evidence that the fully developed heavy plough was a Danish introduction to Britain. To judge from Bede and all the other early Northumbrian writers, the Anglo-Saxons consistently distributed lands in units of the 'hide', that is, enough to support a family: 'terra unius familiae'.[1] In Scandinavia, clearly in terms of the heavy eight-ox plough, a different type of land division developed: the basic unit was the *bol*, divided into eighths or *åttingar*;[2] the ordinary peasant holding seems to have been thought of as the *mark*, or two *åttingar*, i.e. the equivalent of a yoke of oxen. No text mentions the *bol* earlier than 1085,[3] but since traces of it are to be found in communities settled *c.* 900 by the Norse in Normandy,[4] it must be of the Viking age. In 1936 Homans pointed out that while the Danish terminology is not found in Britain, the regions most subject to Danish settlement and influence show a system of land division which is in complete contrast to the traditional Anglo-Saxon hide system but exactly corresponding to *bol* and *åttingar*, now called 'ploughland' and 'oxgang'. He concluded that this is intelligible only

in most areas this system of distribution eventually fell into disuse, and individuals gained permanent ownership of specific strips, in early times it was apparently very widespread, since, as Trow-Smith, op. cit. 46, points out, late records show that the pattern of ownership in a field is often repeated: 'B's lands always lie between A's and C's.' In 1682 in Westmeath County, Ireland, strips were still being allotted according to the individual's contribution to the plough-team; cf. D. McCort, 'Infield and outfield in Ireland', *Economic History Review*, 2nd series, vii (1954–5), 373.

[1] R. Lennard, 'The origin of the fiscal carrucate', *Economic History Review*, xiv (1944), 58.

[2] D. Hannerberg, *Die älteren skandinavischen Ackermasser* (Lund, 1955), *passim*, indicates that, like all such land measurements, the *bol* eventually lost its relation to its functional origin: because of the change in the ell from $1\frac{1}{2}$ to 2 feet, the *bol* came to consist not of 8 but of 6 *åttingar*.

[3] C. Parain, 'Travaux récents sur l'histoire rurale de Danemark', *Annales de Normandie*, ii (1952), 127.

[4] A. Steensberg, 'Modern research on agrarian history in Denmark', *Laos*, i (1951), 198; Parain, loc. cit.

as a Danish importation.[1] In 1066 the Norman conquerors recognized a type of land division familiar to them in Normandy,[2] and spontaneously applied the latinized term 'carrucate' to the basic unit, which was divided into eight 'bovates', these 'bovates' normally being grouped by pairs to form four 'virgates' in each carrucate. Since this particular form of land division, in contrast to division by hides, depends technologically upon the heavy eight-ox plough operating in open fields in terms of communal agriculture, we must conclude that the *plógr* was in fact a novelty introduced by the Danish invaders of the later ninth and early tenth centuries. Probably the new plough spread quickly to areas where the older land divisions continued to be used despite the novel agrarian technology. It is significant of peasant preference that when, after the fearful devastation of 1069, Yorkshire was resettled in the early twelfth century, the bovates and virgates of the Danelaw, rather than the hide, were used as the customary units of tenements.[3]

What, then, do we now know about the origin of the heavy plough? It came to the Slavs from an unknown source, but apparently they did not yet have it in the early fifth century when they were still in contact with the Goths. However, they had received it by the later sixth century and had completely developed its implications for ploughing not only strips but strips which consisted of ridge-and-furrow. There is every reason to believe that such a development would occur very quickly in a favourable environment. We therefore cannot safely date the heavy plough earlier than the sixth century.

In judging its diffusion, we must recognize that while the new productivity which it made possible would rather quickly increase population, it could only be adopted in areas already enjoying a certain density of settlement.[4] It was costly in itself, and costly to operate.[5] An isolated family could not use it; the normal hamlet of

[1] G. C. Homans, 'Terroirs ordonnés et champs orientés: une hypothèse sur le village anglais', *Annales d'histoire économique et sociale*, viii (1936), 438–48; cf. Steensberg, op. cit. 195.   [2] Lennard, op. cit. 62, n. 3.

[3] A. M. Bishop, 'Assarting and the growth of the open fields', *Economic History Review*, vi (1935), 17.

[4] Thinness of population in the forests of Poland and upon the plains of Hungary may account for the fact that an agriculture of the plough was not thriving even in ninth-century Poland, while there is no evidence of the heavy plough in Hungary until the eleventh century; cf. W. Hensel, 'Agriculture of the Slavs in Poland in the early Middle Ages', *Sprawozdania Państwowe Museum Archeologicniego* (Warsaw), IV. iii (1951), 45; M. Belényesi, 'Die Grundfragen der Entwicklung des Ackerbaues im XIV. Jahrhundert', *Ethnographia*, lxv (1954), 415.

[5] The fact that no medieval picture shows a plough being drawn by more than four

four to ten families would find it difficult to manage such a venture. Only in areas already having some village settlement was the new plough likely to be adopted. And even here there was a great psychological obstacle: for its most efficient use the new plough demanded open fields, and, to establish these, all previous rights of ownership in specific blocks or strips must be abolished.

In recent years German historical geographers have concluded that probably towards the end of the sixth century, and certainly in the seventh century, in central and south-western Germany and the Rhineland there began a remarkable increase of population, assarting and colonization which gradually spread to other regions,[1] and that this expansion seems connected with the growth of open fields.[2] In one area it is estimated that by the end of the seventh century the population was quadruple that under the Roman Empire.[3] The shift which we have noted in the meaning of the word *carruca* in the Rhine basin at about this time indicates that the heavy plough was an essential element in this process of growth, and does much to account for the bursting vitality of the Carolingian realm in the eighth century. While the arrival of the new plough in Scandinavia cannot yet be dated, one suspects that its effect upon population may be seen in the Viking outpouring which began *c.* 800. In any case, the Norse took the heavy plough and the method of land division most appropriate to it with them when, in the later ninth century, they settled the Danelaw in England, and then in Normandy.

While doubtless strip-fields were common before the heavy plough,

---

oxen has led some scholars to consider the eight-ox plough a fiction. However, granting that often ploughs were drawn by smaller—and larger—teams, the widespread division of the basic ploughland unit into eight sections, and the reversed-S curve of so many strips (*infra*, p. 55, n. 2), which is scarcely intelligible in terms of a team of less than four yokes, makes it probable that the eight-ox plough was normal in the early period after the introduction of the heavy plough.

[1] F. Steinbach, 'Geschichtliche Siedlungsformen in der Rheinprovinz', *Zeitschrift des Rheinischen Vereins für Denkmalspflege und Heimatschutz*, xxx. ii (1937), 19; L. Franz, 'Zur Bevölkerungsgeschichte des frühen Mittelalters', *Deutsches Archiv für Landes- und Volksforschung*, ii (1938), 404-16; F. Firbas, *Spät- und nacheiszeitliche Waldgeschichte Mitteleuropas nördlich der Alpen* (Jena, 1949), i. 366; H. Dannenbauer, 'Bevölkerung und Besiedlung Alemanniens in der fränkischen Zeit', *Zeitschrift für württembergische Landesgeschichte*, xiii (1954), 13-14; A. Timm, *Studien zur Siedlungs- und Agrargeschichte Mitteldeutschlands* (Cologne, 1956), 17-18; J. C. Russell, 'Late ancient and medieval population', *Transactions of the American Philosophical Society*, XLVIII. iii (1958), 42, 140.

[2] H. Mortensen, 'Die mittelalterliche deutsche Kulturlandschaft und ihr Verhältnis zur Gegenwart', *Vierteljahrschrift für Sozial- und Wirtschaftsgeschichte*, xlv (1958), 31-32.

[3] H. Stoll, 'Bevölkerungszahlen aus frühgeschichtliche Zeit', *Die Welt als Geschichte*, viii (1942), 72.

it is unlikely that the lighter plough normally produced the ridge-and-furrow form of acre which, in soils needing drainage, was characteristic of the improved type of cultivation. If fossil fields of such ridges could be dated archaeologically, our knowledge of the plough's diffusion would be aided.[1] In particular the dating of any strips slightly curved in S-shape would be helpful, since this curve was produced by manœuvring the large team of a plough as it approached the end of the strip.[2] If they were spread over the whole of northern Europe, the methods of English local historians might teach us much about the exact diffusion of the system of open fields, and why in certain areas the plan was not adopted.[3]

But as Sardinia shows,[4] the heavy plough may not have been the sole impulse for setting up open fields. Indeed, in agriculture there are usually at least two reasons for doing everything. One of the chief functions of the open-field system was to increase the facilities for rearing cattle while at the same time putting maximum arable into grain. Even after their migration into Gaul, the Franks continued to favour herding over agriculture.[5] So long as there was a thin population in relation to available land, there was no great competition between the two régimes: the animals were in perpetual pasture. But with growing population, tillage spread at the expense of forest, swamp, and meadow.[6] So long as each peasant was managing his own fields to suit himself, these could not be used for grazing, when fallow, without great expense for fencing, hedging, or herders. The open-field system, by concentrating crops in either one or two big fields at any given moment, made the whole sweep of the fallow available for browsing and at the same time provided maximum protection of crops against cattle. In addition, it assured that the

---

[1] Little progress in this matter has been made since the classic work of C. Frank, *Die Hochäcker* (Kaufbeuren, 1912), summarized in C. Frank, 'Forschungen zur Frage der alten Hochäcker: Zusammenfassung und Ergebnisse', *Deutsche Gaue*, xiii (1912), 35–40, which showed that all ridge-and-furrow in Bavaria is post-Roman.

[2] S. R. Eyre, 'The curving plough-strip and its historical implications', *Agricultural History Review*, iii (1955), 80–94. K. Scharlau, 'S-Formen und umgekehrte S-Formen unter den deutschen und englischen Langstreifenfluren', *Zeitschrift für Agrargeschichte und Agrarsoziologie*, iv (1956), 19–29, offers important supplementary evidence from Germany. F. Imberdis, 'Le Problème des champs courbes', *Annales: économies, sociétés, civilisations*, vi (1951), 77–81, presents an entirely different problem: fields in the region of Langres having irregularly curved boundaries which defy explanation in terms of topography, soils, or ploughing methods.

[3] See p. 155. [4] *Supra*, p. 47, n. 4.

[5] J. Boussard, 'Essai sur le peuplement de la Touraine du Ier au VIIIe siècle', *Moyen âge*, lx (1954), 286–91. [6] See p. 155.

manure would not be wasted on wild pasture but would be deposited on next year's arable.[1]

As noted above, this balanced system of animal and cereal production, in conjunction with the heavy plough, was apparently developed into a normal and accepted system during the seventh century in the Frankish heartland. It helps to account for the relative prosperity and vigour of the Carolingian Age.

Moreover, the heavy plough and its consequence of distribution of strips in the open fields helped to change the northern peasants' attitude towards nature, and thus our own. From time immemorial land was held by peasants in allotments at least theoretically sufficient to support a family. Although most peasants paid rent, usually in produce and services, the assumption was subsistence farming. Then in northern Europe, and there alone, the heavy plough changed the basis of allotment: peasants now held strips of land at least theoretically in proportion to their contribution to the plough-team. Thus the standard of land distribution ceased to be the needs of a family and became the ability of a power-engine to till the earth. No more fundamental change in the idea of man's relation to the soil can be imagined: once man had been part of nature; now he became her exploiter.

We see the emergence of this not only in Charlemagne's effort to re-name the months in terms of human activities—June was to be 'Ploughing Month', July 'Haying Month', August 'Harvest Month'[2] —but more particularly in the change which occurs in illustrated calendars beginning shortly before 830.[3] The old Roman calendars had occasionally shown genre scenes of human activity, but the dominant tradition (which continued in Byzantium) was to depict the months as passive personifications bearing symbols of attributes. The new Carolingian calendars, which set the pattern for the Middle

[1] H. Mortensen, 'Zur Entstehung der Gewannflur', Zeitschrift für Agrargeschichte und Agrarsoziologie, iii (1955), 38–41. W. Abel, Agrarpolitik, 2nd edn. (Göttingen, 1958), 144–5, emphasizes the great advantages of pooling once scattered individual resources in terms of the heavy plough and open fields under group control.

[2] Einhard, Vita Karoli magni, c. 29, ed. H. Pertz, MGH, Scriptores, ii (1829), 458: 'Junium Brachmanoth, Julium Heuvimanoth, Augustum Aranmanoth.'

[3] J. C. Webster, The Labors of the Months in Antique and Mediaeval Art to the End of the Twelfth Century (Evanston, 1938); cf. M. Schapiro in Speculum, xvi (1941), 131–7; also H. Stern, Le Calendrier de 354: étude sur son texte et sur les illustrations (Paris, 1953), 356–7, and his masterly 'Poésies et représentations' (cf. infra, p. 155), esp. 164–6; N. E. Enkvist, The Seasons of the Year: Chapters on a Motif from Beowulf to the Shepherd's Calendar (Helsinki, 1957), 46–47.

Ages, are very different: they show a coercive attitude towards natural resources. They are definitely northern in origin; for the olive, which loomed so large in the Roman cycles, has now vanished.[1] The pictures change to scenes of ploughing, harvesting, wood-chopping, people knocking down acorns for the pigs, pig-slaughtering. Man and nature are now two things, and man is master.

II

The Discovery of Horse-Power

The wide application of the heavy plough in northern Europe was only the first major element in the agricultural revolution of the early Middle Ages. The second step was to develop a harness which, together with the nailed horseshoe, would make the horse an economic as well as a military asset.

For the long haul, a draught animal is only as good as its hooves. Oxen seem to have less hoof-breakage than either horses or mules. The feet of horses are particularly sensitive to moisture: it is said that whereas in dry lands like Spain their hooves remain so hard that they can gallop unshod over rocky terrain, in northern Europe the hoof becomes soft, and is quickly worn and easily damaged.[2]

Recoiling before an appalling bibliography on the horseshoe which he had assembled, the most learned archaeologist in the field of the early Middle Ages, Dom Henri Leclercq, struck his colours, remarking: 'En ce qui regarde la ferrure des chevaux, nous laissons ce sujet à ceux qui ont des loisirs.'[3]

There is no present firm evidence of the nailed horseshoe before the end of the ninth century. The most authoritative statement to the contrary is Sir Mortimer Wheeler's insistence that at Maiden Castle he excavated 'clearly stratified' nailed horseshoes 'incontestably of late fourth and early fifth century date'.[4] Doubt is permissible. Of all archaeological objects, one should be most cautious about the stratification of horseshoes: a horse stepping into a rodent's burrow easily deposits one which the denizen of the burrow may draw still deeper; horses bogging in mud often lose shoes 2 or 3 feet below

[1] Stern, 'Poésies', 166.
[2] L. Palmer, 'Feet and shoeing', in *In My Opinion*, ed. W. E. Lyon (London, 1928), 283. [3] See p. 156.
[4] R. E. M. Wheeler, 'Maiden Castle, Dorset', *Reports of the Society of Antiquaries of London*, xii (1943), 290, pl. 30B.

the surface. In such circumstances the results of excavation must be subject to special control by information from other sources.

There is no literary evidence that the Greeks, Romans, or Franks had the horseshoe: the closest they came were hipposandals and *soleae*[1] attached with thongs or wires either for ornamentation or to help the healing of a broken hoof. Since the veterinary care of horses was of much concern to military writers, their failure to mention the shoe has more force than have most arguments from silence. Likewise there is no ancient or early medieval representation of horseshoes: the famous little statue of Charlemagne mounted, now in the Carnevalet Museum, may be contemporary, but the horse with its nailed shoes is probably a reconstruction of 1507.[2] And surely cavalry was not shod in 873 when a sudden freeze congealed the mud of the roads of Aquitaine and ruined the horses' feet.[3]

As for archaeology, many pagan peoples buried horses with their chieftains, yet in a fairly wide study of such rider-graves in Europe I have found only one supposed horseshoe, a 'Hufeisenstück mit Nagel' listed from grave I at Pfahlheim,[4] probably of the seventh century. One wonders first about the identification of this fragment; second, where the other three shoes are; third, whether some medieval horse may not have intruded it.

The earliest unambiguous excavated evidence of horseshoes comes from nomadic rider-graves of the Yenisei region in Siberia in the ninth to tenth centuries.[5] Simultaneously, nailed horseshoes are mentioned in the Byzantine *Tactica* of the Emperor Leo VI,[6] who reigned from 886 to 911. And in the West we probably hear the first sound of shod hooves in the last decade of the ninth century

---

[1] Despite *History of Technology*, ed. C. Singer, ii (1956), 561, it is merely to a *solea*, and not to a shoe, that Catullus, xvii. l. 26 refers; cf. R. Ellis, *Commentary on Catullus*, 2nd edn. (Oxford, 1889), 66.

[2] P. E. Schramm, *Die zeitgenössischen Bildnisse Karls des Großen* (Leipzig, 1928), 36.

[3] 'Primo quidem pluviarum inundantia plurimarum; deinde humectationem terrae glatiali astringente rigore, quae adeo noxia fuit, ut subtritis pedibus equinis, rarus quisque foret qui vectatione equorum uteretur' (*Vita Hludovici imperatoris*, cap. 47, ed. G. H. Pertz, in *MGH, Scriptores*, ii [1829], 635).

[4] K. M. Kurtz, 'Die alemannischen Grabfunde von Pfalheim', *Mitteilungen des Germanischen Nationalmuseums, Nürnberg*, I. ii (1884–6), 171; cf. W. Veeck, *Die Alamannen in Württemberg* (Berlin, 1931), i. 166.

[5] R. Girshman, in *Artibus Asiae*, xiv (1951), 187.

[6] *Leonis imperatoris Tactica*, v. 3, ed. R. Vári (Budapest, 1917), i. 92: 'πέδικλα, σεληναῖα σιδηρᾶ μετὰ καρφίων αὐτῶν.' The appendix to Book I of the *De ceremoniis* of Constantine Porphyrogenitus (d. 957) likewise mentions them; cf. *Patrologia graeca*, ed. J. P. Migne, cxii. 852. But A. Vogt, *Livre des cérémonies* (Paris, 1935), i, p. xvii, suspects that these appendixes are later accretions.

when Ekkehard's *Waltharius* says 'ferrata sonum daret ungula equorum'.[1] In 973 Gerhard's *Miracula Sancti Oudalrici* speaks of nailed shoes as being habitual for those going on journeys.[2] In 1038 Boniface of Tuscany was exhibiting his status by using silver nails in his horse's shoes.[3] By the later eleventh century they must have been very common, for under Edward the Confessor (d. 1066) six smiths at Hereford annually each produced 120 shoes from the king's iron as part of their taxes.[4] Moreover, clear nailed shoes appear in at least one miniature of the middle eleventh century.[5] We may safely assume that by the eleventh century the virtues of horse-shoeing would be as evident to the peasant as to the lord, and that the peasants could afford the iron for shoes.

But even a shod horse is of little use for ploughing or hauling unless he is harnessed in such a way as to utilize his pulling power. Thanks to the studies of Richard Lefebvre des Noëttes, it is now recognized that Antiquity harnessed horses in a singularly inefficient way. The yoke harness, which was well suited to oxen,[6] was applied to horses in such a way that from each end of the yoke two flexible straps encircled the belly and the neck of the beast. The result was that as soon as the horse began to pull, the neck-strap pressed on its jugular vein and windpipe, tending to suffocate it and to cut off the flow of blood to its head. Moreover, the point of traction came at the withers, mechanically too high for maximum effect. In contrast, the modern harness consists of a rigid padded collar resting on the shoulders of the horse so as to permit free breathing and circulation

[1] *Waltharius*, ed. K. Strecker in *MGH, Poetae aevi carolini*, vi, fasc. 1 (1951), l. 1203; for the date, cf. F. J. E. Raby, *History of Secular Latin Poetry in the Middle Ages*, 2nd edn. (Oxford, 1957), i. 263.

[2] Cap. 29, ed. G. Waitz, *MGH, Scriptores*, iv (1894), 424.

[3] *Vita Matildis, scripta a Donizone presbytero*, c. 10, ed. L. Simonei, in *Rerum italicarum scriptores*, new edn. (Bologna, 1930), 33.

[4] *Herefordshire Domesday, c. 1160–1170*, ed. V. H. Galbraith and J. Tait (London, 1950), 2. While compiled a century later, this document records obligations under Edward.

[5] R. Lefebvre des Noëttes, *L'Attelage et le cheval de selle à travers les âges* (Paris, 1931), fig. 448; the dating of the miniatures in figs. 190, 191, and 446 is in error. For the date of fig. 448, cf. R. Stettiner, *Die illustrierte Prudentius Handschriften* (Berlin, 1895), 130; A. Katzenellenbogen, *Allegories of the Virtues and Vices in Mediaeval Art* (London, 1939), 4.

[6] However, late Antiquity saw an advance with the invention of the horns-yoke, the earliest specimen of which comes from Ireland, but is not exactly datable; cf. W. Jacobeit, 'Ein eisenzeitliches Joch aus Nordirland', *Ethnographisch-archaeologische Forschungen*, i (1953), 95–97; cf. *Cambridge Economic History of Europe*, ed. J. H. Clapham and E. Power, i (Cambridge, 1941), 134.

of the blood. This collar is attached to the load either by lateral traces or by shafts in such a way that the horse can throw its whole weight into the task of pulling. Lefebvre des Noëttes proved experimentally that a team of horses can pull only about 1,000 pounds with the yoke-harness, whereas with collar-harness the same team can pull four or five times that weight.[1] Obviously, until the modern harness was available, peasants could not use the swifter horse in place of the plodding ox for ploughing,[2] harrowing, or heavy hauling.

Lefebvre des Noëttes examined various Roman, Han, and Byzantine efforts to overcome the disadvantage of yoke-harness by means of variations of the breast-strap (which had the defect of chafing), at times combined with lateral shafts.[3] Of particular importance among more recent finds are a Roman bronze fibula from Cologne, probably of the third century, in the form of a withers yoke for a single animal to be harnessed to shafts[4] and a small withers yoke of the second or third century, discovered at Pforzheim, to be used with shafts.[5] Moreover, a late Roman mosaic in Ostia shows a mule attached between shafts with what appears to be a rigid collar, although it rests high upon the neck.[6] That such experiments with harness were gradually perfected is shown by a tapestry of the first half of the ninth century, found in the Oseberg ship near Oslo, illustrating horses harnessed with a single small withers yoke, a breast strap, and lateral traces extending from the junctures of the breast-strap with the yoke.[7] We might thus be confident that the modern harness was the product of a slow development in the Occident, were it not for

---

[1] See p. 156. [2] See p. 156.

[3] e.g. for Gaul, cf. Espérandieu, *Recueil*, nos. 4031, 7685, 7725; H. Dragendorff and E. Krüger, *Das Grabmal von Igel* (Trier, 1924), pl. 12, i.

[4] G. Behrens, 'Die sogenannten Mithras-Symbole', *Germania*, xxiii (1939), 57, fig. 6.

[5] A. Dauber, 'Römische Holzfunde aus Pforzheim', ibid. xxviii (1944–50), 230–4; W. Jacobeit, 'Zur Rekonstruktion der Anschirrweise am Pforzheimer Joch', ibid. xxx (1952), 205–7.

[6] G. Calza and G. Becatti, *Ostia*, 4th edn. (Rome, 1957), 22; 65, fig. 5. Two extant representations from the late second or early third century show a Celtic grain-stripper pushed by a single horse or mule between shafts, but the harness cannot be judged in detail; cf. M. Renard, 'Technique et agriculture en pays trévire et remois', *Latomus*, xviii (1959), 91, fig. 7; pl. XVI. 1; XVII. 1; J. Mertens, 'Eine antike Mähmaschine', *Zeitschrift für Agrargeschichte und Agrarsoziologie*, vii (1959), 1–3.

[7] W. Holmqvist, 'Germanic art during the first millennium A.D.', *Kungl. Vitterhets, Historie och Antikvitets Akademiens Handlingar*, xc (1955), fig. 134. On the basis of the Oseberg material, R. Grand, 'Vues sur l'origine de l'attelage moderne', *Comptes rendus de l'Académie d'Agriculture de France*, xxxiii (1947), 706, and in *Bulletin de la Société Nationale des Antiquaires de France* (1947), 259, suggests a Norse origin for the modern harness.

reports of philological evidence, still too inadequately published to be judged, that English 'hames' and German *Kommut* are of Turkic origin[1] implying a diffusion from Central Asia. It is also asserted that while the breast-strap was borrowed from the Germans by the Slavs before the great Slavic diaspora of the sixth century, the horse-collar (and its Turkic name) was borrowed by the Germans in the eighth–ninth century.[2]

This latter date fits well with other new evidence. While Lefebvre des Noëttes pointed to three Frankish miniatures of the early tenth century[3] as the first indication of the new horse-collar, there is a picture of it a century earlier in the Trier *Apocalypse* (Fig. 3) which was illuminated in the heart of the Frankish realm about the year 800.[4] Metal mountings for horse-collars have been found in Sweden from graves of the middle and later ninth century.[5] Likewise in the late ninth century Alfred the Great notes, clearly with surprise, that on the northern coast of Norway horses were used for ploughing.[6]

What was the advantage to the peasant of having horses rather than oxen for agricultural labour? The studies by modern agronomists on the relative merits of horses and oxen may be slightly misleading because their tests were not made with medieval horses and oxen. Although it cannot yet be proved, it is probable that from the

---

[1] See p. 157.

[2] A. G. Haudricourt and M. J. B. Delamarre, *L'Homme et la charrue à travers le monde* (Paris, 1955), 174, 178; Haudricourt, 'Contribution à la géographie et l'ethnologie de la voiture', *Revue de géographie humaine et d'ethnologie*, i. i (1948), 62. A type of rudimentary horse-collar on the analogy of Siberian reindeer harness and involving bone or horn T-shaped plates with a hole in each extremity, has been reconstructed by L. Gyula, 'Beiträge zur Volkskunde der Avaren, III', *Archaeologiai Értesítő*, 3rd series, iii (1942), 341–6, fig. 4 and pl. LVIII. These are found in seventh–ninth-century Hungary and Bohemia, ninth–tenth-century Ukraine, and tenth–eleventh-century Poland; cf. J. Zak, 'Parties en corne au harnais de cheval', *Slavia antiqua*, iii (1942), 201, fig. 9.

[3] Op. cit. 123, figs. 140–2; cf. *History of Technology*, ed. C. Singer, ii (1956), 554, fig. 508.

[4] Trier, City Library, MS. 31, fol. 58ʳ. For date, cf. P. Clemen, *Die romanische Monumentalmalerei in dem Rheinland* (Düsseldorf, 1916), i. 67; A. Goldschmidt, *Die deutsche Buchmalerei*, i: *Die karolingische Buchmalerei* (Florence, 1928), 50; M. R. James, *The Apocalypse in Art* (London, 1931), 21; W. Neuss, *Die Apocalypse des Hl. Johannes in der altspanischen und altchristlichen Bibel-illustrationen* (Münster i. W., 1931), 249; J. de Borchgrave d'Altena in *Bulletin des Musées Royaux d'Art et d'Histoire, Bruxelles*, xviii (1946), 42; H. Swarzenski, *Monuments of Romanesque Art* (London, 1954), 57. The corresponding folio of the closely related Apocalypse of Cambrai, Municipal Library, MS. 386, is missing; cf. Neuss, op. cit. 262.   [5] See p. 157.

[6] *King Alfred's Orosius*, ed. H. Sweet (London, 1883), i. 18; A. S. C. Ross, *The Terfinnas and Bearmas of Ohthere* (Leeds, 1940), 20.

eighth century onward the increasing weight of armour created a knightly demand for more powerful horses, and that these were bred systematically[1] before any such selective breeding was developed for cattle. While there was a contrast between the *destrier* of the baron and the farm-horse of the peasant, the occasional mixing of the two would soon tend to upgrade the farm-horses. As compared with horses, it is safe to assume that cattle were relatively weaker in the Middle Ages than they are today. We must conclude that any modern advantage which can be shown for the use of the horse in farming should be augmented as applied to the Middle Ages.

Modern experiments show that while horse and ox exert roughly the same pull, the horse moves so much more rapidly that he produces 50 per cent. more foot-pounds per second.[2] Moreover, a horse has more endurance than an ox, and can work one or two hours longer each day.[3] This greater speed and staying-power of the horse is particularly important in the temperamental climate of northern Europe where the success of a crop may depend on plough-ing and planting under favourable circumstances. Moreover, the speed of a horse greatly facilitated harrowing, which was of more importance in the north than near the Mediterranean where cross-ploughing broke up the clods fairly well.

It is these elements which cast suspicion upon the cost-accounting of thirteenth-century agricultural writers like Walter of Henley who favour the ox as plough-beast on the grounds that a horse eats much more than an ox, and whereas an old horse is worth only his hide, an old ox can be fattened up and sold to the butcher.[4] Modern agronomists, aware of the rapid depreciation of the horse as tending to counterbalance its greater efficiency as a worker, nevertheless have calculated that, for a day's work, an ox is thirty per cent. more expensive than a horse.[5] What medieval peasants thought of the

---

[1] I have found no evidence of deliberate selective breeding for the chevalric market earlier than 1341 in Milan, when the contemporary Gualvaneo de la Flamma, *De gestis Azonis vicecomitis*, ed. L. A. Muratori, *Rerum italicarum scriptores*, xii (Milan, 1728), 1038, records that 'equos emissarios equabus magnis commiscuerunt, et procreati sunt in nostro territorio dextrarii nobiles, qui in magno pretio habentur. Item canes Alanos altae staturae, et mirabilis fortitudinis nutrire studuerunt.'

[2] Usher, op. cit. 156; R. J. Forbes, *Studies in Ancient Technology* (Leiden, 1955), ii. 83.

[3] G. Krafft, *Lehrbuch der Landwirtschaft*, iv: *Die Betriebslehre*, 12th edn. rev. by F. Falke (Berlin, 1920), 67.

[4] Walter of Henley, *Husbandry*, ed. E. Lamond (London, 1890), 12. N. Harvey, Walter of Henley and the old farming', *Agriculture, the Journal of the Ministry of Agriculture*, lix (1952–3), 491, is puzzled by Walter's shortsightedness in the matter of plough-teams.   [5] Krafft, op. cit. 70.

matter is shown by the fact that in the twelfth century, in the Slavic lands east of Germany, the ploughland measurement consisted of as much as could be worked by a pair of oxen or by one horse;[1] an advantage of 100 per cent. for the horse.

In view of the evidence from Norway in the late ninth century it is curious that we have no pictures of horses working the fields until 200 years or more later, when two appear: the border of the Bayeux Tapestry, probably made in Kent c. 1077–82,[2] shows a horse pulling a harrow, and a mule harnessed to a wheeled plough; while from the early twelfth century comes a tapestry of the Apocalypse, now in the cathedral of Gerona but showing northern influences, which illustrates the month of April with a team of horses doing the spring ploughing with a wheeled plough.[3]

However, by the end of the eleventh century the plough horse must have been a common sight on Europe's northern plains; for in 1095, at the Council of Claremont which launched the First Crusade, Urban II placed under the protection of the Peace of God 'oxen and plough horses (*equi arantes*) and the men who guide ploughs and harrows, and the horses with which they harrow (*equi de quibus hercant*)'.[4] And a conversation recorded near Kiev in 1103 indicates that in the Ukraine the peasants were doing all of their ploughing with horses[5]—perhaps one key to the precocity of Kievan culture in that period.

Once the world of scholars has realized that the widespread replacement of oxen by horses marked an epoch in the application of power to agriculture, examination of local records will enable us to tell how rapidly, and in exactly what regions, the change took place. The state of the archives in England, for example, is such that much information should emerge; yet thus far we know little. Whether or not the attribution of the Bayeux Tapestry to Kent is correct, the

---

[1] Helmold, *Chronicle of the Slavs*, tr. F. J. Tschan (New York, 1935), 73, 75; but cf. 234. J. Matuszewski, 'Les Origines de l'attelage moderne', *Kwartalnik historii kulturny materialnej*, ii (1954), 836, states that in twelfth-century Poland a farm-horse cost as much as two oxen.

[2] *The Bayeux Tapestry*, ed. F. Stenton (New York, 1957), fig. 12; cf. pp. 11, 33.

[3] C. Zervas, *L'Art de la Catalogne* (Paris, 1937), pl. 4, dates it tenth to eleventh centuries, but cf. Webster, op. cit. 79–84, 165, pls. LI, LII(A); R. Tatlock, *Spanish Art* (New York, 1927), 67–68, pl. 10.   [4] See p. 157.

[5] *The Russian Primary Chronicle, Laurentian Text*, tr. S. H. Cross and O. P. Sherbowitz-Wetzor (Cambridge, Mass., 1953), 200. The *Chronicle* was completed c. 1113; cf. ibid. 21. The earliest Russian reference to the horse-collar appears in twelfth-century letters on birch-bark found at Novgorod; cf. R. Smith, 'Some recent discoveries in Novgorod', *Past and Present*, v (1954), 5.

Tapestry indicates that the Anglo-Normans were familiar with horses in agriculture. Yet in the *Domesday Book* of 1086 there is no hint of plough-horses: with suspicious uniformity the clerks of William the Conqueror's exchequer speak of eight-ox ploughs; but the way they round off fractions indicates that they are using the eight-ox plough as a rather abstract measure of taxable land values.[1] Careful examination shows that in fact English ploughs in 1086 were often drawn by more or fewer oxen, probably according to the prosperity of the specific manor or the variations of soil and topography.[2] In the *Liber niger* of Peterborough, *c.* 1125, Trow-Smith has found a horse harrowing, but none ploughing.[3] In 1167 an Oxfordshire royal manor was restocked with forty-eight oxen for six plough-teams, and five horses[4] who seem destined for carting and harrowing rather than for ploughing. Yet not many years later a description of the Friday horse-market at Smithfield, outside the gates of London, speaks of horses 'for the cart, dray or plough'.[5] Both in the Durham survey of 1183[6] and the Templars' inquest of 1185,[7] we find horses only harrowing, but *c.* 1191 we discover Abbot Samson of Bury St. Edmunds granting lands equipped in one case with a plough of two oxen and three horses (presumably one of them for harrowing), in another case a team of six oxen and two horses, in another manor two more teams similarly made and a third plough-team of eight horses.[8] In the late twelfth century surveys of twenty-three manors of Ramsey Abbey in which one can judge the nature of the plough-teams, nine used oxen only, whereas fourteen used mixed teams.[9]

[1] H. P. R. Finberg, 'The Domesday ploughteam', *English Historical Review*, lxvi (1941), 67-71.

[2] R. Lennard, 'Domesday ploughteams: the southwestern evidence', ibid. lx (1945), 217-33.   [3] Op. cit. 91.

[4] A. L. Poole, *From Domesday Book to Magna Carta*, 2nd edn. (Oxford, 1955), 52.

[5] William Fitzstephen, *Descriptio nobilissimae civitatis Londoniae*, in J. Stow, *Survey of London* (London, 1603), 574.

[6] *Boldon Buke, a Survey of the Possessions of the See of Durham, made by Order of Bishop Hugh Pudsey in the Year 1183*, ed. W. Greenwell (Durham, 1852), 8, 19; 17 mentions a 'molendinum equorum'.

[7] *Records of the Templars in England: the Inquest of 1185* (London, 1935), 11; the six ironshod horses on p. 9 may or may not pull the three ploughs there mentioned; p. cxviii has a 'molendinum chevaleraz'.

[8] *The Kalendar of Abbot Samson of Bury St. Edmunds*, ed. R. H. C. Davis (London, 1954), 119, 127-8.

[9] J. A. Raftis, *The Estates of Ramsey Abbey* (Toronto, 1957), 314. For some thirteenth-century materials, cf. H. G. Richardson, 'The mediaeval plough-team', *History*, xxvi (1942), 288.

These are random notices to which many more will undoubtedly be added as time passes. But their tendency is clear: in late twelfth-century England, at least in some regions which cannot yet be defined,[1] the horse was taking over the plough. Normandy was in advance of Britain: two thirteenth-century documents indicate that in the Duchy peasants were doing all of their ploughing with horses,[2] and a century later Nicholas Oresmus, who died Bishop of Lisieux in 1382, takes it for granted that ploughing is done by horses.[3]

Perhaps one reason for the technological lag in England was that while in France direct exploitation of the demesne dwindled steadily in favour of rents, thirteenth-century England witnessed a decided revival of the demesne and of labour services.[4] Walter of Henley's treatise was one of the textbooks designed to aid this revival,[5] and the real reason for his favouring the ox at the plough emerges when he remarks that 'the malice of the ploughmen does not permit a horse-drawn plough to go any faster than one pulled by oxen'.[6] This kind of 'slow-down' may have affected the ploughing of demesne lands done reluctantly under manorial obligation (it was such plough-ing which, by its nature, was recorded) but it would not apply when the peasants were working their own fields. And in area and produc-tive significance for the total economy, the peasant holdings were far greater than the demesne.

[1] As this book goes to press, R. Lennard, 'The composition of demesne plough-teams in twelfth-century England', *English Historical Review*, lxxv (1960), 193–207, adds con-siderable new evidence of the increasing use of the plough-horse in the later twelfth century, and shows (p. 201) that the change first occurred 'in eastern and east Midland England'.

[2] L. Delisle, *Étude sur la condition de la classe agricole et l'état de l'agriculture en Normandie au moyen âge* (Évreux, 1851), 135, n. 36: 'omnes illi qui associabunt equos ad carucam . . .'. Eudes Rigaud, *Registrum visitationum archiepiscopi Rothomagensis (1248–1269)*, ed. T. Bonnin (Rouen, 1852), 375, records that when, in 1260, he was riding from Meudon to Giset on the feast of St. Matthew, 'invenimus carrucas operantes et arrantes, quarum equos adduci fecimus ad Meullentum, pro eo quod in festo tanti Sancti presumpserint irreverenter operari'.

[3] L. Thorndike, *History of Magic and Experimental Science*, iii (New York, 1934), 466·

[4] R. Grand, 'Les Moyens de résoudre dans le haut moyen âge les problèmes ruraux', *Settimane di Studio del Centro Italiano di Studi sull'Alto Medioevo*, ii (1955), 528–9; M. M. Postan, 'The chronology of labour services', *Transactions of the Royal Historical Society*, 4th series, xx (1937), 186–9.

[5] Cf. D. Oschinsky, 'Medieval treatises on estate management', *Economic History Review*, 2nd series, viii (1955–6), 296–309. Something of the same sort must have been happening in Germany; for the thirteenth-century satirist Seifried Helbling, ed. J. Seemüller (Halle a. S., 1886), 1: 399, 820; 3: 124; 7: 1209; 15: 87, lampoons knights who leave the army to care for their estates, who think about nothing but crops and profits, who worry about cheese, eggs, and the price of grain.   [6] Op. cit. 12.

Not only ploughing but the speed and expense of land transport were profoundly modified in the peasants' favour by the new harness and nailed shoes. In Roman times the overland haulage of bulky goods doubled the price about every hundred miles.[1] The result was that latifundia even close to Rome, but without water transport to compete with Egyptian, North African, and Sicilian shipments, could not afford to raise grain for the Roman market.[2] In contrast, in the thirteenth century the cost of grain seems to have increased only 30 per cent. for each hundred miles of overland carriage[3]—still high, but more than three times better than the Roman situation. Now it was becoming possible for peasants not situated along navigable streams to think less in terms of subsistence and more about a surplus of cash crops.

We still know very little in detail about the improvement of wagons which followed the invention of modern harness—the development of pivoted front axles,[4] adequate brakes, whipple-trees,[5] and the like. Most Roman vehicles, except ceremonial equippages and post-chaises, seem to have been two-wheeled. But beginning with the first half of the twelfth century we find a large, horse-drawn, four-wheeled 'longa caretta' capable of hauling heavy loads,[6] and by the middle of the thirteenth century a wagon normally had four wheels:[7] Friar Salimbene records that in 1248, at Hyères in Provence, Friar Peter of Apulia replied when asked what he thought of Joachim of Flora's teachings, 'I care as little for Joachim as for the

[1] C. A. Yeo, 'Land and sea transportation in Imperial Italy', *Transactions and Proceedings of the American Philological Society*, lxxvii (1946), 222.

[2] Ibid. 224; cf. E. R. Grosser, 'The significance of two new fragments of the Edict of Diocletian', ibid. lxxi (1940), 162.

[3] R. J. Forbes, 'Land transport and road-building (1000–1900)', *Janus*, xlvi (1957), 109.

[4] The fact that the front wheels in the Trier *Apocalypse* of *c.* 800 (*supra*, p. 61, n. 4 and Fig. 3) are smaller than the rear wheels indicates a pivoted front axle. For the later medieval evidence, see M. N. Boyer, 'Medieval pivoted axles', *Technology and Culture*, i (1960), 128–38, and *infra*, n. 7.

[5] I know of no whipple-tree earlier than those on the bronze doors of Novgorod Cathedral made at Magdeburg in Saxony in 1152–4; cf. A. Goldschmidt, *Die Bronzetüren von Novgorod und Gnesen* (Marburg a. L., 1932), 8, pl. 26.

[6] Cf. A. L. Kellogg, 'Langland and two scriptural texts', *Traditio*, xiv (1958), 392–6.

[7] *A Book of Old Testament Illustrations of the Middle of the Thirteenth-Century sent by Cardinal Bernard Maciejowski to Shah Abbas the Great, King of Persia, now in the Pierpont Morgan Library*, ed. S. C. Cockerell, M. R. James, and C. J. ffoulkes (Cambridge, 1927), a manuscript of *c.* 1250, probably Parisian, which is very detailed in technical matters (showing, for example, fol. 21*b*, pivoted front axle, whipple-tree, and horn-harness for oxen), illustrates four-wheeled wagons on fols. 5*b*, 6*b*, 9*a*, 12*a*, 21*b*, 23*a*, 27*b*, 39*a*, and 44*b*, but no two-wheeled carts.

fifth wheel of a wagon'.[1] Not only merchants but peasants were now able to get more goods to better markets.

In still another way the new harness affected the life of the northern peasants. When historical geographers began to study abandoned fields and settlements in Germany, they assumed that these had been deserted either during the Thirty Years War or after the Black Death of 1348–50. To their astonishment they found that abandonment of settlements, but not of fields, began in the eleventh century and occurred with great frequency in the thirteenth.[2] Not only were peasants moving to neighbouring cities while still going out each day to their fields: villages were absorbing the inhabitants of the hamlets in their vicinity. In a period when the total population of Europe was increasing rapidly,[3] places long inhabited[4] were losing their identity because of a 'balling' of peasants into larger and larger villages.

Despite the fact that one scholar has bewailed the resulting 'spiritual urbanization' of the peasants of the thirteenth century,[5] the personal advantages of such concentration are evident: a hamlet with five to ten cottages led a restricted life. In a big village of two or three hundred families there would be not only better defence in emergency, but a tavern, a fine big church, maybe a school run by the priest in which the boys could learn their letters, certainly more suitors for your daughters, and not merely peddlers with packs but merchants with wagons and news of distant parts. But these virtues of a more 'urban' life would always have attracted countrymen. How

[1] 'Tantum curo de Ioachym quantum de quinta rota plaustri', *Cronica Fratris Salimbene de Adam*, ed. O. Holder-Egger, *MGH, Scriptores*, xxxii (1905–13), 239. P. Deffontaines, 'Sur la répartition géographique des voitures à deux roues et à quatre roues', *Travaux du Ier Congrès International de Folklore, Paris, 1937* (Tours, 1938), 119, offers puzzling evidence of an early modern reversion to two-wheeled carts in certain areas of France which had used four-wheeled wagons during the later Middle Ages.

[2] See p. 157.

[3] L. Génicot, 'Sur les témoignages d'accroissement de la population en occident du XIe au XIIIe siècle', *Cahiers d'histoire mondiale*, i (1953), 446–62; J. C. Russell, 'Late ancient and medieval population', *Transactions of the American Philosophical Society*, XLVIII. iii (1958), 113.

[4] É. Perroy, *La Terre et les paysans en France au XIIème et XIIIème siècles* (Paris, 1953, mimeographed), 144–5, shows that by the 1280's, in France, some recently reclaimed land was proving unsuitable for agriculture, and was being abandoned. Evidently by that time assarting had reached the point of diminishing returns.

[5] B. Huppertz, *Räume und Schichten bäuerlicher Kulturformen in Deutschland* (Bonn, 1939), 131–9. When H. Stoob, 'Minderstädte: Formen der Stadtentstehung im Spätmittelalter', *Vierteljahrschrift für Sozial- und Wirtschaftsgeschichte*, xlvi (1959), 22, says, of the myriad little cities which arose during the later Middle Ages, 'bürgerliches Leben wird hier zur Miniatur, ja Karikatur', he is looking at the phenomenon from the standpoint of urban man, not with the eyes of the rising peasant.

is it that, beginning in the eleventh century, so many of them were able to act upon their desires?

The answer seems to lie in the shift from ox to horse as the primary farm animal. The ox moved so slowly that peasants using oxen had to live close to their fields. With the employment of the horse both for ploughing and for hauling, the same amount of time spent going to and from the fields would enable the peasant to travel a much greater distance. The mathematical relation of the radius of a circle to its area governed the redistribution of settlement. Even a slight increase in the distance which it was convenient to travel from the village to the farthest field would greatly enlarge the total arable which could be exploited from that village. Thus extensive regions once scattered with tiny hamlets came to be cultivated wildernesses dominated by huge villages which remained economically agrarian, for the most part, but which in architecture and even in mode of life became astonishingly urban.

The phenomenon of 'balling' has thus far been ascertained only for parts of Germany. There is, however, some evidence of it from northern France[1] and England,[2] and doubtless it took place in other areas where it was technically feasible. Deep in the Middle Ages this 'urbanization' of the agricultural workers laid the foundation for the change in the focus of Occidental culture from country to city which has been so conspicuous in recent centuries. It gave the peasantry of northern Europe psychological preparation for that great shift and perhaps enabled them to build up attitudes and spiritual antibodies which reduced the social shock of subsequent developments.

In pondering the relation of horse to ox, we are faced by a curious set of facts. Over much of northern Europe, from Wales to Sweden, the dominance of the heavy plough was such that the arable land had come to be measured in eight sections correlated to its eight oxen,[3] yet it was roughly in this same region—the drainage basins of the North Sea and the Baltic—that the horse eventually became the normal plough animal.[4] What particular affinity developed

---

[1] É. Chantriot, *La Champagne: étude de géographie régionale* (Nancy, 1905), 247.

[2] M. W. Beresford and J. K. S. St. Joseph, *Medieval England: An Aerial Survey* (New York, 1958), 111–13.

[3] R. Mielke, 'Das Pfluggespann', in *Festschrift Eduard Hahn* (Stuttgart, 1917), 194–7, 202.

[4] E. Hahn, 'Das Pfluggespann', in *Festschrift für Marie-Andree Eysn* (Munich, 1928), 90; cf. the map of the area of horse-culture in France *c.* 1650 in R. Musset, *De l'élevage du cheval en France* (Paris, 1917), 137.

between the horse and the heavy plough? And if the modern harness was known in Europe by the year 800, why was there a delay of nearly three centuries in the wide use of the horse in agriculture? The answer is to be found in a new system of crop rotation which, when joined with the heavy plough and the draught-horse, completed the pattern of a new and vastly more productive system of northern agriculture.

III

The Three-field Rotation and Improved Nutrition

The three-field system of crop rotation has been called 'the greatest agricultural novelty of the Middle Ages in Western Europe'.[1] It bursts upon us in the late eighth century, the first secure indication of it being datable in 763;[2] the next comes in 783;[3] the third, in 800.[4] Thereafter the evidence of it is so frequent that those historians who hold the dogma that nothing in rural life can change quickly are required to believe that the three-field system is a much earlier invention[5] which managed to elude the records.

But it would seem that Charlemagne himself thought of the new pattern of the agricultural year—which had been adopted on the imperial manors, if we may judge by the capitulary *De villis*[6]—as something so new and significant that he felt impelled, as has been mentioned, to rename the months in terms of it. In former times, the ploughing for the winter crop had been done in October or November, and the harvest had been reaped in June or July. But in Charlemagne's new nomenclature, June, when the fallow is ploughed,

---

[1] C. Parain in *Cambridge Economic History*, i (1941), 127.

[2] H. Wartmann, *Urkundenbuch der Abtei St. Gallen* (Zürich, 1863), i. 41, no. 39: 'et in primum ver aratro iurnalem unum et in mense Junio brachare alterum et in autumno ipsum arare et seminare.'

[3] O. Dobenecker, *Regesta historiae Thuringiae* (Jena, 1896), i. 15, no. 48: 'in tribus Hoheimis . . . in tribus Geochusis . . . in tribus Percubis.' A document of 771 in *Codex diplomaticus et variarum traditionum antiquissimi Monasterii Lauresheimensis* (Tegernsee, 1766), Part II, 312–13, no. 494, mentioning a 'mansum de terra araturia xxvii jurnales in tribus locis sitos', is often cited as one of the earliest evidences of the three-field system. But W. Fleischmann, *Caesar, Tacitus, Karl der Große und die deutsche Land-wirtschaft* (Berlin, 1911), 53, n. 1, correctly points out that this codex records so many gifts of land located in 2, 4, 5, 6, &c., *loci* that the instance of 3 is ambiguous.

[4] K. Lamprecht, *Deutsches Wirtschaftsleben im Mittelalter* (Leipzig, 1886); i. 545, n. 4.

[5] e.g. K. Weller, 'Die Besiedlung des Alemannenlandes', *Württembergische Viertel-jahrschrift für Landesgeschichte*, vii (1898), 340–1.

[6] Haudricourt and Delamarre, op. cit. 46.

is the 'Ploughing Month', and August is the 'Harvest Month'.[1] Such was the emperor's propaganda for an agricultural novelty which he must have felt was of the first importance to his realm.

There was nothing comparable to three-field rotation in Roman times. Pliny[2] tells us that the people of Trier once sowed grain in March after their winter crop had been destroyed, but this is recounted as a most unusual episode, and there is no indication that it was repeated. Pliny, indeed, knows of summer crops to be sown in the spring, but the very listing of them—millet, panic, sesame, clary, winter-cress (all of which, he says, are winter crops in Greece and Asia, but not in Italy), lentils, chickpeas, alica (?)—as compared with his list of winter crops—wheat, spelt, barley, beans, turnips, and rape—shows how unimportant the spring planting was.[3] He mentions that Virgil had recommended planting beans in the spring, as was done near Padua, but Pliny regards their sowing in the autumn as normal.[4] Peas, on the other hand, in Italy and colder climates, are sown only in the spring.[5] While both Pliny[6] and the Roman agronomists[7] were well aware that legumes enrich the soil, there apparently was no regular and customary system of alternating such crops with cereals.

Much more important anticipations of the triennial rotation are found in the far north. A Danish palaeobotanist has concluded, on the basis of pollen analysis, that the early agriculture of the Baltic region was confined to the spring planting, and that the autumn ploughing and planting was a fairly late medieval innovation in that area.[8] Writing in the sixth century B.C., Hecataeus[9] reports that in Britain two crops were harvested annually. Applebaum has noted[10] that the chief grain of the northern Bronze Age was barley, which in northern climates has usually been a spring crop in the Middle Ages and more recent times; he suggests that the change of climate

---

[1] Supra, p. 56, n. 2.

[2] Naturalis historia, xviii. 20, ed. C. Mayhoff (Leipzig, 1892), iii. 193.

[3] xviii. 7, ed. cit. iii. 155.   [4] xviii. 12, ed. cit. iii. 175.

[5] xviii. 12, ed. cit. iii. 176.

[6] xviii. 12, ed. cit. iii. 175.

[7] F. Harrison, Roman Farm Management: The Treatises of Cato and Varro (New York, 1913), 41–42, 121–2.

[8] V. M. Mikkelsen, 'A contribution to the history of vegetation in the Sub-Arctic period', in A. Steensberg, Farms and Watermills in Denmark during Two Thousand Years (Copenhagen, 1952), 302.

[9] As preserved in Diodorus Siculus, ii. 47, ed. C. H. Oldfather (London, 1935), ii. 38.

[10] S. Applebaum, 'The agriculture of the British Early Iron Age as exemplified at Figheldean Down', Proceedings of the Prehistoric Society, xx (1954), 104.

c. 500 B.C. may have led to concentration on winter plantings, but with vestigial spring plantings in certain areas.

It seems probable, then, that as the Carolingians marched their armies into barbarian Germany, as St. Boniface and his Benedictine legions replaced pagan shrines with cathedrals and cloisters, as Teuton and Latin began to fuse their talents in the building of a new European culture, at that same moment the Baltic–North Sea spring planting was married to the Mediterranean autumn planting to create a new agricultural system far more productive than either of its progenitors.

How did the three-field system work, as compared with the older Mediterranean two-field rotation?

Under the two-field plan about half the land was planted with winter grain while the other half was left fallow. The next year the two fields simply exchanged functions.

Under the three-field plan the arable was divided roughly into thirds. One section was planted in the autumn with winter wheat or rye. The following spring the second field was planted with oats, barley, peas, chickpeas, lentils, or broad beans. The third field was left fallow. The next year the first field was planted to summer crops; the second field was left fallow; the third field was put into winter grains.

		1st year		*2nd year*		*3rd year*		*1st year*
1st field		- - - -		. . . . .				- - - -
2nd field	AUTUMN	. . . . .	AUTUMN		AUTUMN	- - - -	AUTUMN	. . . . .
3rd field				- - - -		. . . . .		

Winter planting = - - - - -   Spring planting = · · · · ·

In the eighth, ninth, and tenth centuries there were only three ploughings for the entire three-year cycle: winter field in October or November; summer field in March, or whenever the ground was beginning to warm; fallow towards the end of June.[1] Thus in this earlier period a manor of 600 acres under the two-field system would plough 600 acres for 300 acres in crops, whereas the same 600 acres under the three-field system would have 400 acres under crops for the same ploughing, or an increase of one-third.

[1] G. Hanssen, *Agrarhistorische Abhandlungen* (Leipzig, 1880), i. 163.

But by the twelfth century at latest[1] it had been found profitable both in the two- and three-field systems to plough the fallow twice in order to keep down weeds and to improve fertility. This change increased the advantage of the triennial rotation even further. Peasants handling 600 acres under the two-field plan, and ploughing the fallow twice, would plough annually 300+600 = 900 acres for 300 acres in crops. Managing 600 acres on the three-field system, again with double ploughing of the fallow, they would plough annually only 200+200+400 = 800 acres for 400 acres in crops. In terms of 600 acres, the increase of production in adopting the new rotation would still be only one-third. But since the change involved 100 acres less of annual ploughing, 75 acres (ploughed as 25+25+50) might be added without additional labour,[2] if such land could be secured by reclamation. The same peasants would thus be cultivating not 600 but 675 acres (450 in crops), and their production advantage over the two-field rotation would be 50 per cent. The spread of the triennial system thus gave a major impulse to assarting: forests fell; swamps were drained; dykes stole polders from the sea.

The new plan of rotation, then, had several advantages. First, as has just been said, it increased the area which a peasant could cultivate by one-eighth and it pushed up his productivity by one-half. Second, the new plan distributed the labour of ploughing, sowing, and harvesting more evenly over the year, and thus increased efficiency. Third, it much reduced the chance of famine by diversifying crops and subjecting them to different conditions of germination, growth, and harvest. But fourth, and perhaps most important, the spring planting, which was the essence of the new rotation, greatly stepped up the production of certain crops which had particular significance.

Oats had entered Europe in prehistoric times from Asia Minor, probably as a weed accompanying wheat, but the Romans had not developed it.[3] Oats is the best possible food for horses.[4] The ox is

---

[1] M. Bloch, *Caractères*, 25; K. Lamprecht, op. cit. i. 558.

[2] On Walter of Henley's unnecessarily intricate calculations to discover that one-eighth more area could be handled under the new system, cf. *Cambridge Economic History*, i. 129. It is significant that this passage is omitted from one of the Henley MSS.: cf. E. Power, 'On the need for a new edition of Walter of Henley', *Transactions of the Royal Historical Society*, xvii (1934), 101–16.

[3] D. R. Sampson, 'On the origin of oats', *Harvard University Botanical Museum Leaflets*, xvi (1954), 295–8; F. A. Cofman, '*Avena sativa* L. probably of Asiatic origin', *Agronomy Journal*, xlvii (1955), 281; F. Schwanitz, *Die Entstehung der Kulturpflanzen* (Berlin, 1957), 122.

[4] They are not a modern fad with horses: W. Dugdale, *Baronage of England* (London,

a grass-burning engine; the horse is a much more efficient oats-burning engine. The peasants of southern Europe had no choice between ox and horse as plough-beast because their biennial rotation did not give them a sufficient surplus of grain to keep many horses.[1] As a result of their rotational system, since oats was one of the major spring crops, the northern peasantry had both the quantity and quality of surplus food needed for horses.[2] By the end of the Middle Ages there appears to be a clear correlation between the triennial rotation and the use of the horse in agriculture.

It may be that the 300-year delay between the arrival of the modern harness and the widespread use of the horse for non-military purposes can be explained by the practical difficulties of switching a village from the biennial to the triennial rotation. We know of a few cases in which it took place,[3] but unless an entirely new third field could be assarted,[4] or unless by sheer accident individual holdings were so arranged that what had been two could now be cut into three without drastic reallotment of strips, such a change must have run into the opposition of vested rights.

Arrangements of this sort are much more easily effected when new land is being settled, or when devastated areas are being repopulated after a time of chaos. The later ninth and early tenth centuries were an age of dismay. The parts of northern Europe which were not overrun by the Hungarian horsemen were put to the torch by Viking raiders. Only after the Northmen were domesticated at the mouth of

1675), i. 183–4, cites an agreement of 1317–18 providing regularly 'hay and oats for four horses . . . hay and oats for eight horses'.

[1] A survey made in 1338 of 123 estates of the priory of the Hospitalers at Saint Gilles, near the mouths of the Rhone, shows that all but three were using oxen for ploughing, despite the fact that twenty-four of these properties, because of favourable circumstances, had been able to develop rhythms of cultivation more intensive than the two-year rotation; cf. G. Duby, 'Techniques et rendements agricoles dans les Alpes du Sud en 1338', *Annales du Midi*, lxx (1958), 404, 407. In 1422 an effort was made to use horses to operate Brunelleschi's great hoist erected to help build the dome of the cathedral at Florence, but power from horses proved at least 50 per cent. more expensive than from oxen; cf. F. D. Prager, 'Brunelleschi's inventions', *Osiris*, ix (1950), 516, n. 146.

[2] J. Boussard, 'La vie en Anjou au XIe et XIIe siècles', *Moyen âge*, lvi (1950), 57, 67, says that oats are first mentioned in Anjou in 1129, and that during the second half of the twelfth century oats and wheat tended to replace barley and rye as the basic crops. Since Anjou lies on the border between the horse and the ox areas, the triennial and the biennial areas, and the open-field and the enclosure areas, it would be very interesting to know the exact local relationships and changes involved in this shift of crops.

[3] See p. 158.

[4] As occurred before 1220 at one village in Yorkshire; cf. T. A. M. Bishop, 'Assarting and the growth of the open fields', *Economic History Review*, vi (1935), 19.

the Seine and in the Danelaw, and after the Magyar might had been crushed on the Lechfeld, did the second wave of invasions—more destructive than the Teutonic incursions which had toppled Rome—come to an end. At once the reconstruction began, and in the north it seems likely that the new agricultural communities would be eager to organize themselves according to the superior new technology of crop rotation.[1] This in turn would gradually supply the oats which permitted the building up of the stock of horses. In terms of such a sequence, it is not surprising that the farm-horse began to come into much more general use in the eleventh century.

The question of the spread of the three-field system from its point of origin in the Frankish area between the Seine and the Rhine has not been studied systematically. Like the answers to so many other fundamental questions in agricultural history, it must await far more careful local documentary and field investigation than has thus far been accomplished.[2] Even in Germany, where more such research has been done than elsewhere, no one can yet be more definite than to say that its diffusion took several centuries after its start shortly before 800.[3] Hungary is puzzling: one abbey seems to have three fields on its estates in 1086; then there is no mention of a triennial rotation until 1355.[4] In the thirteenth century it appears among the southern Slavs,[5] in Poland,[6] and in southern Sweden.[7] On the other side of Europe it seems not to have reached England until the twelfth

[1] A large proportion of the communities in the area of summer rains which could not redivide their lands, so as to exploit the new system to the full, compromised: their lands remained divided into two fields, but half of each year's arable was planted in the autumn, half in the spring. While obviously less productive than the perfected system, this plan would have many of its advantages, and was perhaps particularly suited to regions with relatively poor soil which would become depleted with the more intensive rotation; cf. Gray, op. cit. 71; C. S. and C. S. Orwin, *The Open Fields* (Oxford, 1938), 49.

[2] See p. 158.

[3] H. Mortensen, 'Zur deutschen Wüstungsforschung', *Göttingische gelehrte Anzeigen*, ccvi (1944), 210.

[4] M. Belényesy, 'Angaben über die Verbreitung der Zwei- und Dreifeldwirtschaft im mittelalterlichen Ungarn', *Acta ethnographica Academiae Scientiarum Hungaricae*, v (1956), 185.

[5] J. K. Jireček, *Geschichte der Serben* (Gotha, 1918), ii. 54; J. Sakazov, *Bulgarische Wirtschaftsgeschichte* (Berlin, 1929), 105.

[6] D. Warriner, 'Some controversial issues in the history of agrarian Europe', *Slavic and East European Review*, xxxii (1953), 105; S. Chmielewski, 'Notes on farm tools and implements in early Polish agriculture', *Kwartalnik historii kultury materialnej*, iii (1955), 282.

[7] *Zeitschrift für Agrargeschichte und Agrarsoziologie*, v (1957), 206, citing D. Hannerberg, 'Byamål', *Kungl. Humanistiska Vetenskaps Samfundets i Lund, Årsberättelse* (1954–5), 19–62.

century,[1] whence it was probably taken to Ireland towards the end of the same century by Anglo-Norman colonists.[2]

We have seen how greatly the new supply of oats made available by the three-field system increased the numbers and prowess of horses. But people likewise were shaped by the new food resources.

In addition to oats and barley, the spring planting was habitually composed of legumes. We have already noted that the Romans knew peas, chickpeas, lentils, and broad beans, and that they were aware that legumes help the soil. But the Mediterranean emphasis on the autumn planting appears to have been so strong that even in the northern area of summer rains these crops were not grown by the Romans in great quantity, in proportion to cereals. At last, however, beginning in the late eighth century, legumes as field-crops came to play a vast and integral part in the new triennial rotation. Indeed, their role in its success has not been sufficiently emphasized; the nitrogen-fixing properties of these plants were fundamental to the maintenance of fertility under the more rigorous cultivation.

Malthus was no dietician: he assumed that population is dictated by the available food supply. The matter is much more complex. Food is not food unless it forms a balanced ration, the chief element in which is a relation between carbohydrates and proteins. A diet overloaded with carbohydrates quickly becomes as bad as starvation, and is, in fact, amino-starvation. A society may theoretically be able to produce great amounts of carbohydrates which it has no practical reason to produce until it finds an increased supply of proteins. Anything affecting the quantity of proteins available will quickly be felt in terms of population.[3]

Under the three-field rotation the autumn planting was largely carbohydrates, but the spring planting held a large amount of vegetable proteins. That by the end of the eleventh century these latter loomed as large as the cereals is indicated by Ordericus Vitalis's lament over the fearful drought which struck Normandy and France in the summer of 1094, searing 'the grain and pulse (*segetes et legumina*)'.[4] The normal picture of the summer fields is seen in the old English game song:

[1] G. Duby, 'La Révolution agricole médiévale', *Revue de géographie de Lyon*, xxix (1954), 362.

[2] J. Otway-Ruthven, 'The organization of Anglo-Irish agriculture in the Middle Ages', *Journal of the Royal Society of Antiquaries of Ireland*, lxxxi (1951), 9.

[3] Cf. R. Linton, 'Crops, soils and culture in America', in *The Maya and their Neighbors* (New York, 1940), 36.   [4] Ed. A. Le Prevost (Paris, 1845), 461; cf. 463.

Do you, do I, does anyone know,
How oats, peas, beans and barley grow?

And in the thirteenth century St. Albertus Magnus tells us how the eel leaves rivers for the fields where he will find peas or chickpeas sown.[1] Cato's slaves had been fed cereals, but no beans,[2] and Pliny had praised pulse above grain as food.[3] A Carolingian sacramentary provided a *Benedictio favae*:[4] now the prayers were answered.

Our recently acquired knowledge of nutrition, then, provides us with new insight into the dynamics of the later Middle Ages. While the legumes available to medieval Europe did not in themselves supply a complete series of the biologically necessary amino-acids, by a happy coincidence the smaller quantities of proteins found in the common grains were the perfect dietary supplement to those present in legumes, and particularly in field peas.[5] It was not merely the new quantity of food produced by improved agricultural methods, but the new type of food supply[6] which goes far towards explaining, for northern Europe at least,[7] the startling expansion of population, the growth and multiplication of cities, the rise in industrial production, the outreach of commerce, and the new exuberance of spirits which enlivened that age. In the full sense of the vernacular, the Middle Ages, from the tenth century onward, were full of beans.[8]

IV

The Northward Shift of Europe's Focus

In 1937 there appeared posthumously the masterpiece of the Belgian historian Henri Pirenne, *Mahomet et Charlemagne*.[9] Since then it has

[1] 'Nonnumquam [anguilla] etiam de aqua egreditur ad agrum in quo pisa vel cicer seminatur', *De animalibus*, Lib. XXIV, cap. 8, ed. H. Stadler (Münster i. W., 1920).

[2] N. Jasny, 'The daily bread of the ancient Greeks and Romans', *Osiris*, ix (1950), 228.

[3] 'Fortiora contra hiemes frumenta, legumina in cibo', *Naturalis historia*, xviii. 7, ed. C. Mayhoff, iii. 159.

[4] *The Gregorian Sacramentary under Charles the Great*, ed. H. A. Wilson (London, 1915), 221.

[5] E. Woods, W. M. Beeson, and D. W. Bolin, 'Field peas (*pisum sativum*) as a source of protein for growth', *Journal of Nutrition*, xxvi (1943), 327–35; J. S. Lester and W. J. Darby, *Nutrition and diet*, 6th edn. (Philadelphia, 1952), 193. For detailed analysis of the protein content of legumes and grains, cf. M. L. Orr and B. K. Watt, *Amino Acid Content of Foods* (U.S. Department of Agriculture, Home Economics Bureau Research Department, report 4) (Washington, 1957) 16–21, 24–33, 54–59.

[6] See p. 158.   [7] See p. 159.

[8] L. White, jr., &c., 'Symposium on the tenth century', *Medievalia et humanistica*, ix (1955), 3–29.   [9] (Paris, 1937); English tr. by B. Miall (New York, 1939).

dominated discussion of the economic history of the Mediterranean from the fifth through the tenth centuries. According to Pirenne, the Western Roman world did not 'fall': it slowly disintegrated. Until *c*. 700 the essential unity of the Mediterranean was preserved, despite political chaos. Levantine traders continued to do business as far west as the Merovingian kingdom, and indeed this commerce may have remained as active as in earlier and happier times. But the upsurge of Islam in the seventh century tore apart the seamless robe of the Middle Sea. Commercial connexions with the East were severed, and the conquest of Visigothic Spain by the Muslims in the eighth century left the Frankish king as the only considerable power in what was left of the Latin West. Cut off from the great currents of the continuing life of the Mediterranean, the Frankish realm turned inward upon itself and became the nucleus of a new kind of civilization. The Islamic smashing of Mediterranean cultural and commercial unity was, according to Pirenne, 'the most essential event of European history that had occurred since the Punic Wars. It was the end of the classic tradition. It was the beginning of the Middle Ages. . . . Without Mohammed, Charlemagne would have been inconceivable.'[1]

No other historical work of our century has provoked such an outburst of research, mostly in opposition. His critics have now destroyed Pirenne's thesis in the greatest detail.[2] Mediterranean commerce suffered a long and steady decline; the Islamic conquest did not close the Mediterranean to the meagre trade still existing between the Orient and the West; economic historians can draw no sharp line between Merovingian and Carolingian times as regards contacts with the East.

But this controversy has been misleading. Pirenne's explanations have been cut to bits, but what he was trying to explain has not yet been clarified by other means. The observable fact from which he started was a shift of the focus of Europe, in Carolingian times, from south to north, from the classic lands of the Mediterranean to the great plains drained by the Loire, the Seine, the Rhine, the Elbe, the Upper Danube, and the Thames. The lands of the olive and vine remained vigorous and creative, but who can doubt that, save for

[1] English tr., 164, 234.

[2] The most extensive recent discussion is R. Latouche, *Les Origines de l'économie occidentale (IVᵉ–XIᵉ siècle)* (Paris, 1956). For something briefer, see A. Riising, 'The fate of Henri Pirenne's thesis on the consequences of the Islamic expansion', *Classica et medievalia*, xiii (1952), 87–130.

brief periods, the core of European culture has been north of the Alps and the Loire from the ninth century to our own day? If Pirenne's answer has been refuted, his question remains.

A more durable solution of the historical problem of the change of the gravitational centre of Europe from south to north is to be found in the agricultural revolution of the early Middle Ages. By the early ninth century all the major interlocking elements of this revolution had been developed: the heavy plough, the open fields, the modern harness, the triennial rotation—everything except the nailed horse-shoe, which appears a hundred years later. To be sure, the transition to the three-field system made such an assault on existing peasant properties that its diffusion beyond the Frankish heartland was slow; but Charlemagne's renaming of the months indicates how large the new agricultural cycle loomed in his thinking. We may assume safely that its increased productivity was a major stimulus to the north even in his day.

The agricultural revolution of the early Middle Ages was limited to the northern plains where the heavy plough was appropriate to the rich soils, where the summer rains permitted a large spring plant-ing, and where the oats of the summer crop supported the horses to pull the heavy plough. It was on those plains that the distinctive features both of the late medieval and of the modern worlds developed. The increased returns from the labour of the northern peasant raised his standard of living and consequently his ability to buy manu-factured goods. It provided surplus food which, from the tenth century on, permitted rapid urbanization. In the new cities there arose a class of skilled artisans and merchants, the burghers who speedily got control of their communities and created a novel and characteristic way of life, democratic capitalism. And in this new environment germinated the dominant feature of the modern world: power technology.

CHAPTER III

The Medieval Exploration of Mechanical Power and Devices

THE later Middle Ages, that is roughly from A.D. 1000 to the close of the fifteenth century, is the period of decisive development in the history of the effort to use the forces of nature mechanically for human purposes. What had been, up to that time, an empirical groping, was converted with increasing rapidity into a conscious and widespread programme designed to harness and direct the energies observable around us. The labour-saving power technology which has been one of the distinctive characteristics of the Occident in modern times depends not only upon a medieval mutation in men's attitudes towards the exploitation of nature but also, to a great extent, upon specific medieval achievements. The famous passage towards the end of Descartes's *Discourse on Method* (1637)[1] in which he says that 'we can have useful knowledge by which, cognizant of the force and actions of fire, water, air, the stars, the heavens and all the other bodies which surround us—knowing them as distinctly as we know the various crafts of the artisans—we may be able to apply them in the same fashion to every use to which they are suited, and thus make ourselves masters and possessors of nature', was not a novel proposal. On the contrary, it stated a programme which had already dominated the ambitions of many generations of engineers[2] and which had long since produced notable results.

I

The Sources of Power

Inasmuch as the Hellenistic age invented not only the cam[3] but also gearing in its three basic forms—star, crown, and worm[4]—and was

[1] R. Descartes, *Œuvres*, ed. C. Adam and P. Tannery, vi (Paris, 1902), 61-62.
[2] See p. 160.
[3] B. Gille, 'La Came et sa découverte', *Techniques et civilisations*, iii (1954), 8-9; A. P. Usher, *History of Mechanical Inventions*, 2nd edn. (Cambridge, Mass., 1954), 140.
[4] F. M. Feldhaus, *Die geschichtliche Entwicklung des Zahnrades* (Berlin–Reinickendorf,

producing very elaborate geared mechanisms by the first century B.C.,[1] it is strange that its ingenious technicians did not make greater progress in developing sources of power. Hero of Alexandria's toy steam reaction turbine[2] and his rather doubtful little windmill[3] seem to have had no influence upon technology until the Renaissance.[4]

However, the turbulent decades during which Rome was extending her sway over the Levant were marked by a conquest far more enduring than the *pax Romana*: the beginnings of the mastery of water-power. A papyrus of the second century B.C. speaks of a *noria* or automatic irrigation wheel in Egypt,[5] while about 18 B.C. Strabo mentions a water-driven grain-mill in the palace which Mithradates, King of Pontus, had completed in 63 B.C.[6] A contemporary of Strabo, Antipater,[7] celebrates the water-mill as freeing the maidservants from drudgery. Doubtless the earliest water-wheels were horizontal, revolving on a vertical axle fixed in the millstone. However, Vitruvius, who is generally dated in the late first century before Christ, gives instructions for building a vertical undershot water-wheel which involves gearing to connect the wheel's horizontal axle with the vertical axle of the stones.[8] Since such gearing permits a much higher speed of rotation in the stones than in the wheel, the Vitruvian mill

1911), 5–11; C. Matschoss, *Geschichte des Zahnrades* (Berlin, 1940), 6–9; W. Treue, *Kulturgeschichte der Schraube* (Munich, 1955), 39–43, 57, 109.

[1] D. J. Price, 'Clockwork before the clock', *Horological Journal*, xcvii (1955), 32–34; in *History of Technology*, ed. C. Singer, iii (1957), 618, fig. 364; and 'An ancient Greek computer', *Scientific American*, cc (June, 1959), 60–67.

[2] *Pneumatikon*, ed. W. Schmidt (Leipzig, 1899), i. 230; cf. A. G. Drachmann, *Ktesibios, Philon and Heron: a study of ancient pneumatics* (Copenhagen, 1948), 128.

[3] Ibid. i. 205. For doubts that this is really a windmill, cf. R. J. Forbes in Singer, op. cit. ii (1956), 615, and Forbes, *Studies in Ancient Technology*, ii (Leiden, 1955), 111–12; H. P. Vowles, *The Quest for Power* (London, 1931), 123–4.

[4] M. Boas, 'Hero's *Pneumatica*: a study of its transmission and influence', *Isis*, xl (1949), 38–48.

[5] M. Rostovtzeff, *Social and Economic History of the Hellenistic World* (Oxford, 1941), 363; cf. Strabo, *Geographica*, xvii. 807, ed. A. Meinecke (Leipzig, 1899), iii. 1125. The only surviving ancient picture of such a noria comes from the middle second century of our era; cf. F. Mayence, 'La Troisième campagne de fouilles à Apamée', *Bulletin des Musées Royaux d'Art et d'Histoire*, v (1933), 6, fig. 5; Singer, op. cit. ii (1956), 637, fig. 577. It is probably to a noria rather than to a water-mill that Lucretius refers, *De rerum natura*, v. 516, ed. J. Martini (Leipzig, 1934), 205.

[6] Strabo, xii. 556, ed. cit. ii. 781. Rostovtzeff, op. cit. 365, points out that the papyri do not mention water-mills in Egypt during ancient times.

[7] *Anthologia palatina graeca*, ix. 418, ed. H. Stadtmueller (Leipzig, 1906), iii. 402–3.

[8] *De architectura*, x. 5, ed. V. Rose (Leipzig, 1899), 253–4. For the earliest picture of such a water-mill, from a fifth-century mosaic, see G. Brett, 'Byzantine watermill', *Antiquity*, xiii (1939), 354–6.

is the first great achievement in the design of continuously powered machinery.

Probably the original horizontal water-wheel was a barbarian invention. In scrupulously careful excavations of two dams in Jutland, one dating from the time of Christ and the other from a little later, the pattern of silt deposits was intelligible only in terms of vertical-axle mills.[1] Moreover, in A.D. 31 a similar horizontal water-wheel is found in China: it turned a vertical shaft carrying an upper wheel which, by means of an eccentric peg and a cord, worked the bellows of a furnace for smelting iron.[2] The almost simultaneous appearance of this first power machine in regions as widely separated as the Mediterranean, northern Denmark, and China argues diffusion from some still unknown centre, presumably north and east of the Roman Empire.

Indeed, even the so-called Vitruvian mill may be an import to the Mediterranean. Within a century of Vitruvius a water-driven trip-hammer mechanism for milling rice was known in China.[3] Trip-hammers can be operated by a vertical axle provided with helical fins, but the first machine certainly of such design appears in 1578 in France,[4] and no form of screw mechanism ever reached China before modern times.[5] We must therefore conclude that these Chinese trip-hammers were set in motion by cams fixed in the horizontal axle of a vertical water-wheel. The diffusion of so novel and complex a device as the vertical water-wheel from Rome to China in the two or three generations between Vitruvius and the *Hou Han-shu* is so improbable that we should look for some still mysterious middle point of radiation.

[1] See p. 160.

[2] H. Chatley, 'The development of mechanisms in ancient China', *Engineering*, cliii (1942), 175, gives the date *c*. A.D. 50; but Dr. Annaliese Bulling, in a letter to me, dates the source, *Hou Han-shu*, ch. 61, in A.D. 31; J. Needham, 'L'Unité de la science: l'apport indispensable de l'Asie', *Archives internationales d'histoire des sciences*, II. i (1949), 579, confirms this dating.

[3] J. Needham, L. Wang, and D. J. Price, *Heavenly Clockwork* (Cambridge, 1959), 104, 109-11, 129. In A.D. 290 a vertical undershot water-wheel operating trip-hammers for hulling rice so efficiently that it knocked the bottom out of the rice market, is found in China; cf. Chatley, loc. cit. In view of such evidence, it is puzzling that in the early ninth century Ennin seems to have regarded water-mills as uncommon; cf. E. A. Reischauer, *Ennin's Travels in China* (New York, 1955), 156.

[4] J. Besson, *Theatrum instrumentorum et machinarum* (Lyons, 1578), pl. 46; for a related device, cf. A. Ramelli, *Le Diverse et artificiose machine* (Paris, 1588), fig. 57.

[5] H. Chatley, 'Engynes: the eotechnic phase of mechanical development', *Engineering*, clxii (1946), 388; and his 'The development of mechanisms in ancient China', *Transactions of the Newcomen Society*, xxii (1941-2), 137.

Yet despite the water-mill's potential usefulness, and the fact that the more powerful overshot wheel was known in the Mediterranean possibly by the fourth[1] and certainly by the fifth century,[2] neither Rome nor China showed imagination in its application to industrial processes. The sole indication that the Romans may have used it for anything but grinding grain[3] is found in Ausonius's *Mosella*,[4] supposedly written about A.D. 369, which speaks of the strident noise of water-driven saws cutting marble on the banks of the Ruwar, a tributary to the Moselle. The fact that no other water-driven saw is known until Villard de Honnecourt's notebook[5] of *c.* 1235 would merely underscore the paucity of our sources for the early history of technology were it not for other puzzling circumstances surrounding the *Mosella*.

The only marketable stone in the region of the Ruwar is a blue roofing slate which breaks so easily that it need not and cannot be sawn.[6] The transportation of rough marble to so obscure a streamlet for sawing is inconceivable, since there was no scarcity of good mill sites in northern Gaul. Moreover, Pliny[7] tells us that (as in modern times) marble was sawn not with toothed saws but with a smooth saw and an abrasive. This means that a marble saw in Ausonius's time must have been horizontal. Yet a horizontal water-driven saw would involve mechanisms for the conversion of motion far more complex than those of the next comparable device, Villard's vertical wood-saw, nearly nine centuries later.

---

[1] C. L. Sagui, 'La Meunerie de Barbegal (France) et les roues hydrauliques chez les anciens et au moyen âge', *Isis*, xxxviii (1948), 225–31, goes far beyond the available evidence in claiming diversified industrial applications of water-power in Roman times.

[2] A. W. Parsons, 'A Roman water-mill in the Athenian Agora', *Hesperia*, v (1936), 70–90. The sole surviving ancient picture of an overshot water-wheel, from a cemetery near St. Agnes's in Rome, has apparently been neither published nor dated, cf. A. Profumo, in *Nuovo bulletino di archeologia cristiana*, xxiii (1907), 108.

[3] See p. 160.

[4] Ed. H. G. E. White (London, 1919), i. 252, ll. 362–4:
> Praecipiti torquens cerealia saxa rotatu
> Stridensque trahens per levia marmora serras
> Audit perpetuos ripa ex utraque tumultus.

[5] See p. 161.

[6] *Mosella*, ed. E. Böcking (Berlin, 1828), 60. Forbes, *Studies*, ii (1955), 104, states that the presence of these marble mills is confirmed by Venantius Fortunatus (d. *c.* A.D. 600). However, his source, *Carmina*, iii. 12, ll. 37–38 (*MGH, Auct. antiq.* iv. 65), mentions merely mills for grinding grain:
> Ducitur inriguis sinuosa canalibus unda,
> Ex qua fert populo hic mola rapta cibum.

[7] *Naturalis historia*, xxxvi. 6, ed. C. Mayhoff (Leipzig, 1897), v. 325.

In addition, the manuscript tradition of the *Mosella* is curious.[1] The poem never appears in the major collections of Ausonius's writings, and a 'validating' letter, supposedly from Symmachus, which is always appended to it, is not found in the regular collections of Ausonius's letters in which correspondence with Symmachus looms large. This letter does, indeed, appear in Symmachus's collection of his own correspondence. However, no manuscript of this section is older than the eleventh century, and the letter may be an insertion by a learned copyist who knew it from the *Mosella*. Ermenricus of St. Gall, *c*. A.D. 850, has left a letter in verse and an epigram which are supposed to appropriate and modify certain verses of the *Mosella*. But are we sure that Ermenricus was not the looted rather than the looter? The earliest manuscript containing the *Mosella* (Codex Sancti Galli 899) is credited to the tenth century and emerged from the scriptorium of his abbey. In other words, the *Mosella*, a poem notably and suspiciously above the level of Ausonius's certainly authentic works both in literary style and in sensibility towards nature, occurs only in late and marginal manuscripts of that author. Can it be the work of some early medieval humanist? We have only to remember the anonymous 'O, tu qui servas armis ista moenia' to recognize that in the later ninth and tenth centuries there were Latin poets of a very high order. Until the anomalies surrounding the *Mosella* are clarified, we must be cautious in accepting its water-driven saws as of the late fourth rather than of the tenth century.

And in fact in the very late tenth or eleventh century we begin to get evidence that water-power was being used for processes other than grinding grain. By 983 there may have been a fulling mill—the first useful application of the cam in the Occident—on the banks of the Serchio in Tuscany.[2] In 1008 a donation of properties to a monastery in Milan mentions not only mills for grinding grain, but, adjacent to them along the streams, *fullae* which were probably fulling mills.[3] In 1010 the place-name Schmidmülen in the

---

[1] *La Moselle d'Ausone*, ed. H. de la Ville de Mirmont (Paris, 1889), pp. ix, xi, xv.

[2] A. Uccelli, *Storia della tecnica dal medio evo ai nostri giorni* (Milan, 1945), 132. R. Meringer, 'Die Werkzeuge der *pinsere*-Reihe und ihre Namen (Keule, Stampfe, Hammer, Anke)', *Wörter und Sachen*, i (1909), 23–24, V. Geramb, 'Ein Beitrag zur Geschichte der Walkerei', ibid. xii (1929), 37–46, and A. Dopsch, *Die Wirtschaftsentwicklung der Karolingerzeit* (Weimar, 1913), ii. 145, strain the evidence in discovering fulling mills in the abbey of St. Gall in the ninth century.

[3] G. Giulini, *Memorie spettanti alla storia di Milano* (Milan, 1760), iii. 67.

Oberpfalz[1] indicates that water-driven trip-hammers were at work in the forges of Germany. About 1040 to 1050 at Grenoble there was a fulling mill, and c. 1085 one for treating hemp.[2] By 1080 the Abbey of Saint Wandrille near Rouen was receiving the tithes of a fulling mill,[3] and by 1086 two mills in England were paying rent with blooms of iron,[4] indicating that water-power was used at forges. Before the end of the eleventh century, iron mills were likewise found near Bayonne in Gascony.[5]

While to the modern mind, which accepts power technology as axiomatic, the millennium between the first appearance of the water-mill and its wider application seems incomprehensible, those thousand years were far from static as regards the diffusion of water-power. Even in the most crepuscular periods of the early Middle Ages—generations for which our sources are considerably less rich than for Roman times—recorded occurrences of water-mills are much more frequent and widespread than formerly.[6] In 1086 the *Domesday Book* lists 5,624 mills for some 3,000 English communities.[7] There is no reason to believe that England was technologically in advance of the continent. By the eleventh century the whole population of Europe was living so constantly in the presence of one major item of power technology that its implications were beginning to be recognized.

In the eleventh century the first sign of an interest in additional sources of power appears in the form of tidal mills. The tidal mill may seem a small step beyond the mill run by a flowing stream, but

[1] F. M. Ress, 'Der Eisenhandel der Oberpfalz in alter Zeit', *Deutsches Museum Abhandlungen und Berichte*, XIX. i (1951), 9.

[2] K. Lamprecht, *Beiträge zur Geschichte der französische Wirtschaftsleben im elften Jahrhundert* (Leipzig, 1878), 105, n. 28.

[3] R. V. Lennard, 'An early fulling-mill', *Economic History Review*, xvii (1947), 150.

[4] H. James, *Domesday Book Facsimile, Somersetshire* (Southampton, 1862), p. xii: 'ii molini reddentes ii plumbas ferri.' The other mills in the *Domesday Book* pay cash or eels, or both.

[5] 'Problème du moulin à eau', *Techniques et civilisations*, ii (1951), 34.

[6] M. Bloch, 'Avènement et conquêtes du moulin à eau', *Annales d'histoire économique et sociale*, vii (1935), 545; B. Gille, 'Le Moulin à eau: une révolution technique médiévale', *Techniques et civilisations*, iii (1954), 2-3.

[7] M. T. Hodgen, 'Domesday water mills', *Antiquity*, xiii (1939), 266. R. Lennard, *Rural England, 1086-1135* (Oxford, 1959), 278-80, offers reasons for considering this count too low. In the ninth century a mill with three wheels was operating at Old Windsor; cf. *Medieval Archaeology*, ii (1958), 184. By the late eleventh century large sums were sometimes spent on water-power. In 1097 the Emperor Henry IV ordered a difficult and costly flume, the remains of which exist, to be cut into the rock cliffs overhanging the river Klamm in the Tyrol to provide a waterfall for the mills of the Abbey of Viecht near Schwaz; cf. C. Reindl, 'Die Entwicklung der Wasserkraftnutzung und der Wasserkraftmaschinen', *Wasserkraft Jahrbuch*, i (1924), 4, fig. 2.

it is a sign that men who lived on marshy estuaries, or on small harbours where the streams were inadequate, were no longer content to accept their fate. In 1044 a tidal mill was operating in the lagoons at the head of the Adriatic.[1] Sometime between 1066 and 1086 such a mill was built at the entrance of the port of Dover.[2] Because of seasonal fluctuation in the height of tides, tidal mills are not satisfactory; nevertheless, they remained fairly common throughout the later Middle Ages.[3] Their invention is important chiefly as an omen of things to come, as the symptom of a new attitude which was to alter the whole pattern of human life.

Some people lived in flat areas where the rivers ran too sluggishly to turn a wheel forcefully, and where the building of a dam flooded too much good agricultural land. Could the streams of air be utilized? The exploratory quality of Western technology announces itself clearly in the twelfth century with the invention of the windmill rotating on an axle tipped slightly above the horizon to secure a turbine action in its vanes.

Since in the shamanistic areas fluttering flags are a form of prayer, it has sometimes been assumed that the Tibetan wind-driven prayer-cylinder, constructed like an anemometer and rotating on a vertical axis, is not only very early but also, perhaps, the inspiration of windmills in general.[4] But the origin of this device cannot yet be dated.[5] Indeed, it would seem that the initial idea of acquiring religious merit by the rotation of sacred writings is Chinese rather than Tibetan. Perhaps as early as the sixth century, but certainly by A.D. 823,[6] revolving book-cases, usually octagonal, were sometimes placed in Chinese Buddhist monasteries to store, and facilitate reference to, the *Tripitaka*. Since in 836 one is mentioned at Suchow with a braking device to stop its rotation,[7] the first intention cannot have

[1] G. Zanetti, *Delle origini di alcuni arti principali presso i Veneziani* (Venice, 1841), 65; cf. 66 for another tidal mill at Venice in 1078.

[2] *Domesday Book*, ed. A. Farley (London, 1783), i. 1.

[3] L. Delisle, 'On the origin of windmills in Normandy and England', *Journal of the British Archaeological Association*, vi (1851), 406; Gille, op. cit. 4–5; *Techniques et civilisations*, ii (1951), 34.

[4] H. T. Horwitz, 'Über das Aufkommen, die erste Entwicklung und die Verbreitung von Windrädern', *Beiträge zur Geschichte der Technik und Industrie*, xxii (1933), 99.

[5] The statement of Horwitz, loc. cit., and R. J. Forbes, *Studies in Ancient Technology*, ii (Leiden, 1955), 112, that *c.* A.D. 400 Fa-hsien observed it in Central Asia, rests on a mistranslation; cf. L. C. Goodrich, 'The revolving book-case in China', *Harvard Journal of Asiatic Studies*, vii (1942), 154; cf. *infra*, p. 116, n. 6.   [6] Ibid. 133.

[7] S. Lévi and E. Chavannes, 'Quelques titres énigmatiques dans la hiérarchie ecclésiastique du Bouddhisme indien', *Journal asiatique*, 11th series, vi (1915), 308.

been to gain spiritual reward simply by spinning it. However, in the early twelfth century a new fashion for mechanized piety swept China: Yeh Meng-tê (d. 1148) tells us that 'recently . . . in six or seven out of ten temples, one can hear the sound of the wheels of the revolving cases turning',[1] surely not as a result of scholarly activity. The fact that in modern Mongolia certain large prayer-cylinders are octagonal suggests that in Central Asia such devices, which contain mantras, were inspired by the Chinese revolving book-case.[2]

As has been said, the first application of wind-power to prayer-cylinders is entirely obscure. In Tibet windmills are used only thus, in the technology of prayer;[3] in China they are applied solely to pumping or to hauling canal boats over lock-slides, but not for grinding grain;[4] in Afghanistan they are engaged chiefly in milling flour.[5] This would argue a diffusion of the mechanically simpler Tibetan device in two directions, in each of which it found a different application. Windmills are not found in China before the later thirteenth century.[6] Vertical-axle windmills on a pattern related to those of Tibet and China, however, are definitely attested in southern Afghanistan in the early tenth century,[7] but there is no evidence that mills of this type ever spread to other parts of Islam.[8] As for Europe, the first vertical-axle windmill appears as a scheme in the unpublished notebook of Mariano Jacopo Taccola, datable 1438–50.[9]

---

[1] Goodrich, op. cit. 137; cf. 141–3.

[2] Ibid. 161, n. 59.

[3] Horwitz, op. cit. 99.

[4] G. Bathe, *Horizontal Windmills, Draft Mills and Similar Airflow Engines* (Philadelphia, 1948), 4. In Flanders, perhaps as early as the twelfth century, water-wheels were employed to pull boats over canal inclines; cf. D. H. Tew, 'Canal lifts and inclines', *Transactions of the Newcomen Society*, xxviii (1951–3), 36.

[5] Bathe, loc. cit.

[6] J. Needham, *Science and Civilisation in China*, i (Cambridge, 1954), 245. Chatley, op. cit. 176, believes that the rigging of junks has influenced the form of windmill sails in China.

[7] Al-Mas'ūdi, *Les Prairies d'or*, ed. and tr. C. Barbier de Meynard and P. de Courteille (Paris, 1863), ii. 80; al-Istakhrī, 'Das Buch der Länder', tr. A. D. Mordtmann, *Schriften der Akademie von Hamburg*, I. ii (1845), 110. At-Tabarī, *Selections from the Annals*, ed. M. J. de Goeje (Leiden, 1902), 1, and al-Mas'ūdi, iv (1865), 226–7, give variants of a story of A.D. 644 in which a Persian craftsman-slave was commanded by the Caliph Omar to make a mill operated by the wind. Quite apart from the problems raised by 300 years of oral transmission, this cannot be used to prove the existence of windmills in the seventh century. H. T. Horwitz, op. cit. 96, concludes that, on the contrary, it proves their non-existence: the command seemed so impossible of fulfilment that the desperate slave assassinated the Caliph.   [8] See p. 161.

[9] Munich State Library, Cod. lat. 197, fol. 87ʳ; A. Uccelli, *Storia della tecnica* (Milan,

The typical European windmill was an independent invention, perhaps inspired by the normal water-mill on the so-called Vitruvian pattern. A charter of St. Mary's at Swineshead in Lincolnshire which has been dated 1170, or at least before April 1179, mentions a windmill as though it had long existed there, but ambiguities suggest interpolation.[1] An apparently authentic charter which Léopold Delisle placed c. 1180[2] mentions a windmill in Normandy; but the document is undated and may well be a few years younger. The first certain windmill in the Occident is found in 1185 at Weedley in Yorkshire, where it was rented for 8 shillings a year.[3] Before Henry II's death in 1189, one of his constables gave a windmill near Buckingham to Oseney Abbey.[4] In 1191 or 1192 Jocelin of Brakelond mentions one as though it were no novelty.[5] At the same time, according to Ambroise's eyewitness account of the Third Crusade,

> The German soldiers used their skill
> To build the very first windmill
> That Syria had ever known,[6]

a passage which confirms the belief that the European windmill was not a diffusion from Islam. That within seven years of its appearance the windmill should have been seen from Yorkshire to the Levant is a fact fundamental to our understanding of the technological

---

1945), 10, fig. 28; cf. L. Thorndike, 'Marianus Jacobus Taccola', *Archives internationales d'histoire des sciences*, viii (1955), 7–26.   [1] See p. 162.

[2] Delisle, op. cit. 403. The assertion of S. Lilley, *Men, Machines and History* (London, 1948), 211, that the European windmill first appears in a charter of 1105, is unwarranted: over a century ago Delisle, loc. cit., showed that this charter must be a forgery, since it mentions an Abbot of Savigny seven years before the abbey was founded. The Statutes of the Republic of Arles, dating between 1162 and 1202 and mentioning 'molendina tam aure quam aque', naturally cannot be used to demonstrate the windmill in Provence before 1202; nevertheless, the phrase indicates that by that date it is taken for granted in that Mediterranean land; text in C. J. B. Giraud, *Essai sur l'histoire du droit français au moyen âge* (Paris, 1846), ii. 208.

[3] *Records of the Templars in England in the Twelfth Century: The Inquest of 1185*, ed. B. A. Lees (London, 1935), 131. Ibid. 135 notes an entry slightly later than 1185 of a windmill at Dunwich in Suffolk probably given to the Templars by Richard I, i.e. before 1199.

[4] *Cartulary of Oseney Abbey*, ed. H. E. Salter (Oxford, 1935), v. 209, no. 692.

[5] *The Chronicle of Jocelin of Brakelond*, ed. and tr. H. E. Butler (London, 1949), 59–60. *The Kalendar of Abbot Samson of Bury St. Edmunds and Related Documents*, ed. R. H. C. Davis (London, 1954), does not mention this windmill at Haberdon, but permits us to date with high probability in 1191 (127, n. 2) the lifetime lease of the manors of Semer and Groton which immediately precedes the windmill episode in Jocelin's chronicle.

[6] Ambroise, *L'Estoire de la guerre sainte*, ed. G. Paris (Paris, 1897), ll. 3227–9; tr. M. J. Hubert (New York, 1941).

dynamism of that era. Its complete integration with medieval mores occurred when Pope Celestine III (1191–8) ruled that windmills should pay tithes.[1]

During the next hundred years windmills became one of the most typical features of the landscape of the great plains of northern Europe where they offered obvious advantages in terms of the topography. Moreover in winter, unlike the water-mill, their operation could not be stopped by freezing. As a result, during the thirteenth century, for example, 120 windmills were built in the vicinity of Ypres alone.[2] Moreover, windmills could grind grain for a besieged castle. Krak des Chevaliers in Syria, the mightiest of medieval fortresses, finished about 1240, had a windmill on its walls.[3] Windmills spread more slowly in Mediterranean Europe than in the north, perhaps because the freezing problem was not so great, perhaps also because in general the streams are more rapid there than on the great plains. Nevertheless, by 1319 at latest the windmill was familiar enough in Italy to permit Dante to use it as a metaphor in describing Satan threshing his arms 'come un molin che il vento gira'.[4] In 1332 a windmill is mentioned at Venice,[5] a terrain where it would be most useful.

Particularly in southern Europe there continued to be technologically retarded pockets: Don Quixote's amazement at windmills was justified: apparently they were introduced into La Mancha only in Cervantes's time.[6] Nevertheless, despite our dearth of fundamental studies of the process, it is clear that by the early fourteenth century Europe had made extraordinary progress towards substituting water- and wind-power for human labour in the basic industries.[7] For

---

[1] P. Jaffé, *Regesta pontificum romanorum* (Leipzig, 1888), no. 17,620, to Archdeacon Bertrand of Dol in Brittany; *Corpus juris canonici*, ed. E. Friedberg (Leipzig, 1881), ii. 563: *Decretales Gregorii IX*, Lib. III, tit. 30, cap. 23.

[2] P. Boissonnade, *Life and Work in Medieval Europe* (London, 1927), 186; cf. also R. Bennett and J. Elton, *History of corn milling* (London, 1898), ii. 238.

[3] P. Deschamps, *Crac des chevaliers* (Paris, 1934), 269, and cf. 103.

[4] *Inferno*, xxxiv. 6.

[5] Zanetti, op. cit. 68. In 1341 windmills were known in Milan; cf. *infra*, p. 124, n. 5.

[6] M. de Cervantes Saavedra, *El ingenioso hidalgo Don Quijote de la Mancha*, ed. D. Clemencín (Madrid, 1894), i. 189, n. 1; J. Cejador y Frauca, *La lengua de Cervantes* (Madrid, 1906), ii. 745; cf. *infra*, p. 161.

[7] The best-documented general survey is B. Gille, 'Le Moulin à eau, une révolution technique médiévale', *Techniques et civilisations*, iii (1954), 1–15; cf. his summary 'Le Machinisme au moyen âge', *Archives internationales d'histoire des sciences*, vi (1953), 281–6. As an example of the study of one industry, cf. O. Johannsen, *Geschichte des Eisens*, 3rd edn. (Düsseldorf, 1953), 92–93, which, however, lacks documentation. Unfortunately, there are as yet few monographs like G. Sicard, *Les Moulins de Toulouse*

example, in England during the thirteenth century mechanical fulling of cloth, in place of the older method of fulling by hand or foot, was decisive in shifting the centre of textile manufacturing from the south-eastern to the north-western region where water-power was more easily available.[1] Nor was England especially advanced: the guild regulations of Speyer in 1298 show that fulling mills had completely displaced earlier techniques in that area as well.[2] Similarly, mills for tanning or laundering, mills for sawing, for crushing anything from olives to ore, mills for operating the bellows of blast furnaces, the hammers of the forge, or the grindstones to finish and polish weapons and armour, mills for reducing pigments for paint or pulp for paper or the mash for beer, were increasingly to be found all over Europe. This medieval industrial revolution based on water and wind would seem to have reached its final sophistication when, in 1534, the Italian Matteo dal Nassaro set up a mill on the Seine at Paris for the polishing of precious stones,[3] only to have it taken over in 1552 by the royal mint for the production of the first 'milled' coins.[4]

Our present concern is not to demonstrate this astonishing rise in productivity, but rather to examine the new exploratory attitude towards the forces of nature which enabled medieval Europe to discover and to try to harness other sources of power which have been culturally effective chiefly in modern times.

As Hero's aeolipyle and several other ancient devices show,[5] the expansive force of heated vapour had been noted in Hellenistic times, but for more than a thousand years little effort was made to use it. From sixth-century Byzantium comes the tale of how Anthemius of Tralles, who was not only architect of Hagia Sophia,

au moyen âge (Paris, 1953), exploiting not only the published but also archival material.

[1] E. M. Carus-Wilson, 'An industrial revolution of the thirteenth century', *Economic History Review*, xi (1941), 39–60; R. Lennard, 'Early English fulling mills: additional examples', ibid., 2nd series, iii (1951), 342–3.

[2] Edited by F. Mone in 'Zunftorganisation vom 13. bis 16. Jahrhundert', *Zeitschrift für die Geschichte des Oberrheins*, xv (1863), 280.

[3] E. Babelon, *Histoire de la gravure sur gemmes en France* (Paris, 1902), 132: 'un moulin porté par basteaulx pour pollir dyamans, aymerauds, agattes et aultres espèces de pierres.' In the fourteenth century better cutting methods for precious stones began to shift the focus of jewellery from gold and enamel to gems; cf. J. Evans, *History of Jewelry, 1100–1870* (New York, 1953), 71–72, 141–2; P. Grozinski, 'History of diamond polishing', *Transactions of the Newcomen Society*, xxviii (1951–3), 203.

[4] W. J. Hocking, 'Some notes on the early history of coinage by machinery', *Numismatic Chronicle*, 4th series, ix (1909), 68–69.

[5] A. Neuburger, *Die Technik des Altertums*, 2nd edn. (Leipzig, 1921), 232–4; H. Diels, *Antike Technik*, 2nd edn. (Leipzig, 1920), 57–61; *supra*, p. 80, n. 2.

mathematician, and author of a treatise on parabolic mirrors but also
a practical joker, terrified his bothersome neighbour Zeno with a
simulated earthquake produced by steam-pressure.[1] William of
Malmesbury's twelfth-century description[2] of the organ constructed
by Gerbert in the tenth century has been taken to mean that the
future Pope Sylvester II built a steam calliope, but the interpretation
is probably incorrect.[3]

Yet there was one very simple contrivance of Antiquity which
captured the imagination of learned men during the later Middle
Ages and led them to an increasing concern with the power of steam.
Vitruvius[4] describes 'aeolipilae aereae cavae; hae habent punctum
angustissimum, quo aqua infunduntur, collocanturque ad ignem, et
antequam calescant, non habent ullum spiritum; simul autem ut
fervere coeperint, efficiunt ad ignem vehementem flatum'. After
Roman times we have no further record of this steam-bellows until
the thirteenth century, when Albert the Great tells us[5] to 'take a
strong earthen vessel with two holes in it. Fill it with water, plug
the holes tightly and set it near a hot fire. Soon the steam will burst
the plugged holes and spray hot water over the surroundings. For
this reason such a vessel is called a *sufflator*, or blower, and it is
usually made in the form of a man.'

Albert's final words are significant: Vitruvius had thought of his
blower as illustrating the force of the winds, and by the thirteenth
century clearly the shape of the boiler is being assimilated to the
stereotype of the Aeolian heads from whose mouths the winds issue.[6]
In the early thirteenth century[7] popular imagination, feeding on such

---

[1] Agathias, *De imperio et rebus gestis Justiniani imperatoris*, v, ed. B. Vulcano in *Corpus historiae byzantinae*, iii (Venice, 1729), 105.

[2] *Gesta regum Anglorum*, ii. 168, ed. W. Stubbs (London, 1887), i. 196.

[3] W. Apel, 'Early history of the organ', *Speculum*, xxiii (1948), 193.

[4] *De architectura*, Lib. I, cap. 6, ed. V. Rose and H. Müller-Strübing (Leipzig, 1867), 24. In the next century Hero's *Pneumatikon*, ed. W. Schmidt, i. 312, describes a samovar for producing hot water to be mixed with wine in which a jet of steam serves as bellows; cf. Drachmann, *Ktesibios*, 131. No such device is visible in the earliest pictures (twelfth century) of samovars which I have found: Bibliotheca Vaticana, Cod. graecus 747, fol. 249ʳ, and nine specimens in Bibliothèque Nationale, MS. grec 74; photographs in Princeton Index of Christian Art.

[5] *Alberti Magni opera omnia* (Paris, 1890), iv. 634: *De meteoris*, Lib. IV, cap. 17, which also credits earthquakes to the force of subterranean steam.

[6] A similar device is used in Tibet, but Dr. Douglas Barrett of the British Museum's Department of Oriental Antiquities informs me that all such objects in that collection are in the shape of birds. In Europe we have no indication until G. B. Isaachi, *Inventioni* (Parma, 1579), 18–20, that *sufflatores* were made in the shapes of animals.

[7] L. Thorndike, *History of Magic and Experimental Science* (New York, 1929), i. 705.

devices, began to endow Gerbert with a magical golden head which whispered secrets to him. The same tale was eventually applied to Roger Bacon, Robert Grosseteste, Albert the Great, Guido Bonatti, and even to Virgil,[1] although now the head is usually of brass and must be heated in order to whisper.

Fortunately, several such blowers in the form of human heads survive from the thirteenth century onward.[2] They were so useful that they attracted the attention of military engineers. When they were placed close to a fire, the jet of steam from the mouth was directed into the fire, and since far more air than water-vapour was carried in the rush, they were particularly helpful with green wood or for camp-fires in wet weather. Konrad Kyeser pictures one in 1405;[3] in 1464 Filarete describes a pair of andirons equipped with blowers in human shape;[4] and between c. 1478 and c. 1495 Leonardo da Vinci sketches three such brazen-headed bellows.[5] The beginnings of a more abstract form are found in Cesariano's 1521 translation of Vitruvius,[6] in Lazarus Ercker's work of 1574 illustrating an alembic-like *sufflator* to blow the fire under a small furnace,[7] and, five years later, in Isaachi's spherical blower which, he says, 'will blow with so mighty a wind that it exceeds any big bellows'.[8] But the medieval

[1] Ibid. ii. 680, 825; J. W. Spargo, *Virgil the necromancer* (Cambridge, Mass., 1934), 132–3; J. C. Russell, 'Richard of Bardney's account of Robert Grosseteste's early and middle life', *Medievalia et humanistica*, ii (1944), 46, 48; A. C. Crombie, *Robert Grosseteste and the Origins of Experimental Science, 1100–1700* (Oxford, 1953), 187, n. 3; J. Voskuil, 'The speaking machine through the ages', *Transactions of the Newcomen Society*, xxvi (1947–9 [1953]), 259–61.

[2] F. M. Feldhaus, 'Ein Dampfapparat von vor tausend Jahren', *Prometheus*, xxv (1913–14), 69–73.

[3] F. M. Feldhaus, *Die Technik der Vorzeit* (Leipzig, 1914), 845, fig. 553.

[4] A. A. Filarete, *Trattato dell'architettura*, written in 1464, ed. and tr. by W. von Oettingen, *Traktat über die Baukunst* (Vienna, 1896), 309–10.

[5] *Codice atlantico*, fols. 80ᵉ b, 380ᵛ a, 400ᵛ a; for dates, cf. C. Pedretti, 'Saggio di una cronologia dei fogli del "Codice atlantico" ', in his *Studi vinciani* (Geneva, 1957), 268, 285, 286; L. Reti, 'Leonardo da Vinci nella storia della machina a vapore', *Rivista di ingegneria*, vii (1957), 778–9, figs. 10–12.

[6] *Di Lucio Vitruvio Pollione de architectura libri dece traducti de latino in vulgare* (Como, 1521), 23; Feldhaus, op. cit. 26, fig. 10.

[7] L. Ercker, *Allefürnemsten mineralischen Erzt unnd Berckwerksorten* (Prague, 1574), title-page and fol. 98ᵛ; cf. *Treatise on Ores and Assaying*, tr. A. G. Sisco and C. S. Smith (Chicago, 1951), frontispiece, 219, fig. 30; 326.

[8] *Supra*, p. 90, n. 6. For other such *sufflatores*, cf. H. Platte, *Jewell House of Art and Nature* (London, 1594), 25; J. Bate, *Mysteries of Art and Nature* (London, 1634), 23, 27–28, 158. D. Schwenter, *Deliciae Physico-mathematicae* (Nuremberg, 1636), i. 458, and J. French, *Art of Destillation* (London, 1653), 150, illustrate the difficulty of abstracting the 'philosophical bellows' from the medieval brazen head by depicting globular *sufflatores* equipped with human faces.

brazen head remained the normal form of boiler, and directly inspired the earliest steam-turbines.

In a note independent of his three sketches, Leonardo suggests
that such a blower be used to turn a spit on the hearth.[1] In 1629
Giovanni Branca[2] pictures the next steam-driven engine designed
for work. Its boiler is a *sufflator* in the shape of a human head from
the mouth of which issues a jet of steam turning a turbine operating
a stamp. It is clear from the text accompanying the plate that in his
time even so responsible an engineer as Branca—he was in charge
of the fabric of the favourite shrine of his age, the Santa Casa at
Loretto—thought of a steam-boiler as being naturally in human
shape: the machine 'è fatta per pestare le materie per far la polvere;
ma con un motore meraviglioso, che non è altro che una testa di
metallo con il suo busto empito d'acqua, posto sopra carboni accesi,
che non possa esalare in altro luoco che nella bocca'. Again, in 1641
Athanasius Kircher[3] shows a small windmill turned by jets of steam
issuing from two blowers in the shape of human heads, which are
clearly related in his mind to Aeolian heads.[4] Although Branca considered such 'enclosed air' to be on a par with water, wind, and
animals as a source of power,[5] this line of effort to harness steam
proved of little profit until much later when the steam-turbine was
achieved. Yet the Branca and Kircher pictures expose the medieval
roots of the seventeenth century's experiments.[6]

As we have seen from St. Albert's *De meteoris*, the explosive force
of steam had been observed in the Middle Ages. There is no sign,
however, of an effort to use it until Leonardo's sketch of a remarkable, if abortive, steam-cannon:[7] one-third of the length of the barrel
is encased in glowing coals; when it is white hot, water is introduced
from a reservoir, and its instantaneous conversion into steam fires
a ball. In 1521 Cesariano pictures grenades apparently exploded by
steam.[8]

---

[1] *Codice Leicester*, fol. 28ᵛ; cf. Reti, op. cit. 778; cf. J. Wilkins, *Mathematicall Magick*
(London, 1648), 149, for the same suggestion; also, 151–2 for aeolipiles to ring bells,
rock cradles, wind yarn, &c.

[2] *Le Machine* (Rome, 1629), fig. 25.

[3] *Magnes, sive de arte magnetica* (Rome, 1641), 616: 'Ego plurimas quoque machinas
huius ope circumago.'

[4] Ibid. 599, shows a pump operated by a horizontal wind-turbine, the wind being
symbolized by a puffing Aeolian head.

[5] Op. cit., in his note preceding fig. 41.   [6] See p. 162.

[7] MS. B, 33ʳ, ed. C. Ravaisson-Mollien (Paris, 1883); cf. Reti, op. cit. 779–83, fig. 14.

[8] *Supra*, p. 91, n. 6.

Related to the force of steam and to the confusion between steam and air, were experiments with hot air[1] and air under pressure. Noticing the upward blast of hot air in chimneys, by the late fifteenth century technicians were setting in the flues small turbines geared to turn a spit.[2] This was a particularly ingenious form of automation, since the hotter the fire, the faster the roast would twirl. In 1845 Father Huc saw nomadic Tibetans placing turbine-operated prayer-cylinders in the draught above the fire in their tents.[3] If, as seems likely, this device is considerably older, it may have been diffused to Europe, where certain Tibetan art motifs are detectable during the later Middle Ages.[4] Whatever their origin, the extent to which such apparatus intrigued engineers is indicated by Branca's design (1629) of a small rolling mill powered by the heat rising from a forge.[5] Such experiments failed to develop a major source of power, but they had a curious by-product: the screw-propeller for ships, and thus eventually the aeroplane propeller, seems to have been inspired by the form of the metal hot-air turbines in chimneys rather than by the wooden, and often spoon-bladed, water-turbines.

The study of air pressures in terms of the air-gun proved more important. Apparently in ancient times the blow-gun was used in India under the name *nālīka* (or 'reed') to shoot small arrows or iron pellets.[6] It is significant that in modern India the word has come to mean 'musket'.[7] However, if the *nālīka* is indigenous to India, it is curious that the blow-guns still used in south India with both darts and clay pellets bear names in Malayālam (*tūmbitān*) and Tamil (*sungutān*) which are clearly derived from the Malay *sumpitan*, and which seem, together with the blow-gun, to have been introduced from Malaya by Muslims.[8] The puzzle is intensified by a casual

[1] See p. 162.

[2] Leonardo, *Codice atlantico*, fol. 51ᵛ a, datable c. 1485; cf. Pedretti, op. cit. 267; Uccelli, op. cit. 13, figs. 37, 38.

[3] E. R. Huc, *Travels in Tartary*, tr. W. Hazlitt (New York, 1927), 195.

[4] Cf. J. Baltrušaitis, *Le Moyen Âge fantastique: antiquités et exotismes dans l'art gothique* (Paris, 1955), 247.

[5] Op. cit., fig. 2. Branca tried to step up the effective power by reducing the speed of rotation through a series of six gears.

[6] B. P. Sinha, 'Art of war in ancient India, 600 B.C.–300 A.D.', *Journal of World History*, iv (1957), 155; cf. *Mahābhārata*, tr. P. C. Ray (Calcutta, 1887), iii. 413.

[7] E. W. Hopkins, 'The social and military position of the ruling caste in ancient India', *Journal of the American Oriental Society*, xiii (1888), 279.

[8] J. Hornell, 'South Indian blow-guns, boomerangs, and crossbows', *Journal of the Royal Anthropological Society of Great Britain and Ireland*, liv (1924), 326, n. 1, 333. R. Heine-Geldern of the Anthropological Institute of the University of Vienna informs

reference, in Apollodoros of Damascus's book on siege machinery dedicated to Hadrian in the early second century, to the use of hollow reeds for hunting birds.[1] While the Byzantines used tubes with which to shoot Greek fire, these were syringes or proto-cannon rather than blow-pipes.[2] In the late twelfth century an Arabic treatise describes a lance from which a small projectile shoots, and calls it *madfa'*,[3] a term which came to mean 'firearm'. Not later than *c.* 1260, blow-guns shooting arrows are found in Persia under the name *nāwak* or 'tube'.[4] In Mameluke Egypt the blow-gun shot small pellets (*bunduq*) in bird hunting; its Arabic name *zabaṭāna* or *zabṭānīya*, later came to mean 'arquebus'.[5]

Despite enigmatic objects, which may be pea-shooters or popguns, in two thirteenth-century illuminations of the Mocking of Christ,[6] we lack evidence (after Appollodoros) of the blow-gun in Europe until a French manuscript of *c.* 1320 showing a grotesque figure aiming what seems to be a blow-gun at a rabbit.[7] In two manuscripts of *c.* 1475, one French, the other Flemish, there is no ambiguity: a blow-gun is being used to shoot a bird.[8] However, by 1425 its name,

---

me by letter that in his opinion all forms of the blow-gun were introduced to India from Malaya, and that Hornell, 335, is in error in believing the Kādar type to be indigenous.

[1] Lib. VII, 7, tr. E. Lacoste, 'La Poliorcétique de Appolodore de Damas', *Revue des études grecques*, iii (1890), 268. Since the passage deals with pipes for fire-fighting, these cannot be simply reeds covered with bird-lime.

[2] M. Mercier, *Le Feu grégeois* (Paris, 1952), 27.

[3] C. Cahen, 'Un traité d'armurerie composé pour Saladin', *Bulletin d'études orientales de l'Institut Française de Damas*, xii (1948), 136, 155, n. 3.

[4] Jalalu'd Dīn Rūmī, *Mathnawī*, Bk VI, l. 4578, tr. R. A. Nicholson (London, 1934), 511; cf. A. K. Coomaraswamy, 'The blowpipe in Persia and India', *American Anthropologist*, xlv (1943), 311; K. A. Creswell, *Bibliography of Arms and Armour in Islam* (Bristol, 1956), 51–52.

[5] D. Ayalon, *Gunpowder and Firearms in the Mamluk Kingdom* (London, 1956), 24, 59, 61, 118, n. 75. Ibid. 61, Ayalon believes that another word for 'arquebus' or handgun in general, *bunduqīya*, is derived from *bunduq*, 'bullet', rather than from *al-Bunduqīya* 'Venice'.

[6] H. T. Horwitz, 'Feuerlanze oder Spritze?', *Zeitschrift für historische Waffenkunde*, vii (1915–17), 344–5.

[7] B. A. L. Cranstone, 'The blowgun in Europe', *Man*, xlix (1949), 119, referring to British Museum, Add. MS. 36684, fol. 44.

[8] Ibid., fig. 1, from Bibliothèque de l'Arsenal, MS. 5064 (cf. also *Le Livre des saisons* [Geneva, 1942], plate unnumbered), and *Life*, xxii. iii (26 May 1947), 77, from the Morgan Library. Both manuscripts are of Petrus de Crescentiis, *Liber ruralium commodorum* (*c.* 1306), and an examination of the tradition of illuminations of the 132 extant manuscripts of the work (listed by L. Frati in the symposium *Pier de' Crescenzi: studi e documenti*, ed. T. Alfonsi, &c. [Bologna, 1933] 265–306) might throw light on the European blow-gun.

cerbottana, is found in Italy,[1] and by 1440 it was being applied in Catalonia to a long cannon of small bore.[2] The name is important because it shows the line of diffusion: it comes from the Arabic *zabaṭāna* which is in turn derived from the Malay *sumpitan*.[3]

European inventors of the sixteenth century are credited with various air-guns, but on doubtful evidence.[4] In 1607, however, Bartolomeo Crescentio described an air-gun equipped with a powerful spiral spring,[5] a device so complex that it must have had predecessors. In 1644 Mersenne spoke in detail of 'sclopeti pneumatici constructio',[6] and four years later Wilkins wrote enthusiastically of 'that late ingenious invention the wind-gun' as being 'almost equall to our powder-guns'.[7] In the 1650's Otto von Guericke, famed for his experiments with vacua and pressures, built the *Madeburger Windbüchse*, one of the technical wonders of its time.[8] In 1686 Denis Papin, whose work on the steam engine was of prime importance, described an air-gun in the *Philosophical Transactions*.[9] Thus a chain of technological stimuli may be traced back from some of the major figures of early modern science and technology through the later Middle Ages to the jungles of Malaya.[10]

[1] C. Battiste and G. Alessio, *Dizionario etimologico italiano* (Florence, 1951), ii. 863.

[2] *Enciclopedia universal illustrada*, xii. 1192, s.v. 'cerbatana'.

[3] Hornell, op. cit. 334; K. Kokotsch, *Etymologisches Wörterbuch der europäischen Wörter orientalischen Ursprungs* (Heidelberg, 1927), no. 2201.

[4] F. M. Feldhaus, 'Zur Geschichte der Windbüchse', *Zeitschrift für historische Waffenkunde*, iii (1902–5), 271–2. For the later history of the air-gun, see Feldhaus, 'Das Luftgewehr als Kriegswaffe', ibid. iii (1902–5), 368, and cf. 334; iv (1906–8), 153.

[5] *Nautica mediterranea* (Rome, 1607), 521.

[6] M. Mersenne, *Cogitata physico-mathematica* (Paris, 1644), 149–53.

[7] J. Wilkins, *Mathematicall Magick* (London, 1648), 153.

[8] O. von Guericke, *Neue 'Magdeburgische' Versuche über den leeren Raum (1672)*, tr. F. Dannemann (Leipzig, 1894), 82–84, with fig.

[9] D. Papin, 'An account of an experiment, shown before the Royal Society, of shooting, by the rarefication of air', *Philosophical Transactions*, xvi (1686), no. 179, pp. 21–22, tab. 1, fig. 5.

[10] A second, and related, Malay invention, the fire piston, may have had significant influence upon the European understanding of air pressure and its applications. H. Balfour, 'The fire piston', in *Anthropological Essays presented to E. B. Tylor* (Oxford, 1907), 17–49, reprinted in the *Annual Report of the Smithsonian Institution* (1907), 565–93, presents a map of its distribution in south-east Asia which proves that it cannot have been introduced from Europe. On the other hand, so many Europeans had been trading, fighting, and ruling in the Indies for so long that although no instances have been cited, they must have observed the fire-piston in that area before it appears in Europe in the late eighteenth century. The most notable technological application of adiabatic heat has been the Diesel engine.

The development of rockets[1] is still another aspect of the late medieval interest in the force of expanding vapours and gases. Burning substances and noxious smokes had long been employed in warfare, and they continued in use throughout the Middle Ages.[2] When, shortly before 673, the Syrian refugee architect Kallinikos invented Greek fire,[3] he started the military technicians not merely of Byzantium but also of Islam, China, and the West on the trail of ever more combustible mixtures. Some were highly inflammable liquids; others were powders. Among the latter a combination of carbon, sulphur, and saltpetre increasingly came into favour, that is, gunpowder. It suffered, however, from two defects: first, the methods of purifying saltpetre[4] were deficient; second, the powder contained no airspaces to permit a combustion so rapid as to become an explosion. Experiments with such mixtures, and improved methods of producing saltpetre, however, reached a point during the thirteenth century throughout Eurasia at which the conversion of the powder into gas occurred at a rate which made the invention of fireworks inevitable. The 'flying fire spears' used in 1232 in the siege of Loyang and K'ai-feng-fu must have been no more than Roman candles, since they shot flame only some ten paces.[5] In 1258 what were probably true rockets are mentioned at Cologne,[6] while c. 1260 Roger

[1] The later development of rocketry seems in no way to have been influenced by classical knowledge of the principle of reaction, such as (perhaps) Archytas's mechanical flying bird or Hero's aeolipyle; cf. P. Tasch, 'Conservation of momentum in antiquity: a note on the prehistory of the principle of jet-propulsion', *Isis*, xliii (1952), 251–2; E. C. Watson, 'Heron's "ball on a jet" experiment', *American Journal of Physics*, xxii (1954), 175–6; *supra*, p. 80, n. 4.

[2] Cf. G. Guy, 'Le Pape Alexandre VI a-t-il employé les armes chimiques?', *Mémoires et documents publiés par la Société de l'École des Chartes*, XII. ii (1955), 321–34, for a letter, probably of 1495 or 1496, from the commander of the French forces in the castle of Ostia, accusing Alexander VI of using 'feu ardant et fumee empoisonnant, qui sont chouses donnans mors plus honteusez et abhominablez que glaive'.

[3] C. Zenghelis, 'Le Feu grégeois et les armes à feu des Byzantins', *Byzantion*, vii (1932), 265–86; M. Mercier, *Le Feu grégeois: les feux de guerre depuis l'antiquité; la poudre à canon* (Paris, 1952), 14. In A.D. 399 Claudian, *De Flavii Malii Theodori consulatu*, ll. 325–30, ed. M. Platnauer (London, 1922), i. 362, mentions theatrical fireworks in the form of flares; similar pyrotechnics are found in Chinese poems of A.D. 605–16; cf. Wang Ling, 'On the invention and use of gunpowder and firearms in China', *Isis*, xxxvii (1947), 164. By A.D. 919 Arabian naphtha, probably mixed with quicklime to help its combustion, was used by the Chinese armies (ibid. 167), and by A.D. 1004 this was being shot from a metal syringe or tube much like that used earlier by the Byzantines; ibid., fig. 2; *infra*, p. 98, n. 5.

[4] E. Rust, 'Aus der Geschichte des Saltpeters', *Technik für Alle*, vii (1916–17), 151–4; for the developments of the later period, cf. F. Baillot, 'Pyrotechnie militaire au 16e siècle', *Science et la vie*, xi (1916–17), 349–58.   [5] See p. 163.

[6] A. Hausenstein, 'Zur Entwicklungsgeschichte der Rakete', *Zeitschrift für das*

Bacon knew them.[1] As regards rockets, however, Islam seems to have been dependent on the Far East rather than upon the West: by 1248 saltpetre was known as 'Chinese snow' in Egypt,[2] and about 1280–95 the Syrian al-Ḥasan al-Rammāh, who even proposes a rocket-propelled torpedo, calls rockets 'Chinese arrows'.[3] Yet there is no evidence of Chinese stimulus to, or precedence over, the European developments. Indeed, one of the earliest Muslim formulae for gunpowder indicates a Frankish source.[4] Although the Chinese are reputed to have perfected festival fireworks of extraordinary quality the elaborate pyrotechnics described in 1540 by Vannoccio Biringuccio[5] show no signs of Chinese inspiration.[6] The confused history of the emergence of explosives and fire-arms is intelligible as a complex of parallel regional experiments resting essentially on the various forms of Greek fire, with occasional interchange of improved techniques as chemical methods became perfected.[7]

gesamte Schiess- und Sprengstoffwesen, xxxiv (1939), 172; W. Ley, 'Rockets in battle', *Technology Review*, xlix (1946), 96. Mercier, op. cit. 26–27, holds that by the late ninth century the Byzantines were using rockets containing Greek fire and propelled by it.

[1] The earliest European reference to an explosive powder containing saltpetre is that of Roger Bacon, *De secretis operibus*, cap. 6, in *Opera inedita*, ed. J. S. Brewer (London, 1859), 536, which speaks of fire-crackers and what appear to be rockets; on the date, cf. *infra*, p. 133, n. 4; cf. also S. J. von Romocki, *Geschichte der Explosivstoffe* (Berlin, 1895), i. 103; Hausenstein, op. cit. 139; R. Sterzel, 'Die Vorläufer des Schießpulvers', in *Beiträge zur Geschichte der Handfeuerwaffen: Festschrift Moritz Thierbach* (Dresden, 1905), 20.

[2] G. Sarton, *Introduction to the History of Science*, ii (Baltimore, 1931), 1036, denies that this *bārūd* was necessarily saltpetre, but overlooks the evidence of al-Ḥasan al-Rammāh. [3] Romocki, op. cit. i. 70–71, fig. 14.

[4] M. Berthelot, *La Chimie au moyen âge* (Paris, 1893), ii. 198.

[5] *La Pirotechnia* (Venice, 1540), 166; tr. C. S. Smith and M. T. Gnudi (New York, 1942), 442–3. For later Western developments, cf. Hanzelet Lorrain (Jean Appier), *La Pirotechnie* (Pont à Mousson, 1630), 224–5, 234–9; F. Malthus, *Traité des feux artificiels pour la guerre et pour la récréation* (Paris, 1629), 57–125. The great elaboration of fireworks in the Baroque Age is indicated by a four-page printed pamphlet bound in Vatican Library Vat. lat. 7495, *Explication du feu d'artifice dressé devant l'Hostel de Ville par les ordres de Messieurs les Prevost des Marchands et Echevins de la Ville de Paris au sujet de la paix concluë entre la France et la Savoye* (Paris, 1696), explaining the Latin and Greek inscriptions on the set pieces.

[6] I find no evidence of Chinese influence on Western fireworks earlier than G. B. della Porta, *Magia Naturalis* (Naples, 1589), Bk. 20, ch. x, facsimile of English tr. (London, 1658), ed. D. J. Price (New York, 1957), 409, who describes a kite with fire-crackers on the tail; cf. also J. Bate, *Mysteries of Art and Nature* (London, 1634), 80–82. Kites had been known in China since Han times at least; cf. Wang Ch'ung, *Lun-hêng*, tr. A. Forke (Berlin, 1907), i. 499. According to A. S. Brock, *History of Fireworks* (London, 1949), 25, festival fireworks were introduced to Japan not by the Chinese but *c.* 1600 by the Dutch.

[7] Cf. especially O. Guttmann, *The Manufacture of Explosives* (London, 1895), i. 2–11. Such efforts as H. J. Rieckenberg, 'Bertold, der Erfinder des Schießpulvers: eine

Despite al-Ḥasan al-Rammāh's suggestion, jet propulsion for anything save fire-arrows was not developed until the fifteenth century when Italian engineers started to speculate about its possibilities. About 1420 or a bit later, Giovanni da Fontana sketched a naval ram and a military tank pushed respectively by two and three rockets. He designed, likewise, a swimming fish, a flying bird, and a running rabbit, all jet-propelled.[1] These are models for his *Tractatus de pisce, ave et lepore* in which he proposes a plan for measuring surfaces, depths of water, and altitudes in the air by means of jet-propelled rabbits, fish, and birds.[2] That Fontana was seriously pondering the problems implicit in such devices is indicated by his supplying the tank not with wheels but with rollers, and providing the ram with a stabilizing tail. Moreover, by a series of experiments he measured the amount of explosive needed to shoot rockets to different heights.[3] At the end of the century (1495–1501) Francesco di Giorgio designed jet-operated petards both on wheels for attacking fortifications and on floats for sinking ships.[4] The practicability of such engines is of less interest than the mentality which they display—the determination to exploit a new source of energy.

Indeed, a culture becoming so power-conscious as the later Middle Ages could not fail to explore to the utmost the strength of the fiery dragons which had made possible the rocket. While gunpowder and rockets were apparently an international development, guns are Occidental in origin, springing from the Byzantine technique of shooting Greek fire from copper tubes.[5] That such tubes were used

Studie zu seiner Lebensgeschichte', *Archiv für Kulturgeschichte*, xxxvi (1954), 316–32, entirely misconstrue the problem. Moreover, the legend of Berthold Schwarz was destroyed by F. M. Feldhaus, 'Berthold der Schwarze, anno 1380', *Zeitschrift für das gesamte Schiess- und Sprengstoffwesen*, i (1906), 413–15; iii (1908), 118; and 'Was wissen wir von Berthold Schwarz?', *Zeitschrift für historische Waffenkunde*, iv (1906–8), 65–69, 113–18, 286.

[1] Munich, State Library, Codex icon. 242, fols. 16ᵛ, 37ʳ, 40ʳ; Romocki, op. cit. i. 231–40, figs. 47–49, dates it *c.* 1420; A. Birkenmajer, 'Zur Lebensgeschichte und wissenschaftlichen Tätigkeit von Giovanni Fontana (1395?–1455?)', *Isis*, xvii (1932), 34–53, attempts to date it slightly later. Cf. also M. Jähns, *Geschichte der Kriegswissenschaften* (Munich, 1889), i. 276, and, on Fontana's jets, F. M. Feldhaus, *Modernste Kriegswaffen, alter Erfindungen* (Leipzig, 1915), 81–82; L. Thorndike, *History of Magic and Experimental Science*, iv (New York, 1934), 156, dates it 1410–49.

[2] L. Thorndike, op. cit. iv (1934), 156, 172–3, 665–6.   [3] Ibid. 174.

[4] M. Salmi, *Disegni di Francesco di Giorgio nella Collezione Chigi Saracini* (Siena, 1947), figs. 13, 14, and p. 43 for dates.

[5] In the late ninth century, *Leonis imperatoris Tactica*, v. 3, ed. R. Vári (Budapest, 1917), i. 92, mentions flame-throwing tubes even as equipment for horsemen. For an extraordinary eleventh-century picture of a 'hand-gun' for shooting Greek fire, cf.

in the West even after the invention of gunpowder is indicated by the distinction between *bastons à feu* and *bastons à pouldre*, the latter using the more explosive *fewe volant* rather than *fewe gregois*.[1] It was the Westerners who began to shoot balls of stone and iron from such tubes in place of fire,[2] although the first pictures of a cannon (1327) show it shooting a huge arrow rather than a ball.[3]

This innovation of cannon balls caused technical difficulties: the metallurgy of the age was not equal to its chemistry. One of the earliest extant exact recipes for gunpowder, that of the end of the thirteenth century given by Marcus Graecus,[4] describes a mixture of great ballistic power. Later the proportion of saltpetre was reduced, presumably to prevent the shooting tubes from bursting so often.[5] Not only the miniature of 1327 but our next secure reference to a gun, a 'pot de fer à traire garros de feu' at Rouen in 1338,[6] shows how long it took for the cannon ball to develop. However, iron shot appear at Lucca in 1341; in 1346 in England there were two calibres of guns firing lead-shot; and balls appear at Toulouse in 1347.[7] Thereafter the evidence of guns of very large calibre, as well as of rudimentary hand-guns, becomes common.

The earliest indication of cannon in China is extant examples clearly dated 1356, 1357, and 1377.[8] It is not necessary to assume the miracle of an almost contemporary Asian development. Enough

Diels, *Antike Technik*, pl. VIII. Wang Ling, op. cit. 172, adduces two passages from A.D. 1274 and 1281 to prove the use of cannon with metal barrels by the Chinese. The former, however, may be interpreted as a trebuchet firing gunpowder grenades; the latter, as a metal tube for shooting Greek fire.

[1] R. C. Clephan, 'A sketch of the history and evolution of the hand gun up to the close of the fifteenth century', *Beiträge zur Geschichte der Handfeuerwaffen: Festschrift M. Thierbach* (Dresden, 1905), 34. In 1380 the city of Saint-Flour made bombs of Greek fire to be thrown by trebuchets against the English, and added to these bombs containers of gunpowder to explode and spread the incendiary; cf. M. Boudet, 'Note sur la fabrication du feu grégois en Auvergne au XIVe siècle', *Bulletin historique et scientifique de l'Auvergne* (1906), 288.

[2] Zenghelis, op. cit. 285. This may have been suggested by the blow-gun if the first medieval sarbacands shot pellets rather than darts; cf. *supra*, p. 94. Another development paving the way for the cannon-ball was the exact calibration, according to an engineer's specifications, of stones for trebuchets, in England as early as 1244; cf. J. Harvey, *English Mediaeval Architects* (London, 1954), 111.

[3] See p. 163.

[4] Ed. and tr. Berthelot, op. cit. 119, §§ 32-33, which also speaks of rockets and fire-crackers.   [5] R. C. Clephan, op. cit. 35.   [6] See p. 163.

[7] Rathgen, op. cit. 42, 30.

[8] L. C. Goodrich, 'Note on a few early Chinese bombards', *Isis*, xxxv (1944), 211, figs. 1 and 2; ibid. xxxvi (1946), 122, n. 27; 120, 251; Wang Ling, op. cit. 175; *supra*, p. 98, n. 5.

Europeans were wandering the Yüan realm[1] to have carried the new technology eastward. Strangely, there is no evidence of cannon in India until the sixteenth century, when they were introduced by the Portuguese and, in the north-western region, by the Muslims.[2]

The problem of the spread of fire-arms in Islam is complicated by the fact that in Arabic *naft* means either 'Greek fire' or 'gunpowder'.[3] The earliest certain use of gunpowder artillery by Saracens comes from Cairo in 1366 and Alexandria in 1376; by 1389 it is common in both Egypt and Syria.[4] Thus there was, roughly, a forty-year lag in Islam behind Europe.

The cannon is not only important in itself as a power-machine applied to warfare: it is a one-cylinder internal combustion engine, and all of our more modern motors of this type are descended from it. The first effort to substitute a piston for a cannon ball, that of Leonardo da Vinci,[5] used powder for fuel, as did Samuel Moreland's patent of 1661,[6] Huygens's experimental piston-engine of 1673,[7] and a Parisian air-pump of 1674.[8] Indeed, the conscious derivation of such devices from the cannon continued to handicap their development until the nineteenth century, when liquid fuels were substituted for powdered.

The chief difficulty of the gun-masters of the later Middle Ages was that their gunpowder was a loose mixture of carbon, sulphur, and saltpetre: any shaking during transport sent the heavier saltpetre to the bottom and the light carbon to the top. Likewise, the lack of sufficient air-spaces between the particles retarded the explosion. Slow and relatively inefficient combustion forced gunners to pack the powder into the gun with a wooden block, and then to pack the

[1] For a list of Occidentals known to have been in China and India, 1261–1349, cf. R. Gallo, 'Marco Polo, la sua famiglia e il suo libro', in *Nel VII centenario della nascità di Marco Polo* (Venice, 1955), 147–9; cf. also R. S. Lopez, 'Nuove luci sugli italiani in Estremo Oriente prima di Colombo', *Studi Colombiani: pubblicazioni del Civico Istituto Colombiano*, Genova, iii (1952), 337–98.

[2] B. Rathgen, 'Die Pulverwaffe in Indien: die europäische Herkunft derselben', *Ostasiatische Zeitschrift*, xii (1925), 11–30; H. Goetz, 'Das Aufkommen der Feuerwaffen in Indien', ibid. 226–9; *infra*, p. 164.

[3] Ayalon, op. cit., p. xv; cf. 10–24.   [4] See p. 164.

[5] L. Reti, 'Leonardo da Vinci nella storia della macchina a vapore', *Rivista di ingegneria*, vii (1957), 778, fig. 20.

[6] R. Jenkins, *Collected Papers* (Cambridge, 1936), 44.

[7] A. K. Bruce, 'On the origin of the internal combustion engine', *Engineer*, clxxiv (1942), 383, incorrectly dates this 1680; cf. C. Huygens, *Œuvres complètes*, vii (The Hague, 1897), 356–8; xxii (1950), 241.

[8] Jenkins, loc. cit. For developments from 1678 onward, cf. Y. Le Gallec, 'Les Origines du moteur à combustion interne', *Techniques et civilisations*, ii (1951), 28–33.

shot with rags or clay to contain the gas until enough had been generated to reach shooting pressure.[1] This exasperating problem was largely solved in the 1420's by the invention of corned gunpowder.[2] By holding the three components in even relationship throughout the mass of the powder, and by providing an equal distribution of larger air-spaces, corned powder made the explosion uniform and practically instantaneous. The cannon became an efficient engine of war, and the fact that packing could be less elaborate raised the hand-gun from the level of a psychological weapon to that of an instrument of slaughter.[3]

The force of flowing water and of wind, the energy of expanding gases and vapours: these captured the imagination of the technicians of the later Middle Ages and in turn were partly taken captive by their skill. But as all Aristotelians well knew, every tangible object naturally tends towards the centre of our globe with the same homing instinct which makes water flow downhill. Was it conceivable that this power too might be made to run machines?

The very violence of gravity was the chief obstacle to its use. To be sure, the automata which graced the shrines and courts of the Hellenistic age, Old Iran, Byzantium, and Islam[4] had normally been operated by the weight of water which flowed into a vessel until it was sufficiently heavy to sink and trip a lever; and in conjunction with such devices, metal weights were used as counterbalances and to maintain the tension on ropes wound around axles. But the lack of any escapement mechanism other than water or mercury to control the flow of power through an engine had discouraged more extensive use of the force of gravitational attraction.

Graeco-Roman Antiquity had developed an artillery based on torsion, that is, the twisting of fibres, usually hair.[5] While this was

[1] P. Reimer, 'Das Pulver und die ballistischen Anschauungen im 14. und 15. Jahrhundert', *Zeitschrift für historische Waffenkunde*, i (1897–9), 164–6.

[2] A. von Essenwein, *Quellen zur Geschichte der Feuerwaffen* (Leipzig, 1872), 25, states that Munich State Library, Cod. germ. 4902, Konrad Kauder's *Feuerwerkbuch*, written in 1429, mentions corned powder.   [3] See p. 164.

[4] A. Chapuis and E. Gélis, *Le Monde des automates: étude historique et technique* (Paris, 1928), 31–47; A. Chapuis, *Les Automates* (Neuchâtel, 1949), 35–45; E. Herzfeld, 'Der Thron des Khosrô', *Jahrbuch der preußische Kunstsammlungen*, xli (1920), 1–24, 103–47; G. von Grunebaum, *Medieval Islam*, 2nd edn. (Chicago, 1954), 29, n. 68; 30, n. 69; V. Raghavan, *Yantras or Mechanical Contrivances in Ancient India* (Bangalore, 1952), 12–30; G. Brett, 'The automata in the Byzantine "Throne of Solomon"', *Speculum*, xxix (1954), 477–87; J. W. Perkins, 'Nero's Golden House', *Antiquity*, xxx (1956), 209–19.

[5] The attempt of E. Sander, 'Der Verfall der römischen Belagerungskunst',

fairly satisfactory for summer campaigns in the dry climate of the Mediterranean, it was of little use in the rains of northern Europe where the wet fibres too easily lost their elastic qualities.

Europe owes to China the initial inspiration for a new kind of artillery. Under the name *huo-p'ao* it first appears in A.D. 1004.[1] It consisted of a large sling-beam pivoted on a frame and actuated by men pulling in unison on ropes attached to the end of the beam away from the sling. It makes its European debut in a Mozarabic manuscript of the early twelfth century,[2] and appears again in 1147 during the northern Crusaders' assault on Lisbon.[3]

The development of this machine was rapid and international. An Arabic treatise written in Syria between 1187 and 1192 not only speaks of Arab, Turkish, and Frankish forms of it, but also describes and illustrates a much more complex version powered by a swinging counterweight which is credited to Persia.[4] In Europe it was known by 1199[5] under the name *trebuchet*.[6] It is strange that this remarkable substitution of gravity for manpower should be ascribed by a Syrian to Iran, since from *c.* 1220 onward oriental sources frequently call such engines *magribī*, i.e. 'Western' and probably 'Frankish'.[7] Moreover, while trebuchets spread with great rapidity in Europe and quickly displaced the older torsion machines,[8] the new and more powerful artillery appears to have become dominant in the Mameluke army only in the second half of the thirteenth century.[9] In 1276 a German artisan and a Nestorian Christian, at the instance of the

---

Historische Zeitschrift, cxlix (1934), 457–76, to show that from the fourth century the art of siege-craft fell into decay, is refuted as regards both Byzantium and the West by F. Lammert, 'Die antike Poliorketik und ihr Weiterwirken', *Klio*, xxxi (1938), 389–411.

[1] See p. 165.

[2] Turin National Library, MS. lat. 93, fol. 181ʳ; G. G. King, 'Divigations on the Beatus', *Art Bulletin*, viii (1930), 57, fig. 3.   [3] See p. 165.

[4] C. Cahen, op. cit. 141–2, fig. 14.

[5] Johannes Codagnellus, *Annales placentini*, ed. A. Holder-Egger (Hannover, 1901), 25, writing before 1235, mentions a trebuchet at Cremona in 1199.

[6] Although the word is apparently derived from the term for 'ducking-stool', I have not found the latter earlier than 1205–6, in an agreement reached 'de libertatibus 1rancorum plegiorum et furcarum et Trebucheti' at Warlington in Suffolk; cf. *The Kalendar of Abbot Samson of Bury St. Edmunds*, ed. R. H. C. Davis (London, 1954), 135–6. P. Bonenfant, 'Le "Marais" Saint Jean où l' "on noyait les adultères" ', *Société Royale d'Archéologie de Bruxelles, Annales*, xlvi (1942–3), 247, offers continental material on the ducking-stool to supplement J. W. Spargo, *Judicial Folklore in England Illustrated by the Ducking Stool* (Durham, N.C., 1944), 87.

[7] *Infra*, p. 164.

[8] Huuri, op. cit. 64, n. 1; however, torsion artillery is still illustrated in 1327 in Walter de Milimete, op. cit., pl. 156.

[9] Ayalon, op. cit. 33, n. 29.

Polos, introduced counterweight artillery to China, and delighted the Great Khan by forcing a city's surrender by means of it.[1]

Whether its origin was Near Eastern or European, the trebuchet is significant as the first important mechanical utilization of the force of weights. The lack of an escapement here was no obstacle: violence is appropriate to war. Modern experiments have shown that while a trebuchet with a 50-foot arm and a 10-ton counterweight can throw a 200–300-pound stone about 300 yards, the best that a Roman-style catapult can do is to fling a 40–60-pound stone in a flatter trajectory for about 450 yards.[2] Since for siege purposes distance was less important than projectile weight, the trebuchet marked a vast improvement in artillery.[3]

With so spectacular a use of the force of gravity before their eyes, technicians of the thirteenth century went on to attempt to harness it to meet one of their most pressing problems: the invention of an adequate clock. The water clocks invented in Antiquity were difficult to manage in the north, where they froze in winter. Sand clocks,[4] developed in an effort to get away from this defect, proved a nuisance save for measuring brief periods, since the sand slowly enlarged the opening through which it flowed, and did not lie level in the lower container. A weight-driven, mechanical time-keeper seemed to be the best solution; so the contemporaries of St. Thomas Aquinas very deliberately determined to make one.

The task was not easy. As one contemplates the superb results, one realizes that the Middle Ages mark an epoch not only in the exploration of the sources of power but also in the invention of means by which power may be guided and controlled. Before we consider the mechanical clock we must examine some of these; for they help to explain the new technological atmosphere of the later thirteenth century which made the clock possible.

II

The Development of Machine Design

Next to the wheel, the crank[5] is the most important single mechanical device, since it is the chief means of transforming continuous rotary

---

[1] See p. 165.

[2] R. Payne-Gallwey, *Projectile-throwing Engines of the Ancients* (London, 1907), 27.

[3] By the second quarter of the fourteenth century, John Buridan tells us that such a machine can throw a projectile of 1,000 lb.; cf. A. Maier, *Zwei Grundprobleme der scholastischen Naturphilosophie*, 2nd edn. (Rome, 1951), 209, l. 85.

[4] See p. 165.   [5] See p. 166.

motion into reciprocating motion, and the reverse. The crank is profoundly puzzling not only historically but psychologically: the human mind seems to shy away from it. The earliest certain example of crank motion occurs in the previously mentioned water-powered bellows in A.D. 31 in China[1] and the first crank is in a Han-dynasty model (Fig. 4) from north-western Honan, now in the William Rockhill Nelson Gallery in Kansas City, which dates from not later than the end of the second Christian century.[2] It shows a farmyard machine for winnowing husked rice with a cranked rotary fan. This device is still used in China,[3] and very curiously turns up in 1768 among the peasantry of upper Austria and the Siebenbürgen.[4] Yet a student of the Chinese technology of the early twentieth century remarks that even a generation ago the Chinese had not 'reached that stage where continuous rotary motion is substituted for reciprocating motion in technical contrivances such as the drill, lathe, saw, etc. To take this step familiarity with the crank is necessary. The crank in its simple rudimentary form we find in the [modern] Chinese windlass, which use of the device, however, has apparently not given the impulse to change reciprocating into circular motion in other contrivances'.[5] In China the crank was known, but remained dormant for at least nineteen centuries, its explosive potential for applied mechanics being unrecognized and unexploited. Can it have been similarly known but neglected in the ancient West?

James H. Breasted insisted that the crank, like conscience, was born in early Egypt[6] in the form of a weighted borer which he believed was cranked. However, the curved upper part of this borer has now been more probably identified as an animal's horn held in the left hand to keep the borer steady while the right hand pushes the lateral weights.[7]

[1] *Supra*, p. 81, n. 2.

[2] I am grateful to Dr. Annaliese Bulling, and to Dr. Laurence Sickman of Kansas City, for information and photographs. The style and glaze are such that the authenticity of the piece can scarcely be doubted. The Nelson Gallery also has a Han tomb model of a rotary quern with a hole for a single vertical peg-handle, as does the Seattle Museum of Art.

[3] F. C. Ma, T. Takasaka, C. W. Yang, *A Preliminary Study of Farm Implements used in Taiwan Province* (Taipei, 1955), 207; F. M. Feldhaus, *Die Maschine im Leben der Völker* (Basel, 1954), fig. 28.

[4] L. Makkai, 'Hadik András az erdélyi mezögazdaságrol', *Agrártörténeti szemle*, i (1957), 42.

[5] R. P. Hommel, *China at Work* (New York, 1937), 247; cf. 238.

[6] *Scientific Monthly*, ix (1919), 571–2; L. Klebs, 'Die Reliefs des Alten Reiches (2980–2475 v. Chr.)', *Abhandlungen der Heidelberger Akademie der Wissenschaften, Phil.-hist. Kl.* (1915), 83, fig. 66.

[7] V. G. Childe, 'Rotary motion', in Singer, *History of Technology*, i (1954), 192. The

No representation of any form of crank survives directly from the Greeks or Romans.[1] Nevertheless, many modern scholars have re-constructed such items as Hero's dioptra with a small crank on the adjustment screw at its base simply because that is the way a sensible man would make it, in their opinion, and not because of evidence of such a crank.[2] Similarly, Renaissance and modern sketches of the so-called Archimedes screw generally show it cranked, whereas all extant remains, texts, and ancient pictures indicate that such water-raising devices were worked by treading in Antiquity.[3]

The most formidable claim for the discovery of cranks in classical times comes from the Nemi ships. Beginning in 1929, Mussolini drained Lake Nemi sufficiently to expose the hulks of two ceremonial barges perhaps built under Caligula (A.D. 37–41). Remains were dis-covered of an endless chain of cups[4] to raise bilge-water. This was reconstructed not only with cranks but with cranks mounted on fly-wheels.[5] If the reconstruction is correct, it is epochal for the history of technology: it produces the Occident's first crank, and the world's first flywheel applied to a complex operation.[6]

The archaeologists in charge of the Nemi enterprise published a scrupulously careful inventory showing where and when every object was discovered. On each of the two ships they found a single wooden chute to send bilge-water overboard after it had been raised to deck level. This probably means that each barge had only one water-lifting apparatus. Considering that the vessels were moored on a tiny lake (1·67 sq. km.), sheltered in an old crater lacking natural outlet, such provision would have been sufficient. In 1929, close to the bilge-chute of the first ship, a toothed wheel was found which may legiti-mately be interpreted as part of a chain of bailers.[7] In 1931, when the second ship was examined, the piston of a pump was found close

screw-thread scorings inside stone vases noted by F. Petrie, *Tools and Weapons* (London, 1917), 44, could have been produced by the unidirectional, but not necessarily con-tinuous, motion of such a borer. Petrie, pl. LXXVIII, M3, goes far beyond the evidence in identifying two 'iron pivots of a brace' in a trove of Assyrian tools found in Egypt.

[1] See p. 167.

[2] e.g. A. P. Usher, *History of Mechanical Inventions*, 2nd edn. (Cambridge, Mass., 1954), 149, fig. 38; it is correctly reconstructed by A. G. Drachmann, 'Heron and Ptolemaios', *Centaurus*, i (1950), 127, fig. 4.

[3] See p. 167.   [4] See p. 168.

[5] G. Ucelli, *Le Navi di Nemi*, 2nd edn. (Rome, 1950), 181, fig. 199; A. Uccelli, *Enciclopedia storica delle scienze e delle loro applicazioni* (Milan, 1942), II. i. 618, fig. 130.

[6] As distinct from the potter's wheel, on which cf. Childe in Singer, *History of Technology*, i (1954), 195–204, and spindle-whorls; ibid. 433, fig. 273.

[7] G. Ucelli, op. cit. 428, nos. 407, 408.

to the bilge-chute of that vessel.[1] On this second ship, but at a considerable distance from the remains of the pump and chute, was found a disk of wood with a square hole in the centre and, close to the edge, a single square hole in which what seemed to be a handle was inserted.[2] Despite the improbability that they had anything to do with a water-raising machine even on the second ship, these fragments were arbitrarily combined with the toothed wheel found two years earlier on the first ship, and thus was reconstructed a cranked chain of bailers which is entirely plausible to a twentieth-century mind, but which is archaeologically a fantasy. Before we accept this pivoted disk and its eccentric peg as flywheel and crank, we must learn much more about the changing technology of the Roman Empire.[3] In judging the purpose of these fragments, it is important to note that the wooden peg has a total length of 15 inches from the point of its emergence from the disk, and that at its thinnest part this peg has a thickness of only one-third of an inch (Fig. 5): it is so slender that it would quickly snap if force sufficient to raise even a small weight were put upon it.

Lacking firm archaeological testimony of the crank in Western Antiquity, we must resort to the texts, from which such evidence has been claimed.[4] The problem consists of the meaning of the word χειρολάβη (or χειρολαβίς) in certain mechanical treatises, and of the related problem of whether Byzantine and Renaissance copyists modified the diagrams in these treatises by adding cranks where they seemed needed.

While χειρολάβη etymologically might indicate any handle, it had a specific meaning of 'plough-tail' which has led most scholars to give it the meaning 'crank' in mechanical contexts. Cohen and Drabkin thus translate it in a passage from Hero's *Mechanics* and in another from his *Dioptra*, while in the first instance they reproduce the customary reconstruction showing a crank.[5] However, in each of these passages χειρολάβη may be construed not as a crank but as

---

[1] G. Ucelli, op. cit. nos. 406, 410.   [2] Ibid., no. 409.   [3] See p. 168.

[4] The statements of T. Beck, *Beiträge zur Geschichte des Maschinenbaues* (Berlin, 1899), 2, of F. M. Feldhaus, *Technik der Vorzeit, der geschichtlichen Zeit und der Naturvölker* (Leipzig, 1914), 592, and of Neuburger, op. cit. 206, that the crank is discussed in the pseudo-Aristotelian *Mechanical Problems*, ch. 29, is not confirmed by any portion of that work.

[5] M. R. Cohen and J. E. Drabkin, *Source Book in Greek Science* (New York, 1948), 228, 230; cf. P. Ver Eecke, *Pappus d'Alexandrie, la collection mathématique* (Paris, 1933), 841, n. 3; 879, n. 4. In his translation of the *Dioptra* (Leipzig, 1903), 312-13, H. Schöne uses 'Handhabe' rather than 'Kurbel'.

a T-handle to be fitted over the squared end of an axle as an alternative to boring holes through the end of the axle for the insertion of spokes for turning it. It is of central importance that the diagram related to the sole occurrence of χειρολαβίς in Hero's *Pneumatics* clearly shows not a crank but exactly such a T-shaped handle.[1] This may well represent the earliest stratum of 'unimproved' diagrams. Unfortunately, most scholars, save for art historians and archaeologists, have been taught to look carefully at words rather than at things or pictures.[2] Editors have concentrated attention upon the textual rather than upon the visual variants in the transmission of the Greek mechanical treatises. All extant manuscripts of such works come from ages when the crank was known. Until the tradition of their illustration has been analysed properly,[3] these diagrams cannot be used as proof that the classical Mediterranean knew the crank.

If not the crank itself, can we at least find crank motion in Antiquity, apart from China?

The first certain appearance of crank motion is found in the use of hand-querns.[4] The two earliest milling devices, the mortar and the metate, both involve reciprocating motion: pounding or rubbing. In the Aegean–Black Sea region the upper stone of the metate gradually was hollowed to serve as a hopper. From this emerged the lever-mill, in which the upper stone's handle was pivoted at one end so that the operator could exert better leverage by pushing and pulling at the other end. By about the eighth century B.C. various experiments with hopper metates shifted the pivot to the middle of the upper stone, thus producing the quern and, eventually, the large, hour-glass-shaped mills turned by mules or slaves harnessed to horizontal

---

[1] Ed. W. Schmidt (Leipzig, 1899), 50, 49, fig. 6b.

[2] In the first edition of his *History of Mechanical Inventions* (New York, 1929), 119, A. P. Usher asserts, although without supporting discussion, that 'no form of crank motion appears in any of the evidence' from Antiquity; yet his figs. 13, 15, and 30 show ancient machines reconstructed with cranks. Evidently no reviewer noticed the inconsistency, since it reappeared in the new edition of 1954 (Cambridge, Mass.), 160, figs. 21, 23, 38.

[3] Cf. R. J. Forbes, *Studies in Ancient Technology*, ii (Leiden, 1955), 112; Drachmann, *Ktesibios*, 41–42, 77. F. W. Galpin, 'Notes on a Roman hydraulus', *The Reliquary*, new series, x (1904), 153, asserts that the present drawings attached to descriptions of the water-organ by both Hero and Vitruvius are fanciful representations from the fourteenth century onward.

[4] A Hallstatt urn from Hungary shows a rod, with a crank at each end, for aiding the shedding in weaving; cf. M. Hoernes, *Urgeschichte der bildenden Kunst in Europa* (Vienna, 1898), pl. XXIX; Singer, *History of Technology*, i (1954), 443, fig. 280. This is clearly identical with the Anglo-Saxon *crancstæf* of *c.* A.D. 1000 (*infra*, p. 166), but in neither case is continuous rotary motion indicated.

beam-handles, and walking endlessly in a circle around the mill.[1]

But while continuous rotary motion was used in this large *mola versatilis* and, of course, in the water-mill which appears in the first century B.C.,[2] it is by no means clear how early such a motion was used with querns.[3] Archaeologists have realized only recently that finds of querns are so common that if patterns of development could be worked out they would be most useful for dating and for tracing cultural influences. The few scholars who have touched on the problem customarily bewail the carelessness with which the stratification of querns has often been recorded. Yet not even the enlightened minority of the quern-conscious has recognized the significance of the quern in the history of applied mechanics. Their reconstructions of the vanished wooden parts of querns almost always show a vertical peg-handle, since that is the kind of handle we prefer today. But the actuality was less simple.

During many generations it was not understood that the grain in a quern was ground less by the weight of the upper stone than by its shearing motion, and that the meal tended outwards as efficiently with a flattish as with a conical lower stone. As a result, the earliest querns were fairly heavy, and the handle, or handles, were inserted horizontally in the side of the upper stone, like the lateral beams of a mule-mill. With such querns the millers used a back-and-forth swinging motion: three such querns were found at Vetulonia *in situ* so close to walls that complete rotation would have been impossible even if the operator had changed the position of her hands during rotation.[4]

As the centuries wore on, the stones of querns became always flatter and thinner. At times the hole in the side of the upper stone was curved upward to emerge on top, and a loop of rope through this perforation served as handle. But the way the sides of the holes are worn indicates that the motion was still reciprocating.[5] As the upper stones became lighter, it was harder to insert a rigid peg-handle horizontally: its angle creeps upward, until eventually it stands vertically on top.

Now at last, with a vertical peg-handle, continuous rotation of the

---

[1] A lucid summary of this development is given by J. Stork and W. D. Teague, *Flour for Man's Bread: A History of Milling* (Minneapolis, 1952), 71–79; cf. also L. A. Moritz, *Grain Mills and Flour in Classical Antiquity* (Oxford, 1958), 10–121.

[2] *Supra*, p. 80.

[3] See p. 168.

[4] *Notizie degli scavi* (1894), 358.

[5] See p. 168.

quern with crank motion was possible. But how soon did it in fact occur? Even as late as the nineteenth century, in the Shetland Islands querns frequently were operated by two women with a to-and-fro motion.[1] Moreover, when, as is often the case, there are two vertical holes in the upper stone, or two slots on opposite sides, it is not at all certain that vertical handles were used: more probably a horizontal bar, attached by means of these sockets or slots, extended laterally to furnish handles.[2] Only when we are faced with a complete upper stone having a single vertical peg-hole can we assume that the handle was arranged in such a way as to permit crank motion.

However, the dating of such querns is most uncertain. At the Saalburg in the Limes, more than 100 querns of the first to late third centuries after Christ were found, all having lateral rather than vertical handle sockets.[3] I have seen at Yale University an unpublished quern with a single vertical peg-hole found at Dura Europos, and therefore presumably from A.D. 256 at latest. One would wish to be certain of its stratification, and that it was not left in Dura by travellers camping among the ruins; for one authority insists that such querns were unknown in Palestine and Syria until Muslim times.[4] Subsequent discussion has not invalidated Cecil Curwen's suggestion, made in 1937, that querns with single vertical peg-handles are, in Britain at least, 'late or post-Roman types'.[5]

Seated before a quern with a single vertical handle, a person of the twentieth century would give it a continuous rotary motion. It is far

[1] E. C. Curwen, 'More about querns', *Antiquity*, xv (1941), 30. This doubtless illumines the tenth-century Norwegian *Quern song* which tells of a king who kept two giant maidens enslaved to work at a magic quern which ground out gold-dust; cf. A. Olrik, *The Heroic Legends of Denmark* (New York, 1919), 449–60.

[2] See p. 169.

[3] L. Jacobi, *Das Römerkastell Saalburg* (Hamburg v. d. H., 1897), pl. XXVII. Moritz, op. cit. 126–30, correctly rejects certain Saalburg reconstructions of querns involving cranks as 'entirely conjectural' and based on analogy with medieval querns.

[4] P. Thomsen, 'Mühle', in M. Ebert, *Reallexikon der Vorgeschichte*, viii (1927), 325. Such querns were known in China by the end of the second century at latest, *supra*, p. 104, n. 2. H. D. Sankalia, 'Rotary querns from India', *Antiquity*, xxxiii (1959), 128–30, records transverse sockets for handles dating from not later than the second–first centuries B.C. I do not know when the vertical peg handle reached India.

[5] E. C. Curwen, 'Querns', *Antiquity*, xi (1937), 146. R. E. M. Wheeler, 'Maiden Castle, Dorset', *Reports of the Society of Antiquaries of London*, xii (1943), 322, dates A.D. 25–50 a quern in which 'the socket, originally at the side, broke away in the process of grinding, and was replaced by one on the top'. However, his fig. 116, no. 23, illustrating this item, shows that only one-third of the stone survives. It therefore may have had a horizontal handle fixed in two sockets on opposite sides of the circumference. W. E. Griffiths, 'Decorated rotary querns from Wales and Ireland', *Ulster Journal of Archaeology*, xiv (1951), 49–61, rather vaguely dates such querns A.D. 200–600.

less certain that one of the decaying Roman Empire would have done so. Crank motion was a kinetic invention more difficult than we can easily conceive. Yet at some point the sense of the appropriate motion changed; for out of the rotating quern came a new machine, the rotary grindstone, which (as the Latin term for it, *mola fabri*, shows) is the upper stone of a quern turned on edge and adapted to sharpening. And with the rotary grindstone the crank appears in the West.

The Utrecht Psalter, illuminated in the region of Rheims between 816 and 834,[1] shows both the earliest rotary grindstone[2] and the first European crank.

The mechanical crank is extraordinary not only for its late invention, or arrival from China, but also for the almost unbelievable delay, once it was known, in its assimilation to technological thinking. After the grindstone, its next application[3] was in the hurdy-gurdy. A brief musical tract rather dubiously ascribed to Abbot Odo of Cluny (d. 942) describes a fretted stringed instrument which was sounded by a resined wheel turned with a crank.[4] However, no representations of this device have been found earlier than the twelfth century, when two appear.[5] From the twelfth century likewise comes a picture of Fortuna cranking her wheel of destiny which is the more amusing because the illuminator is very uncertain about just how a crank works.[6] The thirteenth century provides nothing but further hurdy-gurdies[7] and another cranking Fortuna,[8] by this time doing better. The fourteenth century offers no innovations for

---

[1] See p. 169.

[2] Wheeler, op. cit. 321, reports three grindstones (presumably not whetstones) at Maiden Castle, but does not attempt an exact dating. Most remains from this site are not later than the first Christian century, but there is fourth-century material and a Saxon grave of *c.* A.D. 600. Considering the probable survival-value of grindstones, one is puzzled by the silence of archaeologists regarding them, if in fact they were known in Roman and early medieval times.

[3] No continuous rotary motion was necessarily involved in the shedding operation of the Anglo-Saxon *crancstæf*; cf. *supra*, p. 107, n. 4.

[4] *Quomodo organistrum construatur*, in M. Gerbert, *Scriptores ecclesiastici de musica* (San Blas, 1784), i. 303; cf. G. Reese, *Music in the Middle Ages* (New York, 1940), 258; C. Sachs, *History of Musical Instruments* (New York, 1940), 271.

[5] E. Millar, *English Illuminated Manuscripts from the Tenth to the Thirteenth Century* (Paris, 1926), pl. 60(a) from Glasgow, Hunterian MS. 229; E. E. Viollet-le-Duc, *Dictionnaire raisonné du mobilier*, ii (Paris, 1871), 248, from a capital at Bascherville.

[6] M. R. James, *Descriptive Catalogue of the Latin Manuscripts in the John Rylands Library* (Manchester, 1921), pl. 110.   [7] See p. 169.

[8] Herrade de Landsberg, op. cit., pl. LV (2); A. Doren, 'Fortuna im Mittelatler und in der Renaissance', *Bibliothek Warburg Vorträge, 1922–23*, i (1924), fig. 7.

ordinary application, despite a revolutionary theoretical development which we shall examine in a moment. The cranked windlass for spanning a heavy steel cross-bow is often credited to the fourteenth century,[1] and, indeed, in thirteenth-century Cambodia we find a large Khmer cross-bow operated by two men on two cranks.[2] However, no secure evidence for it in Europe is found earlier than *c.* 1405 when Konrad Kyeser's unpublished *Bellifortis* pictures five different cranked devices for that purpose.[3] Kyeser illustrates only three other very simple applications of the crank,[4] and otherwise from his time there emerges nothing more spine-tingling than a cranked reel for winding skeins of yarn.[5] At the beginning of the 1400's, at least twelve centuries after it was known in China and six centuries after its first appearance in Europe, the crank was still a dormant element in technology. As for Islam and Byzantium, I find no firm evidence of even the simplest application of the crank until al-Jazarī's book of A.D. 1206.[6]

However, during the fourteenth century a mutation was germinating. The Luttrell Psalter, dating from about 1340, records that a grindstone was then in use rotated by two cranks, one at each end of its axle,[7] as in the case of the Cambodian *balista* just mentioned. In

[1] e.g. by Viollet-le-Duc, op. cit. v (1874), 26; R. Payne-Gallwey, *The Crossbow* (London, 1903, reprinted 1958), 71; H. S. Cowper, *Art of Attack* (Ulverston, 1906), 261, fig. 351; A. Uccelli, *Storia della tecnica* (Milan, 1945), 210, fig. 102. According to F. Deters, *Die englischen Angriffswaffen zur Zeit der Einführung der Feuerwaffen* (*1300–1350*) (Heidelberg, 1913), 119, an 'arwelast off vys' was used in the first half of the century. However, R. Valturio, *De re militari* (Verona, 1472), fol. 161ᵛ, shows a cross-bow spanned by a screw which is not cranked but turned by an X-shaped handle.

[2] P. Mus, 'Les Balistes du Bayon', *Bulletin de l'École Française d'Extrême-Orient*, xxix (1929), 333, pl. XLVII–A. Mus, 335, points out that nothing of the sort is found at Ankor Wat, which indicates a revolution in Khmer armament in the twelfth to thirteenth centuries. H. G. Q. Wales, *Ancient Southeast Asian Warfare* (London, 1952), 102, connects this with a Chinese army officer shipwrecked in Cambodia in 1172 who advised the king on military reforms.

[3] Göttingen University Library, Cod. phil. 63, fols. 74ʳ, 76ʳ and ᵛ, 77ʳ; photographs in my possession; cf. Feldhaus, *Technik der Vorzeit*, fig. 21.

[4] Fol. 56ᵛ, chain of buckets; 63ʳ, Archimedes screw; 64ʳ, grindstone; 133ʳ, wheel of bells.

[5] A. Stange, *Deutsche Malerei der Gothik*, ii (Berlin, 1936), 170, pl. 218; O. Fischer, *Geschichte der deutschen Malerei*, 2nd edn. (Munich, 1943), 108, dates the picture *c.* 1410. C. H. Livingston, *Skein-winding Reels: Studies in Word History and Etymology* (Ann Arbor, 1957), 12, fig. 4, knows of no cranked example until later in the century. By 1462 similar cranked reels are found in China; cf. O. Franke, *Kêng tschi t'u: Ackerbau und Seidengewinnung in China* (Hamburg, 1913), Taf. lxxxiii–lxxxiv, xciii, xcvi; for dating, cf. *infra*, p. 114, n. 5.   [6] See p. 170.

[7] E. Millar, *Luttrell Psalter* (London, 1932), pl. 25b. The geared hand-mill, equipped either with one or two cranks, does not appear before the fifteenth century; cf. A. T.

1335, in his unpublished *Texaurus regis Francie acquisitionis terre sancte* urging Philip VI to a new Crusade, the famous Italian physician Guido da Vigevano, then living in Paris, included a chapter on military machines designed to subdue the paynim, and presumably of Guido's own invention. In two of the accompanying illustrations,[1] by an intuition of genius, he has combined the two cranks at the axle-ends of the Luttrell-type grindstone to form a compound crank in the centre of the axle. Guido had one of the most adventurous minds of his age,[2] and a modern student of him testifies that 'clearly he was well acquainted with craft skills'.[3] There is no evidence that any of his projected machines was ever built; nevertheless, his sketches show that new ideas about the crank were in the air.

For practical purposes, the compound crank was invented about 1420 in the form of the carpenter's brace, by some Flemish artisan.[4] The first representation of it occurs in a panel of Meister Francke's St. Thomas altar commissioned in 1424;[5] the second is in the Master of Flemaille's Mérode altar-piece of 1427–8;[6] the third is in a French or Burgundian miniature of 1430 in the Bedford Missal.[7] From such a distribution it is obvious that the compound crank in the form of the carpenter's brace is of northern European origin. The first indication of it in Italy, in Giovanni da Fontana's notebook of

Nolthenius, 'Les Moulins à main au moyen âge', *Techniques et civilisations*, iv (1955), 149–52.

[1] Bibliothèque Nationale, MS. fonds latin 11015, fols. 10ᵛ, 14ᵛ; cf. Singer, *History of Technology*, ii (1956), figs. 594, 659. A. R. Hall, 'The military inventions of Guido da Vigevano', *Actes du VIIᵉ Congrès International d'Histoire des Sciences* (Florence, 1958), 966, indicates a second manuscript of this work, with the illustrations of compound cranks, copied in 1375 in Cyprus by a Martin of Aachen who is otherwise unknown. Hall, 969, correctly asserts that Guido's work was not entirely neglected: it influenced Valturio by 1463; cf. *infra*, p. 114, n. 3.

[2] Cf. L. Thorndike, *History of Magic and Experimental Science*, iii (New York, 1934), 26–27; E. Wickersheimer, *Dictionnaire biographique des médecins en France au moyen âge* (Paris, 1936), 216–17; G. Sarton, *Introduction to the History of Science*, iii (Baltimore, 1947), 846–7.

[3] A. R. Hall, 'Military technology', in Singer, op. cit. ii. 725–6.

[4] The French *vilebrequin* 'brace' is of Flemish origin, whence Catalan *filabarquí* or *belebarquí*, Spanish *berebiquí*, Portuguese *berebequim*; cf. A. Thomas, *Essais de philologie française* (Paris, 1897), 399–400. H. Gade, *Ursprung und Bedeutung der üblicheren Handwerkzeugnamen im Französischen* (Kiel, 1898), 61, dates the appearance of the Flemish word *wimbrequin* in 1432.

[5] B. Martens, *Meister Francke* (Hamburg, 1929), 111, pl. XXVII; Singer, op. cit., fig. 595.

[6] E. Panofsky, *Early Netherlandish Painting* (Cambridge, Mass., 1953), ii, fig. 204, I, 167; Singer, op. cit., pl. 12; cf. M. Schapiro, ' "Muscipula diaboli": the symbolism of the Mérode altarpiece', *Art Bulletin*, xxvii (1945), 184 and fig. 1.

[7] See p. 171.

c. 1420–49, shows that Fontana had not seen one, but had merely heard of an auger with a crank in it: his sketch is of an unworkable tool (Fig. 6).[1]

But now, at long last, the dormant idea of the crank was very suddenly beginning to awaken in the European mind. By *c.* 1430 the compound crank had been transferred from the carpenter's brace to machine design of a sort without precedent, to judge by the notebook of a German military engineer of the Hussite Wars. First, the connecting-rod, a mechanical substitute for the human arm, was applied to cranks.[2] Second, double compound cranks appeared, also equipped with connecting-rods.[3] Third, the flywheel was applied to these cranks to get them over the 'dead-spot' which is the chief difficulty with mechanized crank motion.[4]

The earliest evidence of compound crank and connecting-rod in Italy is found in a manuscript of Mariano di Jacopo Taccola which is not earlier than 1441 nor later than 1458,[5] but the sketch (Fig. 7) shows a defective understanding of the motion involved. However, a drawing in the Louvre by Pisanello, who died *c.* 1456 and who never travelled outside Italy, depicts lucidly a piston-pump powered by a water-wheel and operated by two simple cranks and two connecting-rods.[6]

[1] Munich, Bayerische Staatsbibliothek, Cod. icon. 242, fol. 40ᵛ; for date, cf. *supra*, p. 98, n. 1.

[2] Munich, Bayerische Staatsbibliothek, Cod. lat. 197, fols. 18ʳ, 42ʳ; cf. B. Gille, 'La Naissance du système bielle-manivelle', *Techniques et civilisations*, ii (1952), fig. 2, and his 'Le Manuscrit dit de la Guerre Hussite', ibid. v (1956), 79–86; Singer, *History of Technology*, ii (1956), fig. 596; F. M. Feldhaus, *Geschichte der Kugel-, Walzen- und Rollenlager* (Schweinfurt a. M., 1914), 11, fig. 3.

[3] Cod. lat. 197, fol. 21ʳ and ᵛ; Gille, 'Bielle-manivelle', fig. 3; Singer, op. cit., fig. 597. A possible origin for the connecting-rod is suggested by P. Tohell, 'Team work on a rotary quern', *Journal of the Royal Society of Antiquaries of Ireland*, lxxxi (1951), 70–71, which describes a large rotary quern operated in County Sligo *c.* 1900: to a single vertical handle were attached four ropes, each pulled in succession by four men around the circle.

[4] Cod. cit.; Kyeser's *Bellifortis* (*supra*, p. 111, n. 3), of *c.* 1405, shows a gigantic trebuchet with what are probably tread-mills rather than fly-wheels on the apparatus for lowering the throwing arm; cf. *Zeitschrift für historische Waffenkunde*, v (1909–11), 385, fig. 41.

[5] Munich, Bayerische Staatsbibliothek, Cod. lat. 197, fol. 82ᵛ; on the date cf. P. Fontana, 'I codici di Giorgio Martini e di Mariano di Jacomo detto il Taccola', *Actes du Congrès d'Histoire de l'Art*, i (1936), 102–3; M. Salmi, *Disegni di Francesco di Giorgio nella Collezione Chigi Saracini* (Siena, 1947), 11, n. 1; L. Thorndike, 'Marianus Jacobus Taccola', *Archives internationales d'histoire des sciences*, viii (1955), 20.

[6] B. Degenhart, *Antonio Pisanello*, 3rd edn. (Vienna, 1942), fig. 147, from Louvre drawing no. 2286.

Indeed the next, and perhaps last fundamental, step in exploring the kinetic possibilities of crank and connecting-rod may be credited to Italy. By *c*. 1430 the German engineer of the Hussite Wars had revived[1] Guido da Vigevano's idea,[2] originally published in France, of a boat with two sets of paddle-wheels turned by men operating a compound crank on the axle of each pair. Only a generation later, in 1463, Roberto Valturio shows that the concept is not only known but improved in Italy: he illustrates a boat with five pairs, but these parallel cranks are now all joined to a single source of power by one connecting-rod.[3] This device for transferring rotary motion to a parallel plane appears likewise in a Florentine manuscript of Francesco di Giorgio's *Trattato di architettura* (Fig. 8), 1482–1501.[4]

While there is no early evidence of the compound crank in China, a single crank with connecting-rod is found there applied to a man-powered rice-hulling mill by 1462, if we may judge from the similar illustrations of a Japanese edition of 1676 and a Chinese edition of 1696, both independently derived from an edition of that date.[5]

Students of applied mechanics are agreed that 'the technical advance which characterizes specifically the modern age is that from reciprocating motions to rotary motions',[6] and the crank is the pre-

---

[1] MS. lat. 197, fol 17ᵛ; cf. A. Uccelli, *Storia della tecnica* (Milan, 1945), 535, fig. 52; G. Canestrini, *Arte militare meccanica medievale* (Milan, n.d.), pl. CXXVIII. Leonardo sketched a military tank designed to be propelled by pairs of wheels connected by axles equipped with compound cranks; but, proving that even Leonardo could nod, B. Dibner, 'Leonardo da Vinci, military engineer', in *Studies and Essays in the History of Science and Learning offered to G. Sarton*, ed. M. F. A. Montague (New York, 1946), 96, n. 7, fig. 6, points out that the gearing is so arranged that the front and rear wheels would rotate in opposite directions.

[2] *Supra*, p. 112, n. 1.

[3] Bibliothèque Nationale, MS. 7236, fol. 170ʳ, cf. Thorndike, 'Marianus', 23. Valturio's *De re militari*, illustrating this boat on fol. 215ʳ, was published at Verona in 1472. For a slightly later Italian example, cf. Uccelli, op. cit. 536, fig. 55; Canestrini, op. cit., pl. CXXXII.

[4] Biblioteca Nazionale, Florence, MS. II. I. 141, fol. 198ᵛ; Library of Congress microfilm MLA 588 f. On the date, cf. A. S. Weller, *Francesco di Giorgio* (Chicago, 1943), 268. The same arrangement appears shortly thereafter in Leonardo da Vinci's sketch of a centrifugal water-lifting machine, MS. F, fol. 13ʳ; cf. F. M. Feldhaus, *Leonardo als Techniker und Erfinder* (Jena, 1913), 47.

[5] O. Franke, *Kêng tschi t'u: Ackerbau und Seidengewinnung in China* (Hamburg, 1913), Taf. l, li, and figs. 35–38. Franke, 78, goes beyond the evidence in claiming that the 1676 Japanese reprint (involving new blocks) of the Chinese edition of 1462 gives us the pictures of the edition of 1237: first, the edition of 1462 involved a reworking of the earlier illustrations (cf. 73–74, 76–77); second, the Japanese edition contains (cf. Taf. xcv) a skein-winding reel which is not found in the Chinese edition of 1696 and which therefore must be a Japanese addition.

[6] L. Mumford, *Technics and Civilization* (New York, 1934), 80.

supposition of that change. The appearance of the bit-and-brace in the 1420's and of the double compound crank and connecting-rod about 1430, marks the most significant single step in the late medieval revolution in machine design. With extraordinary rapidity these devices were absorbed into Europe's technological thinking and used for the widest variety of operations.[1] How can we explain the delay of so many centuries not only in the initial discovery of the simple crank but also in its wide application and elaboration?

Continuous rotary motion is typical of inorganic matter, whereas reciprocating motion is the sole form of movement found in living things. The crank connects these two kinds of motion; therefore we who are organic find that crank motion does not come easily to us. The great physicist and philosopher Ernst Mach noticed that infants find crank motion hard to learn.[2] Despite the rotary grindstone, even today razors are whetted rather than ground: we find rotary motion an impediment to the greatest sensitivity. The hurdy-gurdy soon went out of use as an instrument for serious music, leaving the reciprocating fiddle-bow—an introduction of the tenth century[3]—to become the foundation of modern European musical development. To use a crank, our tendons and muscles must relate themselves to the motion of galaxies and electrons. From this inhuman adventure our race long recoiled.

In working out the problems of continuous rotary motion, technicians found that flywheels and other forms of mechanical governors were needed to smooth out irregularities of impulse and get over 'dead-spots'. The flywheel first appears as an element in machinery in the late eleventh-century treatise on technology of the monk Theophilus, who speaks of a 'rotula sive lignea sive plumbea tornatilis' on the axle of a little pigment-grinding mill equipped with a rotary pestle, and also of a 'rotula plumbi parvula' on the spindle of a boring apparatus.[4] By the second quarter of the fourteenth

---

[1] See p. 171.

[2] H. T. Horwitz, 'Über die Entwicklung der Fähigkeit zum Antreib des Kurbel-mechanismus', *Geschichtsblätter für Technik und Industrie*, xi (1927), 30–31.

[3] Madrid, Biblioteca Nacional, Codex Hh 58, *Beatus in Apocalipsin*, fol. 130ʳ, of the early tenth century, shows four musical bows of very primitive form; photos in Princeton Index of Christian Art; cf. L. Bréhier, *La Sculpture et les arts mineurs byzantins* (Paris, 1936), pl. 36, no. 2, for an ivory coffer of the tenth century.

[4] Theophilus, *Diversarum artium schedula*, ed. W. Theobald (Berlin, 1933), 14, 174; cf. 191. On the date, cf. B. Bischoff, 'Die Überlieferung des Theophilus-Rugerus nach den ältesten Handschriften', *Münchner Jahrbuch der bildenden Kunst*, iii–iv (1952–3), 145–9; E. W. Bulatkin, 'The Spanish word "matiz": its origin and semantic evolution in the technical vocabulary of medieval painters', *Traditio*, x (1954), 487.

century John Buridan was supporting his new theory of impetus with the observation that the rotary grindstone continues to turn long after the hand is removed, indicating that the grindstone stores power or 'vis impressa'.[1] We have already noticed the flywheels on large-scale machinery *c*. 1430 in the notebook of the anonymous engineer of the Hussite Wars.[2] The enthusiasm of Renaissance engineers for the flywheel–crank combination was such that they tried to assimilate the two by frequently bending the central section, or key-seat, of their cranks into half circles. In 1567 Giuseppe Ceredi, in the first theoretical discussion of the crank which I have found, points out that this is mechanically useless;[3] nevertheless, gracefully curved cranks continued to be common deep into the nineteenth century.

Towards the end of the fifteenth century a new type of governor is found in Europe which, like the vertical-axle windmill and the hot-air turbine,[4] was probably brought from Tibet by the Central Asian slaves who were so numerous in Italy at that time.[5] Just as the hand-gun emerged from the cannon, and the wrist watch from the monumental clock, so the hand prayer-cylinder of Tibet was doubtless the individualization of an older device[6] to be operated by a group. But it involved a mechanically important innovation: a small ball-and-chain governor attached to its periphery to maintain rotation. By *c*. 1480 a ball of metal is found in Germany on one of a pair of compound cranks to counterbalance the thrust of a connecting-rod on the second compound crank.[7] In Francesco di Giorgio's manuscript of 1482–1501[8] (Fig. 9) there is a ball-and-chain governor on exactly the Tibetan pattern, in conjunction with compound cranks and connecting rods; while in 1507 we find the rotation of a spit being regularized by three weights turning on a vertical axis.[9]

[1] J. Buridan, *Quaestiones super Libris quatuor de caelo et mundo*, ed. E. A. Moody (Cambridge, Mass., 1942), 180, 242–3; A. Maier, *Zwei Grundprobleme der scholastischen Naturphilosophie* (Rome, 1951), 208, l. 40; 209, ll. 72–76; cf. *infra*, p. 174.

[2] *Supra*, p. 113, n. 4.

[3] G. Ceredi, *Tre discorsi sopra il modo d'alzar acque da' luoghi bassi* (Parma, 1567), 54–68.   [4] *Supra*, pp. 86, 93.

[5] Cf. L. White, jr., 'Tibet, India and Malaya as sources of Western mediaeval technology', *American Historical Review*, lxv (1960), pp. 515–26.

[6] *Supra*, pp. 85–86. The frequent statement that coins of Kushan kings, especially of Huvishka (*c*. A.D. 130–60), show the hand prayer-cylinder is groundless. Dr. John Rosenfield of Harvard University assures me, on the basis of a study of the development of Kushan royal iconography, that this object is a small club, an emblem of power.

[7] *Mittelalterliches Hausbuch*, ed. cit., pl. 47; Feldhaus, *Technik der Vorzeit*, fig. 481.

[8] Florence, Biblioteca Nazionale, MS. II. I. 141, fol. 96ʳ; cf. *supra*, p. 114, n. 4.

[9] Feldhaus, op. cit., fig. 100.

So great was the fifteenth-century technician's drive towards continuous rotary motion that the pendulum, the basic governor for reciprocating motion, was overlooked. In the last decade of the century the genius of Leonardo glimpsed it,[1] but not until Besson's work of 1569 were its potentialities for sawing-machines, bellows, and pumps clearly envisaged.[2]

Closely connected with the crank and the flywheel is another medieval device, the treadle. There is no evidence that Antiquity knew the treadle in any form,[3] save in China, where it was used on looms by the middle of the second century of our era.[4] In Europe the earliest indications of the treadle are found in Alexander Neckam's description of the process of weaving in the very late twelfth century,[5] in archaeological finds of the early thirteenth century,[6] and in a middle-thirteenth-century English picture of a loom.[7] In stained-glass windows and illuminations of the thirteenth century, treadle-looms are frequent,[8] as are lathes operated by treadles.[9] It is strange, in view of all this, that the treadle does not seem to have been applied to the pipe-organ (the most complex engine used by the Middle Ages) in the form of a pedal keyboard until *c.* 1418.[10]

Related to the treadle were the overhead sapling-spring and bow-spring. While the spring was known to Greeks and Romans in bows, traps, and military engines, the only evidence of a spring used in classical times as part of the continuing operation of a machine comes from the water-organ, which had a spring of elastic horn or

[1] See p. 172.

[2] J. Besson, *Theatrum instrumentorum et machinarum* (Lyons, 1569). I have not seen this edition, which contains 49 plates, but have used that of Lyons, 1578, with 60 plates; cf. pls. 10, 11, 14, 44, 47, 48. A pendulum-regulated punka-fan, perhaps reflecting Indian influence, is found in G. A. Böckler, *Theatrum machinarum novum* (Nuremberg, 1661), pl. 83.

[3] *Infra*, p. 167, and F. M. Feldhaus, *Die Geschichte der Schleifmittel* (Hannover, 1919), 12–13. [4] See p. 173.

[5] U. T. Holmes, jr., *Daily Living in the Twelfth Century, Based on Observations of Alexander Neckam in London and Paris* (Madison, 1952), 146–7.

[6] G. Sage, 'Die Gewebe aus dem alten Oppeln', *Altschlesien*, vi (1936), 322–32.

[7] Singer, *History of Technology*, ii (1956), fig. 181; M. R. James, *Catalogue of the Western Manuscripts of Trinity College, Cambridge* (Cambridge, 1902), no. 1446, iii. 489; on date and origin, cf. 482.

[8] Cf. G. Durand, *Monographie de l'église Notre-Dame, cathédrale d'Amiens* (Paris, 1901–3), ii. 561–2, fig. 256; Y. Delaporte, *Les Vitraux de la cathédrale de Chartres* (Chartres, 1926), ii, pl. CXI; P. Clemen, *Die romanische Monumentalmalerei in den Rheinlanden* (Düsseldorf, 1916), pl. XXXI and fig. 347; A. de Laborde, *La Bible moralisée* (Paris, 1912), ii, pl. 213.

[9] Delaporte, op. cit. iii, pl. CLXXXIX.

[10] C. W. Pearce, *The Evolution of the Pedal Organ* (London, 1927), 1.

metal to stop each note after the perforated slide sounding the note had been pressed down.[1] The spring does not enter machine design until *c.* 1235, when Villard de Honnecourt's notebook shows us a sapling-spring effecting the up-stroke of a water-powered sawmill.[2] This drawing, incidentally, presents the first industrial automatic power-machine to involve two motions: in addition to the conversion of the wheel's rotary motion into the reciprocating motion of sawing, there is an automatic feed keeping the log pressed against the saw. Shortly after 1235, at Boppard in the Rhineland,[3] we find such an overhead spring, in conjunction with a treadle, used in place of a pulley to operate the heddles of a loom, and in the carpenters' window at Chartres (1215–40) we see a vertical saw operated by pedal and overhead spring.[4]

By *c.* 1250 overhead springs were used to operate lathes: in earlier times a lathe was turned by a bow, held in the left hand, the bow-cord being wound around the lathe's spindle; now the cord ran from treadle to overhead sapling, freeing both hands of the artisan.[5] This drive is still found *c.* 1500 in the oldest extant machine tool, the favourite lathe of the Emperor Maximilian,[6] even though *c.* 1480–2 Leonardo da Vinci had already sketched a lathe equipped with treadle, compound crank, and flywheel[7] which greatly improved efficiency by substituting continuous rotary motion for the changes of direction of motion involved in the action of spring and treadle.

[1] W. Apel, 'Early history of the organ', *Speculum*, xxiii (1948), 195, fig. 3; cf. 216, fig. 16; W. Chappell, *History of Music* (London, 1874), i. 347; F. W. Galpin, 'Notes on a Roman hydraulus', *The Reliquary*, new series, x (1904), 162; Drachmann, *Ktesibios*, 8–9. R. J. Forbes, 'Food and drink', in Singer, op. cit. ii (1956), 107, suggests that a passage in Polybius, *Histories*, i. 22, ed. W. R. Patton (London, 1922), i. 60, may refer to a pestle suspended from a sapling-spring. More probably this pestle was operated by a pulley.   [2] *Infra*, p. 161.

[3] Clemen, loc. cit.; for date cf. 487.

[4] Delaporte, op. cit. i, pl. CXXXII.

[5] *Supra*, p. 117, n. 9; Bib. Nat., MS. lat. 11560, fol. 84^r, in A. Laborde, op. cit. ii, pl. CCCVIII, and L. F. Salzman, *English Industries in the Middle Ages* (Oxford, 1923), 172; on the date cf. *infra*, p. 120, n. 3; also cf. A. Rieth, 'Die Entwicklung der Drechseltechnik', *Archäologischer Anzeiger* (1940), 615–34; F. Spannagel, *Das Drechslerwerke*, 2nd edn. (Ravensburg, 1940), 16–17; K. Wittmann, *Die Entwicklung der Drehbank* (Berlin, 1941), 12. A miniature of *c.* 1350 shows a sapling-spring used over a mortar for preparing gunpowder; cf. O. Guttman, *Monumenta pulveris pyrii* (London, 1906), pl. 48; cf. pls. 46, 49. For the general medieval use of springs, cf. C. Roth, 'Medieval illustrations of mouse-traps', *Bodleian Library Record*, v (1956), 244–51.

[6] F. M. Feldhaus, 'Die Drehbank des Kaisers Maximilian', *Werkstattstechnik*, x (1917), 293–4.

[7] *Codice atlantico*, fol. 381^r *b*; Feldhaus, *Technik der Vorzeit*, fig. 150; for date cf. C. Pedretti, *Studi vinciani* (Geneva, 1957), 285.

Even more important, in terms of increasing sophistication of machine design, was the spinning wheel. This device appears *c.* 1280 in Speyer, in a regulation permitting wheel-spun yarn to be used in the weft but not in the warp of textiles,[1] and in a prohibition of its use at Abbeville in 1288,[2] presumably because the thread was not sufficiently firm. Various forms of the spinning wheel are used all over Asia, and its origin is habitually ascribed to India.[3] However, thus far its appearance in India and China cannot be dated.

The spinning wheel is mechanically interesting not only because it is the first instance of the belt transmission of power and a notably early example of the flywheel principle, but because it focused attention upon the problem of producing and controlling various rates of speed in different moving parts of the same machine. One turn of the great wheel sent the spindle twirling many times; but, not content with this, by *c.* 1480[4] craftsmen had developed a U-shaped flyer rotating around the spindle and permitting the operations of both spinning and winding the thread on a bobbin to proceed simultaneously. To accomplish this, spindle and flyer had to rotate at different speeds, each driven by a separate belt from the large wheel, which, of course, revolved at a third speed. Finally, by 1524 the crank, connecting-rod, and treadle had been added to the spinning wheel.[5]

The most notable study of differential speeds, however, was carried on in relation to that ingenious medieval invention, the mechanical clock. As has been mentioned, the engineers of the thirteenth century became fascinated by the problem of devising a chronometer operated by the force of gravity. The difficulty was to discover an escapement, that is, a means of obtaining an even flow of energy through the mechanism. The previous history of technology offered no precedent for such an effort, save by a flow of water, which was unsatisfactory in a climate where icing was frequent.

[1] See p. 173.

[2] A. Thierry, *Recueil des monuments inédits de l'histoire du tiers état: Région du Nord* (Paris, 1870), iv. 53: 'que nus ne nule ne filent d'ore en avant à rouet.'

[3] e.g. by W. F. Parish, 'Origin of textiles and the spinning wheel', *Rayon Textile Monthly*, xvi (1936), 570; R. J. Forbes, *Studies in Ancient Technology*, iv (Leiden, 1956), 156.

[4] *Mittelalterliches Hausbuch*, ed. cit., pl. 35. In the 1490's in the *Codice atlantico*, fols. 337ᵛ, 377ʳ, 393ʳ⁻ᵛ, Leonardo is sketching various forms of flyer; cf. F. M. Feldhaus, 'Die Spinnradzeichnungen von Leonardo da Vinci', *Melliand Textilberichte*, vii (1926), 469–70; for the date, cf. Pedretti, op. cit. 282, 285. It may be noted that a water-powered spinning device appears in G. Branca, *Le Machine* (Rome, 1629), fig. 20.

[5] W. Born, 'The spinning wheel', *Ciba Review*, iii (1939), 997.

Even in the late twelfth century the market for water-clocks was so considerable that by 1183 a guild of clockmakers is mentioned at Cologne, while by 1220 they occupied an entire street, the Urlogingasse, in that city.[1] An unpublished thirteenth-century treatise written in France tells us how one of the simple forms was made: a cord, with a float at one end and a counterweight at the other, passed around an axle which rotated the dial and operated the alarm.[2] However, the sole surviving thirteenth-century picture of a Western water-clock (Fig. 10), probably representing one at the royal court in Paris c. 1250, is sufficiently detailed[3] to indicate that such mechanisms might be very intricate, and that they involved cogwheels.

This is a large chamber-clock, essentially a device for ringing the hours, and it lacks a dial. It is mounted in a clock-case such as Villard de Honnecourt illustrates c. 1235 in his sketchbook.[4] Its most conspicuous feature is a wheel composed of fifteen metal cones. Since the *hora equalis* corresponded to fifteen degrees of the equinoctial cycle, the arbitrary division of this wheel into fifteen sections probably indicates that it made one complete rotation in each hour. The holes seen between these cones may well be schematic rather than visually naturalistic. Doubtless they actually ran from cone to cone, rather than through the wheel. This would permit the water to trickle slowly from one cone to another, thus braking the rotation of the axle, the driving power of which seems to be a weight hanging from a cord which is wound around the axle: a similar plan is followed in a clock at the court of Alfonso X of Castile not later than

---

[1] E. Volckmann, *Alte Gewerbe und Gewerbegassen* (Würzburg, 1921), 129.

[2] Codex Vaticanus latinus 5367; cf. E. Zinner, 'Aus der Frühzeit der Räderuhr: von der Gewichtuhr zur Federzuguhr', *Deutsches Museum Abhandlungen und Berichte*, XXII. iii (1954), 6. Since all such devices were activated by the weights of float and counterpoise, they are, strictly speaking, weight driven. But in the history of applied kinematics it is important to distinguish this sort of gravity motor from that involving mechanical escapement. For this reason Hero's Temple of Bacchus puppet show, driven by a weight resting on a container from which millet or mustard seed trickled as a substitute for water, should be regarded as a slight variant of the water-driven apparatus, and not as the ancestor of the true weight drive; cf. *Heronis opera*, ed. W. Schmidt (Leipzig, 1899), i. 361, fig. 86.

[3] Oxford, Bodleian Library MS. 270b, fol. 183ᵛ; cf. C. B. Drover, 'A medieval monastic water-clock', *Antiquarian Horology*, i (1954), 54–59. Since the manuscript was made under the patronage of the French royal family, and since this miniature illustrates the dream of King Hezekiah, probably its clock was not monastic but rather inspired by a clock in the palace at Paris. For this miniature and manuscript, cf. A. de Laborde, *La Bible moralisée* (Paris, 1911–27), i, pl. 183; v, p. 181. *Bibliothèque Nationale: Les Manuscrits à peintures en France du XIIIᵉ au XVIᵉ siècle* (Paris, 1955), 10, no. 6, dates it c. 1250.   [4] Ed. Hahnloser, pl. 12.

1277[1] in which mercury is used instead of water. Behind the braking-wheel, and mounted either on the same axle or on one collared on to it, is a large toothed wheel which appears to control the striking train for the bells. At the left of the clock is a turbine-like wheel of vanes which is probably a fan-escapement to slow the action of the chime, at the striking of the hours, by friction with the air.[2]

This is no mean clock. If the above interpretation of its mechanism is correct, it exhibits *c.* 1250 the first instance of the weight drive in a machine other than the trebuchet, the second example being that of the closely related clock of Alfonso X a quarter-century later. At least in the present state of the evidence, the weight drive appears to be a Western innovation. Doubtless this clock at the court of St. Louis, like that at the court of Castile, was built in more modest emulation of the extraordinary astronomical clock which in 1232 the Sultan of Damascus presented to Frederick II of Hohenstaufen and of which the Emperor was inordinately proud,[3] 'in quo ymagines solis et lune artificialiter mote cursum suum certis et debitis spaciis peragrant et horas diei et noctis infallibiliter indicant'.[4] But there is no indication that a weight drive, as distinct from counterweights to aid the action of floats, was found in Frederick's clock; nor does it appear in Riḍwān's book of 1203 describing his repairs to, and improvements of, the monumental astronomical clock built at Damascus by his father in the late twelfth century.[5]

---

[1] *Libros del saber de astronomia del rey D. Alfonso de Castilla*, ed. M. Rico y Sinobas (Madrid, 1866), iv. 67–76. This section was written by Isaac ben Sid of Toledo between 1252 and 1277; cf. A. Wegener, 'Die astronomische Werke Alfons X', *Bibliotheca mathematica*, vi (1905), 163; E. Wiedemann and F. Hauser, 'Über die Uhren im Bereich der islamischen Kultur', *Nova acta*, c. v (1915), 19; F. M. Feldhaus, 'Die Uhren des Königs Alfonso X von Spanien', *Deutsche Uhrmacher-Zeitung*, liv (1930), 608–12; E. S. Procter, 'The scientific works of the court of Alfonso X of Castile', *Modern Language Review*, xl (1945), 12–29.

[2] A similar shape is found in the blades of the fan escapement of the Dover Castle clock; cf. Feldhaus, *Technik der Vorzeit*, fig. 776; but its date is much in doubt; cf. A. P. Usher, *History of Mechanical Inventions*, 2nd edn. (Cambridge, Mass., 1954), 197.

[3] Cf. Conradus de Fabaria, *Casus Sancti Galli*, in *MGH, Scriptores*, ii (1879), 178.

[4] *Chronica regia Coloniense, continuatio IV*, ed. G. Waitz in *MGH, Scriptores rer. Germ. in usum scholarum*, xii (1880), 263. Trithemius's description, cited by J. Beckmann, *History of Inventions* (London, 1846), i. 350, n. 1, is clearly based on the Cologne Chronicle, with imaginative embellishments.

[5] Wiedemann and Hauser, op. cit. 176–266; Sarton, *Introduction*, ii. 632; Usher, op. cit. 191, fig. 55; cf. L. A. Mayer, *Islamic Astrolabists and their Works* (Geneva, 1956), 62, on Riḍwān's father. H. Schmeller, 'Beiträge zur Geschichte der Technik in der Antike und bei den Arabern', *Abhandlungen zur Geschichte der Naturwissenschaften und der Medizin*, vi (1932), 10–11, publishes a Saracenic chain of buckets for raising water which is powered by two lead weights and which involves gearing. However, since no

Yet the technicians of Europe were not content with the advances illustrated in St. Louis's water-clock: they wanted a purely mechanical chronometer.[1] Fortunately, we possess a treatise written by Robert the Englishman in 1271 which shows not only their attempts and failures, but also the clarity with which they envisaged what they were trying to do.[2] Robert says that while no clock is astronomically accurate, 'nevertheless clockmakers are trying to make a wheel, or disc, which will move exactly as the equinoctial circle does; but they can't quite manage the job (*sed non possunt omnino complere opus eorum*). If they could, however, they would have a really accurate time-piece worth more than the astrolabe or any other astronomical instrument for noting the hours.' He then tells how they are going about their tinkering: a wheel is mounted on an axle so that its rotational balance is even; then a lead weight is suspended from the axle in such a way that the wheel shall revolve once between sunrise and sunset. As for the escapement, in 1271 this is still the unsolved problem.

The main line of development is indicated not only by Robert's astronomical emphasis but by the fact that Alfonso X's mercury clock had an astrolabe as its dial.[3] Most of the first clocks were less chronometers than exhibitions of the pattern of the cosmos. From the time of Archimedes mechanical models of the planetary orbits had been constructed,[4] and there is continuity between those of Antiquity and such a planetarium as was given to Frederick II in 1232. From the first century before Christ we have fragments of a machine of this type which involves very complex gearing.[5] By Ptolemy's time such apparatus was being related to the astrolabe and was becoming a time-measuring device.[6] Al-Bīrūnī (d. A.D. 1048)

escapement is indicated, it is difficult to see how such apparatus would work unless the lead weights and the weight of the water being lifted were very delicately balanced. While this device is found in a group of technological items associated with works of Ridwān, it cannot yet be dated; cf. *infra*, p. 130, n. 4.   [1] See p. 173.

[2] L. Thorndike, 'Invention of the mechanical clock about 1271 A.D.', *Speculum*, xvi (1941), 242–3; also his *Sphere of Sacrobosco and its Commentators* (Chicago, 1949), 180; and 'Robertus Anglicus', *Isis*, xxxiv (1943), 467–9.   [3] *Supra*, p. 121, n. 1.

[4] The evidence is summarized by E. Zinner, 'Entstehung und Ausbreitung der Copernicanischen Lehre', *Sitzungsberichte der Physikalisch-medizinischen Sozietät zu Erlangen*, lxxiv (1943), 48–49. Such machines were early known in China, and reach their culmination in A.D. 1088; cf. J. Needham, Wang Ling, and D. J. Price, 'Chinese astronomical clockwork', *Nature*, clxxvii (1956), 600–2.

[5] *Supra*, p. 80, n. 1.

[6] A. G. Drachmann, 'The plane astrolabe and the anaphoric clock', *Centaurus*, iii (1954), 183–9; cf. also O. Neugebauer, 'The early history of the astrolabe', *Isis*, xl (1949), 240–56.

mentions an intricately geared machine exhibiting the phases of the moon,[1] while al-Battānī (d. A.D. 929) had already given us a diagram of an elaborately geared astrolabe.[2] A specimen from Isfahan survives, dated 1221–2.[3]

That astrolabes had continued to be used in the Latin West throughout the early Middle Ages is made probable by the division of all astrolabes into two families, an eastern Muslim and an Occidental, including the Spanish Muslim specimens. The Occidental variety has a zodiacal circle and operates on the Julian calendar[4] which has no meaning in terms of the lunar months of Islam. Moreover, the division of the hours on the Spanish Muslim *alidades* shows either a Christian derivation or Christian influence.[5] Doubtless the Saracens found astrolabes in use when they conquered Visigothic Spain in the eighth century, and failed to follow eastern Islam's lead in adapting the instrument to the lunar calendar.

The earliest extant Latin astrolabe is of English make, and comes from the late twelfth century.[6] By *c.* 1300 admirable geared astrolabes were being produced in France.[7] Clearly, the origins of the mechanical clock lie in a complex realm of monumental planetaria, equatoria,[8] and geared astrolabes.[9] By the later thirteenth century, scholars were not only theorizing about such things, they were occasionally making them with their own hands: in 1274 the famous Henry Bate of Malines boasts of an astrolabe which 'manu complevi propria'.[10] That

[1] E. Wiedemann, 'Ein Instrument das die Bewegung von Sonne und Mond darstellt nach al-Bīrūnī', *Der Islam*, iv (1913), 5–13.

[2] Price, in *Horological Journal*, 29, fig. 4.

[3] Price, op. cit., figs. 2, 3; Mayer, op. cit. 59; R. T. Gunther, *Astrolabes of the World* (Oxford, 1932), i. 118–20, pls. XXV–XXVI.

[4] H. Michel, 'Un astrolabe latin du XIIe siècle', *Ciel et terre*, lxiv (1948), 73–74. On the difficulties of dating, cf. E. Poulle, 'Peut-on dater les astrolabes médiévaux?', *Revue d'histoire des sciences*, ix (1956), 301–22.

[5] E. Zinner, 'Über die früheste Form des Astrolabs', *Bericht der Naturforschende Gesellschaft, Bamberg*, xxx (1947), 18.   [6] Michel, op. cit. 73–79.

[7] Price, op. cit., figs. 5, 6; also his 'The prehistory of the clock', *Discovery*, xvii (1956), 155, fig. 2.

[8] Cf. *The Equatorie of the Planetis*, ed. D. J. Price (Cambridge, 1955), 119–30.

[9] E. Poulle, 'L'Astrolabe médiéval d'après les manuscrits de la Bibliothèque Nationale', *Bibliothèque de l'École des Chartes*, cxii (1954), 99, emphasizes the great interest in, and development of, the astrolabe in the later thirteenth century as preparation for the notable astronomical advances of the fourteenth century, on which cf. L. Thorndike, 'Pre-Copernican astronomical activity', *Proceedings of the American Philosophical Society*, xciv (1950), 321–6.

[10] R. Levy, 'The authorship of a Latin treatise on the astrolabe', *Speculum*, xvii (1942), 569; cf. E. Poulle, 'La Fabrication des astrolabes au moyen âge', *Techniques et civilisations*, iv (1955), 117–28.

many inventors were working on the problem of a mechanical escapement is best indicated by the emergence in close sequence of two related solutions: the oscillating foliot bar north of the Alps, and the oscillating wheel in Italy.[1] Yet we shall probably never know exactly when the discovery was made. Just as the origins of gunpowder artillery are obscured by the visual and verbal similarity to cannon of Greek fire shot from tubes, so also the absorption of the entire vocabulary of the water-clock[2] by the later mechanical clock, and the fact that some large water-clocks employed chains of gears[3] have hopelessly confused our ability to judge the records of the crucial period, the early fourteenth century.[4] Yet certainly weight-driven mechanical clocks were well known by 1341, when a Milanese chronicle tells us that on the analogy of such clocks, and after many trials, the local technicians had constructed weight-driven mills for grinding grain.[5]

Suddenly, towards the middle of the fourteenth century, the mechanical clock seized the imagination of our ancestors. Something of the civic pride which earlier had expended itself in cathedral-building now was diverted to the construction of astronomical clocks of astounding intricacy and elaboration. No European community felt able to hold up its head unless in its midst the planets wheeled in cycles and epicycles, while angels trumpeted, cocks crew, and apostles, kings, and prophets marched and countermarched at the booming of the hours.[6]

[1] Cf. E. Zinner, *Die ältesten Räderuhren* (Bamberg, 1939), 26; Usher, op. cit. 200, figs. 58–59.

[2] Cf. especially P. Sheridan, 'Les Inscriptions sur ardoise de l'Abbaye de Villers', *Annales de la Société d'Archéologie de Bruxelles*, x (1896), 203–15, 404–51.

[3] *Supra*, p. 120. Dante scholars have wrongly assumed that the poet (d. 1319) thrice refers to mechanical clocks, because he speaks of gears in clocks; cf. G. Boffito, 'Dove e quando potè Dante vedere gli orologi meccanici che descrive in *Par.* X, 139; XXIV, 13; XXXIII, 144?', *Giornale dantesco*, xxxix (1938), 45–61.

[4] Usher, op. cit. 196, followed by W. C. Watson, 'Fourteenth century clocks still in existence', *American Journal of Physics*, xxiv (1956), 209, concludes that the first evidence of a mechanical clock is at Milan in 1335, with fair probability for Modena in 1343, Padua in 1344, and Monza in 1347; but in no case do we have certainty. The first instance outside Italy was probably the clock of Strassburg in 1352.

[5] Gualvaneo de la Flamma, *De gestis Azonis vicecomitis*, ed. L. A. Muratori, *Rerum italicarum scriptores*, xii (Milan, 1728), 1038: 'adinvenerunt facere molendina, quae non aqua aut vento circumferuntur, sed per pondera contra pondera sicut fieri solet in horologiis. Et sunt ibi rotae multae, et non est opus, nisi unius pueri, et moliunt continue quatuor modios tritici, molitura optima nimis. Nec unquam in Italia tali opus fuit adinventum, licet per multos exquisitum.'

[6] The most comprehensive listing and description of these clocks is A. Ungerer, *Les Horloges astronomiques et monumentales les plus remarquables de l'antiquité jusqu'à nos*

It was not only in their diversity, their scale, and their wide diffusion that these automata were unlike those of earlier times. While many were attached to churches, they lacked the element of pious deception found in devices for Hellenistic temples. While many were the ornaments of city halls or palaces, in intent they were far from the Byzantine political use of automata, as described in the tenth century by Liutprand of Cremona,[1] to enhance awe of the emperor. These new great astronomical clocks were presented frankly as mechanical marvels, and the public delighted in them as such.[2] This in itself indicates a shift in the values of European society.

But while they were gargantuan toys, such clocks were far more than toys: they were symbols related to the inmost, and often unverbalized, tendencies of that age. By 1319–20 a novel theory of impetus was emerging, transitional between that of Aristotle and Newton's inertial motion.[3] Under the older concept, nothing moved unless it were constantly pushed by an outside force. Under the new physical theory, things keep moving by means of forces originally imprinted upon them, by *vis impressa*. Moreover, regularity, mathematically predictable relationships, facts quantitatively measurable, were looming larger in men's picture of the universe.[4] And the great clock, partly because its inexorability was so playfully masked, its mechanism so humanized by its whimsicalities, furnished the picture. It is in the works of the great ecclesiastic and mathematician Nicholas Oresmus, who died in 1382 as Bishop of Lisieux, that we first find the metaphore of the universe as a vast mechanical clock created and set running by God so that 'all the wheels move as harmoniously as possible'.[5] It was a notion with a future: eventually the metaphore became a metaphysics.

In 1348 a distinguished physician and astronomer, Giovanni de' Dondi, began work with his own hands on a clock which it took him sixteen years to complete.[6] When it was finished in 1364, Giovanni wrote a treatise describing it, equipped lavishly with diagrams.

jours (Paris, 1931). However, it lacks specific documentation and rests to a suspicious extent upon correspondence with local antiquarians.

[1] *Antapodosis*, vi. 5, tr. F. A. Wright (London, 1930), 207–8.

[2] See p. 174.   [3] See p. 174.

[4] L. Mumford, *Technics and Civilization* (New York, 1934), 12–18.

[5] See p. 174.

[6] As we are told *c.* 1389 by his friend Philippe de Mézières; cf. the Abbé Lebeuf, 'Notice des ouvrages de Philippe de Maizieres', *Histoire de l'Académie Royale des Inscriptions et Belleslettres*, xvi (1751), 228; D. M. Bell, *Étude sur Le Songe du vieil pèlerin de Philippe de Mézières* (Geneva, 1955), 116–17.

Although six manuscripts of the work survive,[1] this monument in the history of machinery has never been published. Giovanni's clock was only incidentally a timepiece: it included the celestial wanderings of sun, moon, and five planets, and provided a perpetual calendar of all religious feasts, both fixed and movable. His sense of the inter-relation of moving parts showed genius: to provide for the eliptical orbits of the Moon and Mercury (as required by the Ptolemaic system) he produced eliptical gears, and likewise made provision for the observed irregularities in the orbit of Venus.[2] In complexity and refinement Giovanni's gearing goes enormously beyond anything which survives from earlier technology, including the fragments of the Hellenistic planetarium found in the Aegean Sea.[3] In this aspect of machine design the fourteenth century marks an epoch. Indeed, no progress in the design of gravity-operated clocks seems to have been made during the next two centuries, for in 1529 when the Emperor Charles V visited Pavia and marvelled at Giovanni's clock, which was then out of order, he could find only one technician, Giovanni Torriani, capable of repairing it.[4]

Yet soon after Giovanni de' Dondi's day, clockmakers were pressing on to technical conquests of a different sort. In 1377 Charles V of France owned an *orloge portative*:[5] this may indeed have been simply a miniature conventional clock. But we have seen that from the middle thirteenth century engineers were interested in springs as elements in automatic machines, and from the time of the earliest spring-trap it had been understood that a spring stores energy. By about A.D. 1400 the coiled spring appears in locks,[6] from which source (as the name indicates) it was transferred to flint-locks for

[1] H. A. Lloyd, *Giovanni de' Dondi's horological masterpiece, 1364* (Hookwood, Limpsfield, Oxted, Surrey, 1956), 1, enumerates them; cf. L. Thorndike, 'Milan manuscripts of Giovanni de' Dondi's *Astronomical Clock* and Jacopo de' Dondi's discussion of tides', *Archeion*, xviii (1936), 308–17, and his *History of Magic and Experimental Science*, iii. 386–92; G. Baillie, 'Giovanni de' Dondi and his planetarium clock of 1364', *Horological Journal*, lxxvi (1934), April: 472–6, May: 8–12, June: 39–43; summarized by A. Simoni, 'Giovanni de' Dondi e il suo orologio dei pianeti', *La Clessidra*, viii (Feb. 1952), 3–12; Usher, op. cit. 198–200.

[2] Lloyd, op. cit., figs. 14–17. Shortly after 1500 Leonardo da Vinci seems to have sketched the gearing for Venus on this clock; cf. D. J. Price, 'Leonardo da Vinci and the clock of Giovanni de' Dondi', *Antiquarian Horology*, ii (1958), 127–8.

[3] *Supra*, p. 80, n. 1.

[4] Lloyd, op. cit. 23. On Torriani, cf. T. Beck, *Beiträge zur Geschichte des Maschinen-baues* (Berlin, 1899), 365–90.

[5] J. D. Robertson, *Evolution of Clockwork* (London, 1931), 44.

[6] Feldhaus, *Technik der Vorzeit*, 289.

fire-arms in the second half of the fifteenth century.[1] The earliest extant example of a spring-driven chronometer is a magnificent chamber clock made c. 1430 for Philip the Good, Duke of Burgundy.[2] Even the sceptics who fear that the works of this clock may not be original admit that springs were used in clocks by c. 1440–50 when such a timepiece is shown in a Burgundian painting.[3] Moreover, in 1459 the King of France bought a 'demi orloge doré de fin or sans contrepoix'.[4] In a letter of 19 July 1488 in the Modena Archive a marvel appears: Ludovico Sforza has ordered three elaborate costumes for himself, his wife, and Galeazzo of San Severino, each to be ornamented with a pendent watch, two of which shall strike the hours.[5] The timepiece had reached the human neck, if not the wrist.

But the spring-drive for small clocks and watches presented an entirely new set of problems as regards escapement: obviously neither the foliot nor the balance-wheel would function well in terms of the motion and jarring of a portable clock; but equally important was the fact that, whereas a weight exerted equal force at all times, a spring loses its energy as it uncoils. An escapement was therefore needed which would exactly compensate for this gradual diminution of power in the drive.

The world of those educated humanistically has not trained itself in the appreciation of the aesthetics of skill. Yet one cannot contemplate the solutions of this pair of difficulties at which the technicians of the fifteenth century arrived without the emotion which should be stirred by any great achievement. The intensity and ingenuity of the effort expended is indicated by the fact that once again, as in the case of the escapements for the weight-driven clock, two devices emerged —the stackfreed and the fusee.

The stackfreed cannot yet definitely be documented earlier than a watch of c. 1535,[6] but since it is a slightly less satisfactory device

[1] M. Thierbach, 'Über die Entwicklung des Steinschlosses', Zeitschrift für historische Waffenkunde, iii (1902–5), 305–11; F. M. Feldhaus, 'Das Radschloss bei Leonardo da Vinci', ibid. iv (1906–8), 153–4.   [2] See p. 175.

[3] Lloyd, loc. cit., Singer, op. cit. iii (1957), pl. 32b.

[4] L. Reverchon, Petite histoire d'horlogerie (Besançon, 1935), 67.

[5] E. Morpurgo, 'L'Orologio da petto prima del Henlein', La Clessidra, viii (Aug. 1952), 5: the costumes are 'ad una Liverea, che è un orologio da sonare hore cum li soi Campanini, excepto che in quella del perfacto S. Lodovico'. Zinner, op. cit. 20–21, thinks, without adequate reason, that these were not pendent watches but only portable clocks.

[6] F. J. Britten, Old Clocks and Watches and their Makers, 2nd edn. (London, 1904), 134, figs. 130–4; E. Hillary, 'The first 100 years of watchmaking', Horological Journal, xcvii (1955), 40. By 1530 the utilization of spring clocks for ascertaining navigational

than the fusee, it may perhaps antedate the latter. The stackfreed[1] consists of two parts: first, a snail-shaped disk cam mounted on a wheel geared to the mainspring's axle; and second, a long, stiff, arched spring anchored firmly at one end, and with the other end exerting a braking pressure on the large part of the snail when the mainspring is tight, but upon the smaller diameters of the snail when the mainspring is running down. Thus the mainspring must overcome the braking friction of the stackfreed-spring in addition to driving the works. Finally, as the clock runs down, a small roller at the free end of the stackfreed-spring slips into the snail's notch and in this position the stackfreed-spring helps the weakened mainspring to do its work.

The fusee was an even more wonderful invention; indeed, a leading historian of horology has said of it: 'Perhaps no problem in mechanics has ever been solved so simply and so perfectly.'[2] It is found in the earliest surviving spring-clock, that of *c.* 1430, and from 1477 we have a diagram of it.[3] The fusee equalizes the changing force of the mainspring by means of a brake of gut or fine chain which is gradually wound spirally around a conical axle, the force of the brake being dependent upon the leverage of the diameter of the cone at any given point and moment. It is a device of great mechanical elegance. Yet the idea did not originate with the clock-makers: it is typical of the interdependence of all aspects of technology that they borrowed it from the military engineers. In Kyeser's *Bellifortis* of *c.* 1405[4] we find such a conical axle in apparatus for spanning a heavy cross-bow. With very medieval humour, this machine was called 'the virgin', presumably because it offered least resistance when the bow was slack, and most when it was taut.

By the latter part of the fifteenth century, Europe was equipped not only with sources of power far more diversified than those known to any previous culture, but also with an arsenal of technical means for grasping, guiding, and utilizing such energies which was immeasurably more varied and skilful than any people of the past had

position was envisaged, if not practised; cf. A. Pogo, 'Gemma Frisius, his method of determining longitude by transporting timepieces', *Isis*, xxii (1935), 469–85.

[1] Diagrams of both stackfreed and fusee may be found in Usher, op. cit., fig. 113, and Singer, op. cit. iii (1957), figs. 392, 394.

[2] G. Baillie, *Watches* (London, 1929), 85.

[3] Zinner, op. cit. 19, fig. 3; Singer, op. cit. iii, fig. 392.

[4] *Bellifortis*, fol. 76ᵛ; cf. *supra*, p. 111, n. 3; F. M. Feldhaus, 'Über den Ursprung von Federzug und Schnecke', *Deutsche Urmacher-Zeitung*, liv (1930), 720–2.

possessed, or than was known to any contemporary society of the Old World or the New.[1] The expansion of Europe from 1492 onward was based in great measure upon Europe's high consumption of energy, with consequent productivity, economic weight, and military might.[2] But mechanical power has no meaning apart from mechanisms to harness it. Beginning probably with the fulling mill on the Serchio in 983, the eleventh and twelfth centuries had applied the cam to a great variety of operations. The thirteenth century discovered spring and treadle; the fourteenth century developed gearing to levels of incredible complexity; the fifteenth century, by elaborating crank, connecting-rod, and governor, vastly facilitated the conversion of reciprocating into continuous rotary motion. Considering the generally slow tempo of human history, this revolution in machine design occurred with startling rapidity. Indeed, the four centuries following Leonardo, that is, until electrical energy demanded a supplementary set of devices, were less technologically engaged in discovering basic principles than in elaborating and refining those established during the four centuries before Leonardo.

III

The Concept of a Power Technology

Did the technicians of the later Middle Ages know what they were doing? Obviously there was a vigorous and even daring effort at innovation,[3] but was it guided by any broader concepts?

The symptom of the emergence of a conscious and generalized lust for natural energy and its application to human purposes, is the enthusiastic adoption by thirteenth-century Europe of an idea which

[1] See p. 175.

[2] About 1444 Bessarion wrote to Constantine Palaeologus, Despot of the Morea and the best hope of Greek resurgence against the Turks, urging him to send young men to Italy to learn the practical arts. He was impressed not only with Western textiles and glass, improved arms, ships, and metallurgy: he speaks more particularly of the use of water-power to eliminate hand labour, for example in sawing timbers and working the bellows of furnaces; cf. A. G. Keller, 'A Byzantine admirer of "Western" progress: Cardinal Bessarion', *Cambridge Historical Journal*, xi (1955), 343–8.

[3] For example, in 1322 a 'Teothonicus ingenerius' in Venice offered to build a new kind of mill for grinding grain, and to submit it to test by the Grand Council; cf. H. Simonsfeld, *Der Fondaco dei Tedeschi in Venedig* (Stuttgart, 1887), ii. 292. Such awareness of change led to the beginning of the modern historiography of technology *c.* 1350 in Gulielmus Pastrengus, *De originibus rerum*, printed at Venice in 1547. On the development of such writings through the sixteenth century, cf. E. Zilsel, *Die Entstehung des Geniebegriffes* (Tübingen, 1926), 130–4.

had originated in twelfth-century India—perpetual motion.[1] Writing about A.D. 1150, the great Hindu astronomer and mathematician Bhāskarā says in his *Siddhānta śiromaṇi*:[2] 'Make a wheel of light wood and in its circumference put hollow rods all having bores of the same diameter, and let them be placed at equal distances from each other; and let them also be all placed at an angle somewhat verging from the perpendicular; then half fill these hollow rods with mercury: the wheel thus filled will, when placed on an axis supported by two posts, turn by itself.' And again he writes: 'Or scoop out a canal in the tire of a wheel; then, plastering leaves of the tála tree over this canal with wax, fill one half of this canal with water and the other half with mercury till the water begins to come out, and then seal up the orifice left open for filling the wheel. The wheel will then revolve of itself, drawn round by the water.'

In India the idea of perpetual motion was entirely consistent with, and was perhaps rooted in, the Hindu concept of the cyclical and self-perpetuating nature of all things.[3] Almost immediately it was picked up in Islam where it amplified the tradition of automata. An Arabic treatise of uncertain date,[4] but which in the manuscripts seems to be associated with works of Riḍwān (*c*. A.D. 1200), contains six *perpetua mobilia*, all gravitational. One of them is identical with Bhāskarā's mercury wheel with slanted rods,[5] whereas two others[6]

---

[1] See p. 175.

[2] *Bibliotheca indica*, XXXII: *Hindu astronomy: Siddhānta śiromaṇi*, tr. L. Wilkinson (Calcutta, 1861), 227–8; cf. M. Winternitz, *Geschichte der indischen Literatur*, iii (Leipzig, 1920), 564. The text mentions other discussions of perpetual motion by Lalla and other astronomers, but of these I find no trace; cf. A. K. Ganguly, 'Bhāskarāchārya's references to previous teachers', *Bulletin of the Calcutta Mathematical Society*, xviii (1927), 65–76.

[3] The suggestion of J. Needham, L. Wang, and D. J. Price, *Heavenly Clockwork: the Great Astronomical Clocks of Medieval China* (Cambridge, 1959), 55, 73, n. 2, 192, that the concept of perpetual motion may have originated from naïve observation of the astonishing water-driven Chinese clocks, the motor of which was concealed, cannot be accepted for two reasons: first, there is no present evidence that the idea of perpetual motion was known in China; second, there is no indication that news of such clocks reached India where in fact the idea emerged.

[4] The manuscripts are Gotha no. 1348; Leiden no. 1414, Cod. 499 Warner; Oxford, cod. arab. 954, and Istanbul, Hagia Sophia no. 2755. B. Carra de Vaux in *Bibliotheca mathematica*, 3rd series, i (1900), 29–34, and *Notices et extraits des manuscrits de la Bibliothèque Nationale*, xxxviii (1903), 29, n. 1, 30, n. 1, considers the treatise 'd'une époque très tardive'. E. Wiedemann in the *Erlangen Sitzungsberichte*, xxxvii (1905), 231, ascribes the treatise to Riḍwān, but ibid. xxxviii (1906) 13 considers the authorship doubtful. H. Schmeller in *Abhandlungen zur Geschichte der Naturschaften und der Medizin*, vi (1922), 16–23, is uncertain of the date or authorship.

[5] Schmeller, op. cit. 16–19; figs. 9, 9a.   [6] Ibid. 20–21, figs. 12, 13.

are identical with the first two perpetual motion devices to appear (c. 1235) in Europe: Villard de Honnecourt's wheels of pivoted hammers and of pivoted tubes of mercury.[1] In an anonymous Latin work of the later fourteenth century[2] we find a perpetual motion machine very like Bhāskarā's second proposal for a wheel with its rim containing mercury. Moreover, a *perpetuum mobile* of radial hinged rods found in the Arabic treatise[3] reappears c. 1440 in the notebook of Mariano di Jacopo Taccola.[4] Thus, while there is no evidence that this particular Arabic collection was known to Latin Europe, we may be sure that about A.D. 1200 Islam served as intermediary in transmitting the Indian concept of perpetual motion to Europe, just as it was transmitting Hindu numerals and positional reckoning at the same moment: Leonard of Pisa's *Liber abaci* appeared in 1202.

To Hindus the universe itself was a perpetual motion machine, and there seemed nothing absurd in an endless and spontaneous flow of energy. Bhāskarā speaks of the siphon as though it were a device for perpetual motion,[5] and his fourteenth-century European imitator insists that his mercury wheel is in perpetual motion, even though when he made it experimentally he applied heat to its lower part, and is quite aware that it turned because the heat made the mercury rise.[6] A windmill on a hill with constant breezes, a water-mill in a stream which never runs dry, were, to the Middle Ages, perpetual motion machines.[7] The significant things about the idea of perpetual motion in late Medieval Europe, in contrast to India and Islam, are the indications of the intense and widespread interest in it, the attempt to diversify its motors, and the effort to make it do something useful.

The thirteenth-century Occident saw two forces, gravity and magnetism, which operated with a constancy unrivalled by wind and water. Attached to his sketch of a gravitational *perpetuum mobile*, Villard de Honnecourt appends a note: 'Many a day have the masters [*maistres*] disputed how to make a wheel turn by itself. Here is how it can be done, either by unequal hammers or by quicksilver.'[8]

[1] Ed. Hahnloser, pl. 9.
[2] Thorndike, op. cit. iii. 578.
[3] Schmeller, op. cit. 22, fig. 14.
[4] Munich, Staatsbibliothek, Cod. lat. 197, fol. 58ʳ; cf. T. Beck, *Beiträge zur Geschichte des Maschinenbaues* (Berlin, 1899), 287, fig. 341. I do not know the nature of what seems to be a proposal for perpetual motion made in 1418 at Florence by Peter 'Fannulla'; cf. F. D. Prager, 'Brunelleschi's inventions', *Osiris*, ix (1950), 523, n. 170.
[5] Op. cit. 227.   [6] Thorndike, loc. cit.
[7] Cf. the quotation from A. Meygret, *infra*, p. 176.   [8] Loc. cit.

Could magnetism similarly be harnessed? Notices of A.D. 1040–4, 1089–93, and 1116 refer to the use of a magnetized needle in China for geomancy, while in 1119 and 1122 the Chinese were using it for navigation.[1] In Europe the mariner's compass appears in Alexander Neckham's *De naturis rerum*,[2] which was in wide circulation by the end of the twelfth century,[3] and in Guiot de Provins's *Bible*[4] composed between 1203 and 1208. By *c.* 1218 Jacques de Vitry considered the compass 'valde necessarius . . . navigantibus in mari'.[5] By *c.* 1225 it was in common use even in Iceland.[6] It did not reach the West by way of Islam, but rather overland, primarily as an astronomical instrument for determining the meridian.[7] The first Muslim reference to the compass comes in a Persian story of 1232–3.[8] The earliest Arabic mention of it, written in 1282 but explicitly referring to an episode of 1242–3, speaks of it as a novelty.[9] Moreover, the Arabic word *al-konbas* indicates that its use reached the Muslim Levant from the West, probably from Italy.[10]

Almost immediately after its introduction, the compass began to stimulate European thinking about magnetic force. In his *De universo creaturarum*, written *c.* 1231–6, the great Bishop of Paris, William of Auvergne, used the analogy of magnetic induction to explain the motion of the celestial spheres.[11] In 1269, in his epochal *Epistola de*

[1] Li Shu-hua, 'Origine de la boussole', *Isis*, xlv (1954), 180, 183, 184, 188, 192.

[2] See p. 175.

[3] G. Sarton, *Introduction to the History of Science*, ii (Baltimore, 1931), 385. Ibid. 349, mentions a Hebrew text written in England *c.* 1194 by Berakya ha-Naqdan in which the compass is found.

[4] Ed. J. F. Wolfort and H. Schulz, *Percival-Studien*, i (Halle, 1861), 50–51, ll. 622–53; for the date, cf. 4.

[5] *Historia hierosolimitana*, cap. 89, in *Gesta Dei per Francos*, ed. J. Bongars (Hannover, 1611), i. 1106. The frequent statement that Jacques says that the compass came from India is incorrect: he simply says that the lodestone is of Indian origin.

[6] A gloss of *c.* 1225 on the *Historia islandica*, written *c.* 1108, speaking of an episode in 868, says that the sailors of that time did not have the compass; cf. G. Beaujouan, *La Science antique et médiévale* (Paris, 1957), 573.

[7] E. G. R. Taylor, 'The south-pointing needle', *Imago mundi*, viii (1951), 1–7, and her *The Haven-finding Art* (New York, 1957), 96.

[8] Balmer, op. cit. 54.

[9] Ibid. 53; Li, op. cit. 195; E. Wiedemann, 'Beiträge zur Geschichte der Naturwissenschaften', *Sitzungsberichte der Physikalisch-medizinischen Sozietät zu Erlangen*, xxxv (1903), 330–1; Taylor, *Haven-finding Art*, 96. However, by 1282 the author had learned that in the Indian Ocean a compass was in use consisting of a thin floating dish of magnetized iron, which is likewise the form mentioned in the Persian source of 1232–3. Since, according to Li, op. cit. 180–1, fig. 5, this is the earliest Chinese type of geomantic compass, it appears that Islam received the compass almost simultaneously from both East and West.

[10] Balmer, loc. cit.

[11] P. Duhem, *Le Système du monde*, iii (Paris, 1915), 259.

magnete, which is the cornerstone of all subsequent work on magnetism, the military engineer Peter of Maricourt, whom Roger Bacon considered the greatest scientist of his age,[1] presents a diagram for a magnetic perpetual motion machine, and incidentally confirms Villard's testimony of the general interest in such matters by adding: 'I have seen many men floundering exhausted in their repeated efforts to invent such a wheel.'[2] Such are the roots of fourteenth-century notions of mills operated by magnetic power.[3]

But by *c.* 1260[4] Peter had already been pondering a second *perpetuum mobile* which is doubly significant because, unlike his magnetic wheel, it was designed to be useful. That his experiments with it may have been generally known in Paris is indicated by John of St. Amand's identification, in the 1260's, of the properties of the magnet with those of Earth itself: 'Dico quod in adamante est vestigium orbis.'[5] In 1269 Peter of Maricourt described his new device: a globular lodestone which, if it were mounted without friction parallel to the celestial axis, would rotate once a day. Properly inscribed with a map of the heavens, it would serve as an automatic armillary sphere for astronomical observations and as a perfect clock, enabling one to dispense with all other chronometers.[6]

By the middle of the thirteenth century, then, a considerable group of active minds, stimulated not only by the technological

---

[1] In *Opus tertium*, cap. 13, in *Opera inedita*, ed. J. S. Brewer (London, 1859), 46–47, Bacon says of Peter: 'He was ashamed if any ordinary person or old crone or soldier or country bumpkin knew something he didn't. So he investigated the methods of metal casters, and what they do with gold, silver, other metals and all minerals; and he learned all about warfare, arms and hunting; he examined everything concerned with agriculture, land surveying, and the work of peasants; he even studied the doings (*experimenta*) of hags, their divinations and incantations, and those of all the sorcerers, and likewise the illusions and tricks of all the jugglers, so that ▪▪thing should escape him which might be learned, and in order that he might be able to expose all fraud and magic.'

[2] *Epistola Petri Peregrini de Maricourt ad Sygerum de Foucaucourt militem*, Pars II, cap. 3, ed. G. Hellmann in *Neudrucke von Schriften und Karten über Meteorologie und Erdmagnetismus*, no. 10: *Rara magnetica* (Berlin, 1898), 11.

[3] Cf. J. L. Lowes, *Geoffrey Chaucer* (Bloomington, 1958), 36.

[4] Bacon's *De secretis operibus*, c. 6, in *Opera inedita*, 537, says that 'experimentator tamen fidelis et magnificus ad hoc anhelat, ut ea [sphera armillaris] tali materia fieret, et tanto artificio, quod naturaliter coelum motu diurno volveretur'. A. G. Little, *Roger Bacon Essays* (Oxford, 1914), 395, suggests a possible date of *c.* 1248 for the composition of the *De secretis operibus*, but on inadequate grounds. S. C. Easton, *Roger Bacon and his Search for a Universal Science* (New York, 1952), 111, more cautiously proposes a date of *c.* 1260.

[5] L. Thorndike, 'John of St. Amand on the magnet', *Isis*, xxxvi (1946), 156. John's work was printed at Venice in 1508.

[6] See p. 176.

successes of recent generations but also led on by the will-o'-the-wisp of perpetual motion, were beginning to generalize the concept of mechanical power. They were coming to think of the cosmos as a vast reservoir of energies to be tapped and used according to human intentions. They were power-conscious to the point of fantasy. But without such fantasy, such soaring imagination, the power technology of the Western world would not have been developed. When Peter of Maricourt's friend Roger Bacon wrote, c. 1260, 'Machines may be made by which the largest ships, with only one man steering them, will be moved faster than if they were filled with rowers; wagons may be built which will move with incredible speed and without the aid of beasts; flying machines can be constructed in which a man . . . may beat the air with wings like a bird . . . machines will make it possible to go to the bottom of seas and rivers',[1] he spoke not alone but for the engineers of his age.

[1] *De secretis operibus*, c. 4, ed. cit. 533; cf. L. Thorndike, *History of Magic and Experimental Science*, ii (1929), 654–5; F. Boll, 'Technische Träume des Mittelalters', *Die Umschau*, xxi (1917), 678–80.

Notes

Note 1, p. 1. Polydore Vergil was the first to note, in *De inventoribus rerum* (Venice, 1499), Lib. III, cap. 13, that the stirrup is post-classical. The idea soon became common: Jan van der Straet (1523-1605) published an engraving celebrating the stirrup as a 'modern' discovery on a par with that of America, the compass, gunpowder, printing, the mechanical clock, guaiacum (a supposed specific against syphilis), distillation, and silk; cf. J. Stradanus, *Nova reperta: New Discoveries of the Middle Ages and Renaissance*, ed. E. Rosen and B. Dibner (Norwalk, Conn., 1953), pl. 9. The early literature on the stirrup is critically summarized by J. Beckmann, *History of Inventions and Discoveries*, 3rd edn. (London, 1817), ii. 255-70. The most exhaustive modern study is by Major A. Schlieben, 'Geschichte der Steigbügel', *Annalen des Vereins für Nassauische Altertumskunde und Geschichtsforschung*, xxiv (1892), 165-231; xxv (1893), 45-52. R. Zschille and R. Forrer, *Die Steigbügel in ihrer Formentwicklung* (Berlin, 1896), depend largely on Schlieben for their historical material. The discussion was renewed by Commandant R. Lefebvre des Noëttes, *L'Attelage et le cheval de selle à travers les âges* (Paris, 1931). For the total problem, as distinct from its detailed aspects, see subsequently R. Reinecke, 'Zur Geschichte des Steigbügels', *Germania*, xvii (1933), 220-2; R. Blomqvist, 'Stigbyglar', *Kulturen*, 1948, 92-124; A. D. H. Bivar, 'The stirrup and its origins', *Oriental Art*, new series, i (1955), 61-65. The frequently cited correspondence in the London *Times* for 24 and 26 Feb., 14, 20, and 31 Mar. 1947, added nothing to the discussion.

Note 2, p. 1. The military and social effects of the introduction of the light chariot are discussed by H. A. Potratz, *Das Pferd der Frühzeit* (Seestadt-Rostock, 1938); cf. also B. P. Sinha, 'Art of war in ancient India, 600 B.C.-300 A.D.', *Journal of World History*, iv (1957), 126-8. For the effects of the displacement of the chariot by riders, see J. Wiesner, 'Fahren und Reiten in Alteuropa und im alten Orient', *Der alte Orient*, xxxviii, Heft 2-4 (1939); E. Erkes, 'Das Pferd im alten China', *T'oung pao*, xxxvi (1940), 26-63. E. D. Phillips, 'New light on the ancient history of the Eurasian steppe', *American Journal of Archaeology*, lxi (1957), 273-4, concludes that horse-riding began probably on the Caucasian plains *c*. 1000 B.C. A. R. Schulman, 'Egyptian representations of horsemen and riding in the New Kingdom', *Journal of Near Eastern Studies*, xvi (1957), 263-71, shows that in Egypt mounted military scouts were used at a time when chariots alone were employed for actual combat. However, M. A. F. Hood, 'A Mycenaean cavalryman', *Annual of the British School at Athens*, xlviii (1953), 84-93, has produced firm evidence of riding *c*. 1300 B.C. In general, see G. G. Simpson, 'Horses and history', *Natural History*, xxxviii (1936), 277-88.

Note 2, p. 3. In an essay which has a significance out of all proportion to its brevity, J. R. Strayer, 'Feudalism in Western Europe', in *Feudalism in History*, ed. R. Coulborn (Princeton, 1956), 15-25, challenges this view, and insists (p. 16) that 'Western European feudalism is essentially political—it is a form of government. . . . Feudalism is not merely the relationship between lord and man, nor the system of dependent land tenures, for either can exist in a non-feudal society. The combination of personal and tenurial dependence brings us close to feudalism, but something is still lacking. It is only when rights of government (not mere political influence) are attached to lordship and fiefs that we can speak of fully developed feudalism in Western Europe. It is the possession of rights of government by feudal lords and the performance of most functions of government through feudal lords which clearly distinguish feudalism from other types of organization.' Admitting (p. 21) that 'vassalage was becoming common and something very like fiefs held of a king or of lords appeared about the middle of the eighth century', nevertheless 'this was not yet feudalism: there was still public authority'; the rise of feudalism as a form of government came in the dynastic chaos of the fifty years after Charlemagne's death.

But Brunner was closer to the violent tone of feudal life, and to the self-image of members of the feudal class, in maintaining that European feudalism was essentially a way of organizing society for instant warfare, with emphasis upon local forces. In the ninth century, when the Carolingian realm decayed, vassals and fief-holders inherited the debris of public authority exactly because their society had already been reorganized in such a military way that they were in a position to pick up the political pieces. Feudalism was a military structure which, after about a century, added political to military functions. Nouns like *feudalism* are crypto-verbs: they describe not so much patterns of institutions as patterns of action and of fluctuating power relationships which became consciously institutionalized and legalized not only after the fact but often after the legalized 'fact' has already changed into something different. On the basis of Far Eastern evidence, O. Lattimore in *Past and Present*, xii (1957), 47–57, similarly rejects Strayer's concept of feudalism, and particularly (p. 50) its inadequate emphasis on 'the nature of the warfare that precedes and helps to produce feudalism'.

Note 4, p. 3. '. . . ut paries inmobiles permanentes sicut et zona rigoris glacialiter manent adstricti, Arabes gladio enecant', *Monumenta Germaniae Historica* (hereafter cited as *MGH*), *Auctores antiqui*, xi. 361. The records of the battle are so unsatisfactory that it cannot be visualized in detail; cf. E. Mercier, 'La Bataille de Poitiers et les vraies causes du recul de l'invasion arabe', *Revue historique*, vii (1878), 1–8; F. Dahn, *Urgeschichte der germanischen und romanischen Völker* (Berlin, 1883), iii. 794–8; M. G. J. L. Lecointre, 'La Bataille de Poitiers entre Charles Martel et les Sarrasins: L'histoire et la legende; origine de celle-ci', *Bulletin de la Société des Antiquaires de l'Ouest*, 3rd series, vii (1924), 632–42; L. Levillain and C. Samaran, 'Sur le lieu et la date de la bataille de Poitiers en 732', *Bibliothèque de l'École des Chartes*, xcix (1938), 243–67; M. Mercier and A. Seguin, *Charles Martel et la bataille de Poitiers* (Paris, 1944). The attempt of G. Roloff, 'Die Umwandlung des fränkischen Heeres von Chlodwig bis Karl den Grossen', *Neue Jahrbücher für das klassische Altertum*, ix (1902), 390, n. 1, to challenge Brunner's view that Martel's men at Poitiers fought primarily on foot has found favour only with A. Dopsch, *Wirtschaftliche und soziale Grundlagen der Europäischen Kulturentwicklung*, 2nd edn. (Vienna, 1924), ii. 297. A charitable editor, however, removed the relevant sentence from the English translation (New York, 1937).

Note 1, p. 4. There is no evidence to support the assertion of H. Delbrück, op. cit. ii. 463, that the change from March to May is irrelevant to military developments, since by 755 the Marchfield was 'nur ein Art Reichstag'. H. von Mangoldt-Gaudlitz, *Die Reiterei in den germanischen und fränkischen Heeren bis zum Ausgang der deutschen Karolinger* (Berlin, 1922), 31, disputes Brunner's explanation on the ground that a Mayfield was held in 612 (Fredegarius, iv. 38; *MGH, Scriptores Merov.* ii. 139) and that after 755 expeditions are known to have been launched in seasons other than the late spring. But whatever may have been the earlier irregularities in the date of the Marchfield, it is clear that Pipin's action impressed contemporaries as a novelty: 'mutaverunt Martis campum in mense Maio' (*MGH, Scriptores*, xvi. 494; cf. ibid. i. 11); 'venit Tassilo ad Martis campum in mense Madio' (ibid. 28). Mangoldt-Gaudlitz, 45, notes the importance of fodder in the later eighth century, when in 782 and 798 expeditions were postponed because of a late season. The ninth-century *Officia XII mensium*, ed. H. Stern, *Revue archéologique*, xlv (1955), 185, explicitly connects the grass of May with the launching of warfare: 'Maius hinc gliscens herbis generat nigra bella.' See also L. Levillain, 'Campus Martius', *Bibliothèque de l'École des Chartes*, cvii (1947-8), 62–68.

Note 2, p. 5. A chapter in the history of historiography might be written about the ridicule poured on what F. Lot in *Histoire du moyen âge, I: Les Destinées de l'empire en Occident de 395 à 888* (Paris, 1928), 664, called the 'théorie explosive de la vassalité'. Presumably under the influence of the Darwinian concept of biological change through the gradual accretion of tiny differences, many historians have held it to be axiomatic that no significant historical change can be sudden. In their studies of the antecedents of feudalism they have therefore tended to reduce emphasis upon the change anticipated. The more recent biological theory of the mutation of genes provides a metaphor at least equally provocative of historical thought. This is especially applicable to military technology, where a sudden innovation may revolutionize an entire society. For example, D. M. Brown, 'The impact of firearms on Japanese warfare, 1543-98', *Far Eastern Quarterly*, vii (1948), 236–53, has shown that the introduction of fire-arms, and of the methods of their manufacture, by Western traders, quickly affected the entire fabric of Japanese life and laid the foundations for the political reunification of Japan under the Tokugawa shogunate.

Note 4, p. 5. Delbrück, op. cit. ii. 424-33, 472; Roloff, op. cit. 389-99; C. Oman, *History of the Art of War in the Middle Ages*, 2nd edn. (London, 1924), i. 22-37, 103-5 (yet, 57–58, he admits that the Franks fought on foot at Zülpich in 612 and at Poitiers in 733); Dopsch, *Grundlagen*, 2nd edn., ii. 294-8; P. Guilhiermoz, *Essai sur l'origine de la noblesse en France au moyen âge* (Paris, 1901), 100; E. Mayer, 'Die Entstehung der Vassalität und des Lehnwesens', *Festgabe für R. Sohm* (Munich, 1914), 66–67; Mangoldt-Gaudlitz, op. cit. 21-24, 36-37, 48-49; Frauenholz, op. cit. 60. The judgement of C. von Schwerin, in *Zeitschrift für die gesamte Staatswissenschaft*, lxxx (1925-6), 719, and in his edition of Brunner's *Deutsche Rechtsgeschichte* (Munich, 1928), ii. 277, n. 30, and 279, n. 33, is justified, that this literature proves no more than that the Merovingians fought to some extent on horseback, which no one had ever doubted; it does not prove that cavalry was the decisive arm among the Franks before the middle of the eighth century.

Note 5, p. 5. Since Brunner did not deny the continued use of infantry by Charlemagne and even occasionally by the later Carolingians (cf. Schwerin, loc. cit.), this school is chiefly a reaction against the extreme claims of Delbrück; cf. W. Erben, 'Zur Geschichte des karolingischen Kriegswesens', *Historische Zeitschrift*, ci (1908), 321–36 (criticism which Delbrück neither refuted nor received gracefully: cf. *Geschichte des Kriegswesens*, 2nd edn., ii. 475–6). H. Fehr, 'Das Waffenrecht der Bauern im Mittelalter', *Zeitschrift der Savigny-Stiftung für Rechtsgeschichte, Germ. Abt.* xxxv (1914), 116–18, supports Erben in holding that Charlemagne's army was both in law and in fact primarily a levy of freemen, but emphasizes (119–20) that even under Charlemagne, as cavalry became more important, property qualifications for military service were introduced, which, in the ninth century, changed the whole basis of the Frankish army. K. Rübel, 'Fränkisches und spätrömisches Kriegswesen', *Bonner Jahrbücher*, cxiv (1906), 136–42, attempts to show that infantry continued to be decisive in the Saxon wars especially, but not to the satisfaction of Mangoldt-Gaudlitz, op. cit. 36.

Note 1, p. 8. In late Antiquity horses continued to become larger and heavier, culminating in the superb charger in the late second-century statue of Marcus Aurelius; cf. H. Friis, *Rytterstatuens historie i Europa fra oldtiden indtil Thorvaldsen* (Copenhagen, 1933), 67, fig. 33. J. C. Ewart, 'On skulls of horses from the Roman fort at Newstead near Melrose', *Transactions of the Royal Society of Edinburgh*, xlv (1907), 576–7, found evidence of three varieties of horse, including one much like the modern Shire breed of heavy horse; cf. G. Nobis, 'Beiträge zur Abstammung und Domestikation des Hauspferdes', *Zeitschrift für Tierzüchtung und Züchtungsbiologie*, lxiv (1955), 201–46, esp. 233. The earliest Western saddles of the first and second centuries, with marked cantle and pommel, usually appear on heavy horses, which are recognizable by the thick fetlocks and wavy mane and tail; cf. E. Espérandieu, *Recueil général des bas-reliefs, statues et bustes de la Gaule Romaine*, iii (Paris, 1910), no. 2150, of a German auxiliary cavalryman; also viii, no. 2465; ix, no. 6589. Similar horses appear in Sassanian Iran and Han China; cf. W. W. Tarn, *Hellenistic Military and Naval Developments* (Cambridge, 1930), 79. Pausanius, *Description of Greece*, x. 19. 10, ed. W. H. S. Jones (London, 1935), iv. 478, tells us that in the old Celtic tongue μάρκα means 'horse'. It would seem that the Germans got the heavy war-horse from a Celtic people, since in the eighth century they called it *marach*: cf. *Lex Bajuvorum*, xiii, 11–12, ed. J. Merkel, *MGH, Leges*, iii. 317, 'Si caudem amputaverit vel aurem, si equus est quod marach dicunt, cum solido componat. Si mediocris fuerit, quod wilz vocant, cum medio solido componat. Et si deterior fuerit, quod angargnago dicimus, qui in hoste utilis non est, cum tremisse componat'; *Lex Alamannorum*, lxxii, § 1, ed. J. Merkel, ibid. iii. 69: 'Si equo quod marach dicunt, oculum excusserit . . .', the fine is six times that for blinding a cheap horse. *Marca* is 'war-horse' in various Celtic tongues; cf. A. Holder, *Alt-celtischer Sprachschatz* (Leipzig, 1904), ii. 417; A. Heiermaier, 'Westeuropäische Heimat und Namen des Pferdes', *Paideia*, vi (1951), 371–5, for the rich Celtic vocabulary regarding horses and vehicles which entered the Romanic and Teutonic tongues; H. Dannenbauer, 'Paraveredus-Pferd', *Zeitschrift der Savigny-Stiftung für Rechtsgeschichte, Germ. Abt.* lxxi (1954), 55–73, for a specific instance and its legal implications.

Note 4, p. 9. Frauenholz, op. cit. 59; Mangoldt-Gaudlitz, op. cit. 84. However, that the two-handed lance had some diffusion to the West is shown by a late Roman relief of an auxiliary cavalryman armed with one, and lacking a shield; cf. J. Barodez, 'Organisation militaire romaine de l'Algérie antique', *Revue internationale d'histoire militaire*, iv (1953), 33. Moreover, Paulus Diaconus, *Historia Langobardorum*, v. 10, in *MGH, Scriptores Langob*. 149, tells us, as an amazing feat, that a Lombard pierced a Byzantine horseman and lifted him from the saddle on the weapon's point. Lacking stirrups (cf. *infra*, p. 145), this could only have been done with a two-handed lance, and then with great difficulty. Perhaps such a lance may also account for the description of Chnodomar, King of the Alemanni, in 357 at the battle of Strassburg given by Ammianus Marcellinus, xvi. 12, 24, ed. C. U. Clark (Berlin, 1910), i. 95: 'Chnodomarius . . . equo spumante sublimior, erectus in iaculum formidandae vastitatis, armorumque nitore conspicuus ante alios.' E. Salin, *La Civilisation mérovingienne*, iv (Paris, 1959), 293, figs. 100, 101, shows a Lombard rider of the late sixth century and a pagan Alemannic warrior of the seventh century, each with a two-handed lance but no shield.

Note 1, p. 14. *Deutsche Altertumskunde*, ii (Munich, 1923), 339, n. 1. Without elaboration or documentation, L. Montross, *War Through the Ages* (New York, 1944), 95, credits the Carolingian development of mounted shock combat to 'the invention of the stirrup, which doubtless ranks as the foremost contribution of the Dark Ages to the science of war'. M. Bloch, *La Société féodale: La Formation des liens de dépendance* (Paris, 1949), 236, explicitly connects the introduction of the stirrup with the shift (which he regards as gradual) from infantry to cavalry in the early Middle Ages, but is prevented by defective information on the diffusion of the stirrup (cf. his remarks in *Annales d'histoire économique et sociale*, vii [1935], 638) from concentrating this technological insight on the eighth century. R. A. Preston, S. F. Wise, and H. O. Werner, *Men in Arms: A History of Warfare and its Interrelationships with Western Society* (New York, 1956), 66–67, credit the origins of feudalism jointly to 'the introduction of the stirrup sometime during the sixth century, and . . . the incursions of mounted Saracens into southern France in the early eighth century'.

Note 4, p. 14. A crude gravestone, perhaps of the late third or early fourth century, from Putačevo in Jugoslavia has at times been thought to show a stirrup, but the object is doubtful; cf. M. Hoernes, 'Altertümer der Herzegovina, II', *Sitzungsberichte der Wiener Akademie der Wissenschaften, Phil.-hist. Classe*, xcix (1881), 895, fig. 13; *Corpus inscriptionum latinorum*, iii (1878), 2765; for the date, cf. O. Kleemann, 'Samländische Funde und die Frage der ältesten Steigbügel in Europa', *Rheinische Forschungen zur Vorgeschichte*, v (1956), 118. An object which has sometimes been interpreted as some sort of stirrup, but which is certainly a bow-case hanging from the horse-pad, appears on coins struck, probably at Antioch, by Q. Labienus Parthicus, about 40 B.C.; cf. J. Eckhel, *Doctrina nummorum veterum* (Vienna, 1828), v. 145–6; H. A. Grueber, *Coins of the Roman Republic in the British Museum* (London, 1910), ii, 500 and n. 1, iii, pl. CXIII, nos. 19–20; M. von Bohrfeldt, *Die römische Geldmunzprägung während der Republik und unter Augustus* (Halle, 1923), 71 and pl. VII, nos. 21–23; E. Babelon, *Monnaies de la république romaine* (Paris, 1885), i. 225;

H. Cohn, *Monnaies frappées sous l'empire romain* (Paris, 1880), i. 30. For similar bow-cases on Kwarazmian coins, cf. *Ars islamica*, vi (1939), 165. L. Sprague de Camp, 'Before stirrups', *Isis*, li (1960), 160, has identified a handle appearing on the neck-strap of a Roman saddle-pad of the time of Marcus Aurelius as a device for securing support for the rider. L. H. Heydenreich, 'Marc Aurel und Regisole', *Festschrift für Erich Meyer zum 60. Geburtstag* (Hamburg, 1959), 146–59, asserts that a bronze equestrian statue, probably of the sixth century, erected first at Ravenna and later at Pavia, had stirrups. By *c.* 1335 it clearly was equipped not only with stirrups but also with rowel spurs, which otherwise are not known earlier than a Spanish illumination of the ninth century; cf. C. Singer, *History of Technology*, ii (1956), 558 (Lefebvre des Noëttes, op. cit., fig. 294, however, interprets these not as rowels but merely as 'éperons à points multiples'). The vicissitudes of this statue make it most improbable that it originally showed such harness. In 1315 it was captured by the Milanese, cut into pieces, and taken to Milan; *c.* 1335 it was recaptured by the Pavians and re-erected in their city. The craftsmen charged with this restoration would have been concerned about the strength of the dangling legs and feet, would probably have reinforced the legs with metal rods disguised as stirrup straps, and the feet with metal straps for the spurs. There would have been no sense of anachronism: as indicated *supra*, p. 135, the first observation that the stirrup was unknown to the Romans was published in 1499.

Note 7, p. 14. J. Marshall, *Guide to Sanchi* (Calcutta, 1918), 138, n. 3; J. E. van Lohuizen-de Leeuwe, 'Heinrich Zimmer and Indian art', *Arts asiatiques*, iv (1957), 228, fig. 4; A. K. Coomaraswamy, 'Early Indian sculptures', *Bulletin of the Museum of Fine Arts, Boston*, xxiv (1926), 59 and fig. 4, and *History of Indian and Indonesian Art* (New York, 1927), 25; J. P. Vogel, *La Sculpture de Mathurâ* (Paris, 1930), pl. VIII*b*; L. L. Fleitmann, *The Horse in Art from Primitive Times to the Present* (London, 1931), 28; L. Bachofer, *Early Indian Sculpture* (New York, n.d.), ii, pl. 72; R. Lefebvre des Noëttes, *L'Attelage et le cheval de selle* (Paris, 1931), fig. 261. It is curious that the stirrup enlarged to receive the foot does not appear in India proper until the tenth century in Orissa (Lefebvre des Noëttes, op. cit., fig. 370) and late eleventh century at Pagan; cf. C. Duroiselle, 'The stone sculptures in the Ananda temple at Pagan', *Archaeological Survey of India, Annual Report* (1913–14), pls. XXXIV–XXXV and pp. 64–65. Such stirrups appear in Java at Borobudur in the eighth century (Lefebvre des Noëttes, figs. 372–3) but are lacking in the Khmer reliefs of the eighth–ninth centuries; ibid., figs. 374–5.

Note 3, p. 15. Dr. C. Carrington Goodrich of Columbia University has called to my attention the archaeological report by Kao Chih-hsi, in *Kaogu Xuebao*, iii (1959), 75–106, showing three Hunan tomb figures (pl. XI. 1; XII. 3; XIII. 5) equipped with stirrups and dating from the Chin period (A.D. 265–420). For the citation of A.D. 47, cf. F. Hirth in *Verhandlungen der Berliner Gesellschaft für Anthropologie* (1890), 209; P. Pelliot in *T'oung pao*, xxiv (1926), 259. W. C. White, *Tomb Tile Pictures of Ancient China* (Toronto, 1939), 33, calls attention to the discovery in Shensi by C. W. Bishop of the stone figure of a kneeling water-buffalo datable 117 B.C. and equipped with stirrups. Before his death Dr. Bishop informed me that the saddle-pad and stirrups are incised on the figure, whereas the other details are in relief; consequently he considered these stirrups a later addition. The assertions of B. Laufer, *Chinese Pottery of the Han Dynasty* (Leiden, 1909), 230, and *Chinese Grave Sculptures of the Han Period* (New York, 1911), pls. V and 23, that stirrups were known in Han times, are refuted by Pelliot, op. cit. 260–1. J. Needham, *Science and Civilisation in China* (Cambridge, 1954), i. 167, fig. 31, reproduces a rubbing made in 1821 of a relief supposedly of A.D. 147 showing a stirrup. E. M. Jope in C. Singer, *History of Technology*, ii (1956), 556, n. 2, understandably registers scepticism.

Note 5, p. 16. W. W. Arendt, 'Sur l'apparition de l'étrier chez les Scythes', *Eurasia septentrionalis antiqua*, ix (1934), 206–8, which produces a pen-sketch of a supposed Scythian saddle with stirrups, reconstructed from the scene on the famous Chertomlyk vase (which depicts a dangling strap, but no stirrups; cf. E. H. Minns, *Scythians and Greeks* [Cambridge, 1913], 75, 116, fig. 48; 277, 279, fig. 202; J. Tolstoi, N. Kondakov, and S. Reinach, *Antiquités de la Russie méridionale* [Paris, 1891], 296 and cf. 397), from unpublished material in the Historical Museum of Moscow found by Zabelin in 1865, and from 'les analogies avec le harnais asiatique du cheval moderne'. M. Ebert, 'Čertomlyk', *Reallexikon*, ii (1925), 298, correctly denies that the nomads of Antiquity had any form of stirrup. Bivar, op. cit. 61, notes that there are no stirrups in the Pazirik tumuli roughly contemporary with the Chertomlyk vase; cf. also J. Haskins, 'Northern origins of "Sassanian" metalwork', *Artibus Asiae*, xv (1952), 263, n. 73. Unfortunately, F. Hančar, 'Stand und historische Bedeutung der Pferdezucht Mittelasiens im 1. Jahrtausend vor Christi', *Kultur und Sprache: Wiener Beiträge zur Kulturgeschichte und Linguistik*, ix (1952), 478–80, has been misled by Rostovtzeff and Arendt regarding the stirrup.

Note 7, p. 17. *Survey of Persian Art*, ed. A. U. Pope (New York, 1938), i. 759, n. 1 and iv. 217; cf. F. Sarre, *Die Kunst des alten Persien* (Berlin, 1923), 70, fig. 112; Bivar, op. cit. 61, n. 11; K. Erdmann, 'Die sassanidischen Jagdschallen', *Jahrbuch der preußischen Kunstsammlung*, lvii (1936), 221, fig. 16. R. Lefebvre des Noëttes, 'Deux plats sassanides du Musée de l'Ermitage', *Aréthuse*, i (1924), 151–2, was deceived by this plate into distorting the history of the stirrup in Iran; cf. his *L'Attelage*, fig. 291, and M. Ebert in *Reallexikon*, xii (1928), 101. M. S. Dimand, 'A review of Sassanian and Islamic metal work', *Ars islamica*, viii (1941), 197, agreed with Pope, on stylistic grounds, that the plate is post-Sassanian. E. Herzfeld, 'Postsassanidische Inschriften', *Archäologische Mitteilungen aus Iran*, iv (1932), 151–4, on the basis of an inscription on the plate, placed it in the first half of the eighth century. According to A. Alföldi, 'A Sassanian silver phalera at Dumbarton Oaks', *Dumbarton Oaks Papers*, xi (1957), 239, n. 19, W. B. Henning has recently challenged this decipherment; nevertheless, Alföldi seems to feel that the plate can scarcely be dated earlier than the second half of the seventh century. J. Kovrig in *Acta archaeologica* (Budapest), vi (1955), 164, n. 3, believes that the non-Persian long soft boots worn by the rider may indicate a Turkish origin for the plate. F. Haskins, op. cit. 346–7, pl. VIII, fig. 4, is doubtless extreme in placing it in the eleventh century.

Care must be used in searching for stirrups in Sassanian art because of a peculiar Iranian boot having a strap around the instep, to be seen on unmounted warriors in J. Smirnoff, *Argenterie orientale* (St. Petersburg, 1909), fig. 308, and C. Trever, *Nouveaux plats sassanides de l'Ermitage* (Moscow, 1937), pl. II.

Note 4, p. 18. Al-Mubarrad, *al-Kāmil*, ed. W. Wright (Leipzig, 1886), 675; cf. F. W. Schwarzlose, *Die Waffen der alten Araber aus ihren Dichtern dargestellt* (Leipzig, 1886), 50; on al-Mubarrad cf. *Encycl. Islam*, iii. 623. Al-Mubarrad's book is doubtless the source of similar statements on the origin of the stirrup made by the twelfth-century Spanish Muslim Ibn el ʿAwwām; cf. Ali ibn ʿAbd al-Raḥmān ibn Huḍail al-Andalusī, *La Parure des cavaliers et l'insigne des preux*, tr. L. Mercier (Paris, 1924), p. x. In the ninth century, as our citations have shown, the stirrup was common in the Muslim East. Zschille and Forrer, op. cit. 16, cite an account of how the Caliph al-Maʾmūn (A.D. 809–33) distributed largesse in Damascus 'without taking his foot out of the stirrup'. Al-Maqdisī (late tenth century) in *Descriptio imperii moslemici*, ed. M. J. de Goege (Leiden, 1877), 325, notes that Samarkand had a flourishing export trade in stirrups; cf. W. Barthold, *Turkestan down to the Mongol Invasion* (London, 1928), 235.

Note 1, p. 19. E.g. on this ground a bas-relief in the church of St. Julien at Brioude (Haute-Loire) showing simple strap-stirrups has often been cited as Merovingian, but, as A. Demmin, *Kriegswaffen* (Leipzig, 1893), 355, points out, the rider's armour better suits the tenth or eleventh century. E. László, 'Der Grabfund von Kornoncó und der altungarische Sattel', *Archaeologia hungarica*, xxvii (1943), 159, believes that an original leather or rope form of stirrup explains a rib under the foot-rest of certain types of stirrups, and likewise the twisting and knotted decoration of some metal forms. However, good craftsmanship and the blacksmith's delight in shaping white-hot iron make such genetic explanations unnecessary.

The *Oxford English Dictionary* derives 'stirrup' from Anglo-Saxon *stig* (climb)+ *rap* (rope), and remarks that 'as the etymology shows, the original "stirrup" must have been a looped rope'. W. Meyer-Lübke, *Etymologisches Wörterbuch der romanischen Sprachen*, 3rd edn. (Heidelberg, 1935) s.v. *estribo*, is dubious, but offers nothing better. The word is more probably derived from ἀστράβη, a pack-saddle sometimes made into a side-saddle for women by the addition on one side of a board, supported by straps, to serve as a foot-rest; cf. A. Mau, 'Astrabe', in Pauly-Wissowa, *Real-Encyclopädie der classischen Altertumswissenschaft* (Stuttgart, 1896), ii. 1792–3; W. Günther, 'Sattel', in *Reallexikon der Vorgeschichte*, xi (1928), 214. Such a saddle appears in Hittite reliefs of *c*. 730 B.C., showing a queen riding (cf. Halet Çambel, 'Karatepe', *Oriens*, i [1948], 155, pl. I); in Gallo-Roman reliefs (cf. E. Espérandieu, *Recueil général des bas-reliefs*, iii [1910], no. 2246; vii [1918], no. 5863); in the early eleventh century Farfa Bible (cf. *Art Bulletin*, x [1928], 311, fig. 6); in the mosaics of the Capella Palatina, Palermo, 1143–70 (cf. O. Demus, *Mosaics of Norman Sicily* [London, 1950], pl. 18); and twice in the miniatures (*c*. 1205) of Herrad of Landsberg's *Hortus deliciarum* (Strassburg, 1900), pl. XXV *ter* and XXVII *bis*. In Carolingian times *astraba* had come to mean not the whole saddle but only the foot-rest: the glossary in Codex leidensis 67F, of the eighth–ninth century, lists 'astraba: tabella ubi pedes requiescunt'; cf. *Corpus glossariorum latinorum*, ed. G. Goetz, iv (1889), 406, xix. When the true stirrup reached the West it was assimilated linguistically to *astraba*, the only form of equestrian foot-support already familiar to the Franks. From this came Spanish *estribo*, Provençal *estreup*, Old French *estrieu*, and Anglo-Saxon *stirap*. The Anglo-Saxon *stigrap* and German *Stegreif* are probably the result of popular etymologizing. John of Garland's *Dictionarius* (after 1218), in T. Wright, *A Volume of Vocabularies from the Tenth Century to the Fifteenth* (London, 1857), 123, glosses *strepae* with the English *styropys*.

Note 2, p. 19. According to L. Mercier, *La Chasse et les sports chez les Arabes* (Paris, 1927), 57, horses, in contrast to camels, were very rare in Arabia as late as the seventh century. The word *gharz* appears at least as early as the second half of the sixth century in the poetry of al-Muthaggib, *Mufaḍḍalīyat*, poem 28, verse 10, ed. C. J. Lyall (Oxford, 1918), ii. 105. J. von Hammer-Purgstall, 'Das Kamel', *Denkschriften der Kaiserlichen Akademie der Wissenschaften zu Wien, Phil.-hist. Cl.* vii (1856), 86, no. 5192, believes that *gharz* is a leather stirrup, whereas *rikāb* is a wooden or iron stirrup. G. Jacob, *Altarabisches Beduinleben nach dem Quellen geschildert* (Berlin, 1897), 69, translates *gharz* as 'camel stirrup', but K. Wittfogel and Fêng Chia-shêng, *History of Chinese Society: Liao (907–1125)* (Philadelphia, 1949), 506, n. 13, think that *gharz* may be simply the cushion on which the normally stirrupless meharist rests a foot. Lyall, however, op. cit. ii. 108, n., points to an old Arab commentator as saying that *gharz* means 'girth', which is intelligible in terms of the early Indian surcingle, and would explain such a passage as that of the poet Labīd (d. A.D. 661): 'When I move my [foot in the] *gharz* [the camel] starts to run quickly', cf. *Die Gedichte des Lebīd*, ed. A. Huber (Leiden, 1891), no. xxix, l. 8, cf. p. 25. The fragment of an Indian statue of about the second century has been found in south Arabia; cf. *Archaeology*, vii (1954), 254, and in the first decade of the fifth century Fa Hsien saw a luxurious hostel for Sabaean merchants at Kandy in Ceylon; cf. S. Beal, *Chinese Accounts of India* (Calcutta, 1957), 47; also G. W. Van Beek, 'Frankincense and myrrh in ancient South Arabia', *Journal of the American Oriental Society*, lxxviii (1958), 141–52. M. Z. Siddiqi, 'India as known to the ancient Arabs', *Indo-Asian Culture*, v (1957), 275, lists pre-Islamic Arabic words of Indian derivation, e.g. those for 'camphor' and 'ginger'.

Note 3, p. 20. H. Stern, 'Quelques œuvres sculptées en bois, os et ivoire de style omeyyade', *Ars orientalis*, i (1954), 128–30, esp. n. 77. There is a related, but cruder, ivory in the Louvre showing stirrups; cf. J. Strzygowski, *Der Dom zu Aachen und sein Entstehung* (Leipzig, 1904), 7, fig. 4, which, in view of Stern's findings about the Aachen ivories, is presumably later. There has likewise been much discussion of carved wooden panels showing stirruped riders in the church of Abu Sarga in Old Cairo. A. J. Butler, *Ancient Coptic Churches of Egypt* (Oxford, 1884), i. 191, fig. 11, dated them eighth-century, since the church was built at that time, but in his *Islamic Pottery* (London, 1925), pl. XXVII, he ascribes them to the sixth century without offering reasons. On stylistic grounds, however, they must be considerably later than the stirrupless rider of the Eton tile (pl. VIII) which he also places in the sixth century. A. Gayet, *L'Art copte* (Paris, 1902), 240, dates the Abu Sarga panels in the tenth century; W. de Grüneisen, *Les Caractéristiques de l'art copte* (Florence, 1922), 92–93, is convinced, by what he regards as clear Muslim influence on costumes, horse harness, and ornamental details, that they are not earlier than the eleventh century;

J. Strzygowski, 'Die koptische Reiterheilige und der hl. Georg', *Zeitschrift für ägyptische Sprache und Altertumskunde*, xl (1902), 55, relegates them to the thirteenth century.

J. Strzygowski, *Hellenistische und koptische Kunst in Alexandria nach Funden aus Aegypten und den Elfenbeinreliefs der Domkanzel zu Aachen* (Vienna, 1902), 23, fig. 15, shows a badly damaged relief of a rider serving as the lintel of the mosque at Dashlut but perhaps coming from Bawit, and asserts that the rider, like that of the Aachen and Louvre ivories, has stirrups. These are not visible in his photograph (also reproduced in his *Koptische Kunst* [Vienna, 1904], 105, fig. 160), nor in the independent photograph in J. Clédat, 'Baouit' in *Dictionnaire d'archéologie chrétienne*, ed. F. Cabrol, ii. i (1907), 225, fig. 1266, and the visible leg and foot of the rider are so badly broken that no convincing identification of a stirrup would seem possible. The surviving frescoes at Bawit show seven riders, all without stirrups; cf. ibid., figs. 1284–6. Since that monastery remained inhabited until the late eleventh century, a late sculpture showing a stirrup is not out of the question: a Coptic miniature of the tenth–eleventh century shows clear stirrups; cf. H. Hyvernat, *Album de paléographie copte* (Paris, 1888), pls. XVI, XVII. A letter from Dr. Walter Till of the University of Manchester, the leading authority on vernacular Coptic, tells me that no Coptic word for *stirrup* is known.

Note 5, p. 20. 'χρὴ . . . ἔχειν δὲ εἰς τὰς σέλλας σκάλας σιδηρᾶς δύο', *Arriani Tactica et Mauricii Artis militaris libri duodecim*, ed. J. Scheffer (Uppsala, 1664), i. 2, p. 22; cf. ii. 8, p. 64. Cf. R. Vári, 'Sylloge tacticorum graecorum', *Byzantion*, vi (1931), 401–3. The manuscripts, of which the earliest extant is of the tenth century, are listed by G. Moravcsik, *Byzantinoturcica* (Budapest, 1942), i. 252. There are two recensions, but iron stirrups are mentioned in both; cf. R. Vári, 'Zur Überlieferung mittelgriechischer Taktiker', *Byzantinische Zeitschrift*, xv 1906), 54, and 'Desiderata der byzantinischen Philologie auf dem Gebiete der mittelgriechischen Kriegswissenschaftlichen Literatur', *Byzantinisch-neugreichische Jahrbücher*, viii (1929–30), 228–9. According to A. Dain, 'La Tradition des stratégistes byzantins', *Byzantion*, xx (1950), 316, a critical edition of this work is much needed.

Note 1, p. 21. The traditional dating of *c.* 600 has been defended by G. Moravcsik, *Byzantinoturcica*, i. 250–3, with rich literature. However, as early as 1877–8, F. Salamon in *Századok*, x. 1–17, 686–733, xi. 124–37, attempted to show that this work cannot be earlier than the ninth century. In 1906 R. Vári, *Byzantinische Zeitschrift*, xv. 47–87 and xix (1910), 552–3, produced important evidence for a period later than the Emperor Maurice; cf. F. Lammert, *Jahresbericht über die Fortschritte der klassischen Altertumswissenschaft*, cclxxiv (1941), 45–47, for a summary of his arguments. His position was notably strengthened by C. M. Patrono, 'Contro la paternità imperiale dell' Οὐρβικίου Τακτικὰ στρατηγικά', *Rivista abruzzese di scienze, lettere ed arti*, xxi (1906), 623–38, by E. Gerland in *Deutsche Literaturzeitung*, xli (1920), 446–9, 468–72, and by R. Grosse, *Römische Militärgeschichte von Gallienus bis zum Beginn der byzantinischen Themenverfassung* (Berlin, 1920), 301. In 1929, when he came to write the article 'Steigbügel' for Pauly-Wissowa, *Real-Encyclopädie*, 2nd series, iii. 2237–8, F. Lammert concluded that the Pseudo-Maurice must be placed in the early eighth century.

Note 2, p. 23. R. Mengarelli, 'La necropoli barbarica di Castel Trosino presso Ascoli Piceno', *Monumenti antichi*, xii (1902), 290, fig. 180; Csallány, *Archaeologische Denkmäler*, 95, no. 143; B. Thordeman, 'The Asiatic splint-armour in Europe', *Acta archaeologica* (Copenhagen), iv (1933), 145. Thordeman, 125, n. 7, says that further splint armour from grave 79 is exhibited in the National Museum in Rome, but is not listed by Mengarelli, 253. Remains of stirrupless saddles were also found in Castel Trosino, grave 90 (Mengarelli, loc. cit.), and in Nocera Umbra, grave 5; cf. R. Paribene, 'Necropoli barbarica di Nocera Umbra', *Monumenti antichi*, xxv (1919), 168–70, figs. 14–17. There are no stirrups from the Lombard cemeteries either of Testona near Turin or of Cividale in Friuli; cf. E. and C. Calandra, 'Di una necropoli barbarica scoperta a Testona', *Atti della Società di Archeologia et Belle Arti per la Provincia di Torino*, iv. i (1880), 17–52; S. Fuchs, 'La Suppellettile rinvenuta nelle tombe della necropoli di San Giovanni a Cividale', *Memorie storiche forogiuliesi*, xxxix (1951), 2–5.

Note 4, p. 23. The assertion by Schlieben, op. cit. 171, and Zschille and Forrer, op. cit. 4, that Isidore of Seville (d. 636) refers to stirrups as 'Scansuae: ferrum per quod equus scanditur' is unwarranted. This definition is found not in the *Etymologies* but in the *Glossae Isidori* compiled by Scaliger in the late sixteenth century; cf. *Corpus glossariorum latinorum*, ed. G. Goetz, v (Leipzig, 1894), 611; cf. i (1923), 249. The silence of Isidore is significant, since in his *Etymologiarum libri XX*, ed. W. M. Lindsay (Oxford, 1911), Lib. xx. xvi, *De instrumentis equorum*, he gives a most detailed inventory of the names of the parts of riding harness. Nor can it be claimed that Isidore was merely a compiler from earlier books, blind to the actualities around him: in the previous section, xx. xv. 3, he gives us the Hispanic Latin slang for 'wellswipe', *ciconia*, a word not elsewhere found in the ancient sources. G. Joly, 'Les Chevaux mérovingiens d'après les données de Grégoire de Tours', *Bulletin trimestriel de la Société Archéologique de Touraine*, xix (1914), 311, finds that the Merovingian authors do not mention stirrups, and Gregory's account (*Historia Francorum*, vi. 31) of the assassination of Chilperic in 584 while he was leaning on a servant's shoulder to dismount, indicates that they were not used at that time.

Note 7, p. 24. F. Kaufmann, *Deutsche Altertumskunde* (Munich, 1923), ii. 669, n. 7; these may be of the ninth century: cf. Lindenschmidt, op. cit. iv (Mainz, 1900), pl. 23. K. M. Kurtz, 'Die alemannischen Gräberfunde von Pfahlheim im Germanischen Nationalmuseum', *Mitteilungen aus dem Germanischen National-museum, Nürnberg*, i (1884–6), 173–4, mentions similar late Merovingian or early Carolingian stirrups from Öhringen and Grossingerheim, but on these I have no further information. A stirrup found at Gabensdorf may be datable as of the later eighth century; cf. K. Dinklage, 'Zur deutschen Frühgeschichte Thüringens', *Mannus*, xxxiii (1941), 496, pl. 6, fig. 2. On purely stylistic grounds, H. J. Hundt, 'Ein tauschierter Steigbügel von Aholfing', *Germania*, xxix (1951), 259–61, attempts to date certain other stirrups in the eighth rather than in the ninth century. Those dredged from the River Ucker are probably of the early eleventh century; cf. K. Raddatz, 'Steigbügel frühgeschichtlicher Zeit aus der Ucker-mark', *Berliner Blätter für Vor- und Frühgeschichte*, iii (1954), 57–60.

Note 11, p. 24. For Danish stirrups from the late eighth century onward, see J. Brønsted, 'Danish inhumation graves of the Viking Age', *Acta archaeologica*

(Copenhagen), vii (1936), 81–228. H. Arbman, *Schweden und das karolingische Reich* (Stockholm, 1937), 221, n. 4, and pl. 69, shows stirrups from a ninth-century grave near Groningen in the Netherlands. Despite H. J. Hundt, loc. cit., the stirrups from Immenstadt in Schleswig are probably ninth-century; cf. H. Handelmann, 'Vorgeschichtliches Burgwerk und Brückwerk in Dithmarschen', *Verhandlungen der Berliner Gesellschaft für Anthropologie* (1883), 25, and L. Lindenschmidt, *Alterthümer*, iv, pl. 23. Similar early stirrups have been found in lakes and rivers: cf. H. J. Hundt, op. cit.; J. Pilloy, 'L'Équitation aux époques franque et carolingienne', *Bulletin archéologique* (1894), 164. For indications of ninth and tenth-century stirrups in Holstein, Posen, East Prussia, and Norway, cf. *Zeitschrift für Geschichte von Schleswig-Holstein*, xvi (1886), 411; B. Engel, 'Steigbügel des 9. Jahrhunderts', *Zeitschrift für historische Waffenkunde*, ii (1900–2), 418; O. Olshausen, 'Bemerkungen über Steigbügel', *Verhandlungen der Berliner Gesellschaft für Anthropologie* (1890), 207–9; P. Paulsen, 'Der Stand der Forschung über die Kultur der Wikingerzeit', *Bericht der Römisch-Germanischen Kommission*, xxii (1932), 228, pls. 30–31; O. Rygh, *Norske oldsager* (Oslo, 1885), nos. 587–90.

Note 7, p. 26. A. Merton, *Die Buchmalerei in St. Gallen vom neunten bis elften Jahrhundert* (Leipzig, 1912), 38 ff., pls. XXVIII, XXIX; Boinet, op. cit., pls. CXLV, CXLVI; A. Bruckner, *Scriptoria medii aevi helvetica, III: St. Gallen II* (Geneva, 1938), 58, pl. XXI. Another Latin manuscript, probably of the ninth century, containing stirrups is the Berne Prudentius, Public Library, Cod. 264, fol. 31ᵛ; cf. R. Stettiner, *Die illustrierten Prudentiushandschriften* (Berlin, 1905), pl. 130; Lefebvre des Noëttes, op. cit., fig. 296. In the tenth century evidences of stirrups increase in the West: they are found in the Leyden *Maccabees*, University Library, Cod. Perizoni 17, fols. 22ʳ, 24ᵛ, 37ʳ (cf. Merton, op. cit. 64–66, pls. LVI, LVII; Lefebvre des Noëttes, op. cit., fig. 298, wrongly dates this early eleventh century); in two Prudentius MSS. at Brussels, Royal Library, MSS. 9987–91, fol. 97ᵛ, and MSS. 10066–77, fol. 112ᵛ (Lefebvre des Noëttes, op. cit., fig. 299; Stettiner, op. cit., pl. 68, 169); in the Beatus, datable 975, of the Cathedral Archives of Gerona, fol. 134ᵛ (Neuss, op. cit. i. 22); in the Codex Epternacensis at Gotha, of *c.* 990, fols. 19ʳ, 77ᵛ (K. Lamprecht, 'Der Bilderschmuck des Cod. Egberti zu Trier und des Cod. Epternacensis zu Gotha', *Jahrbücher des Vereins von Alterthumsfreunden im Rheinlande*, lxx [1881], pl. X); and on a capital of the church of San Celso in Milan, before 998 (C. Ramussi, *Milano ne' suoi monumenti* [Milan, 1893], 158, fig. 115).

Note 2, p. 27. E. A. Gessler, *Die Trutzwaffen der Karolingerzeit vom VIII. bis zum XI. Jahrhundert* (Basel, 1908), 32, 43, 60, 101; Mangoldt-Gaudlitz, op. cit. 75. A. France-Lanord, 'La Fabrication des épées damassées aux époques mérovingienne et carolingienne', *Pays gaumais*, x (1949), 39, finds such swords as early as the sixth century but far more numerous from the eighth century. For the ballistics and evolution of the *francisca*, which was a projectile as well as a weapon for hand-to-hand fighting, cf. E. Salin, *La Civilisation mérovingienne*, *III: Les Techniques* (Paris, 1957), 40–42. In view of his belief that the Western trend, since Roman times, towards longer swords shows the influence of Asian nomad horsemen (ibid. 90–94, 109), it is curious that Salin, 58, asserts the Carolingian sword to have been a footman's rather than a cavalry weapon.

Note 4, p. 27. The spurred or winged spear is found in Roman mosaics showing its use in hunting boars, bears, and leopards; cf. J. Aymard, *Essai sur les chasses romaines des origines à la fin du siècle des Antonins* (Paris, 1951), 312–13, pls. XIIc, XVI, XXXIV; E. Salin, 'Le Mobilier funéraire de La Bussière-Étable', *Monuments et mémoires publiés par l'Académie des Inscriptions et Belles-lettres*, xlv (1951), 93, n. 1. The ferocity of these beasts when wounded is such that spears of this type have normally been used even in recent centuries for hunting them, and we may safely assume that the scattered specimens earlier than the Carolingian age were designed for the chase rather than for war. Salin's Germanic examples should be supplemented by those from the Lombard cemeteries at Castel Trosino, Nocera Umbra, and Testona (cf. R. Mengarelli in *Monumenti antichi*, xii [1902], 198, fig. 35; R. Paribeni in ibid. xxv [1919], 180, fig. 26; E. and C. Calandra in *Atti della Società di Archeologia e Belle Arti per la Provincia di Torino*, iv, i [1880], 28, pl. I, figs. 19, 22), by one of the late fifth century from Hammelburg in Lower Franconia (H. Müller-Karpe, 'Das Hammelburger Kriegergrab der Völkerwanderungzeit', *Mainfränkisches Jahrbuch für Geschichte und Kunst*, vi [1954], 205, fig. 2), another of the later seventh century from Baden (A. Dauber, 'Ein fränkisches Grab mit Prunklänze aus Bargen, Ldkr. Sinsheim, Baden', *Germania*, xxxiii [1955], 381–90), another of about the same date from Bülach (J. Werner, *Das alamannische Gräberfeld von Bülach* [Basel, 1953], pl. XXXV. 11), another of the late seventh or early eighth century on a curious terracotta plaque from Issoire (R. Lentier, 'Plaque funéraire de terre cuite mérovingienne', *Jahrbuch des Römisch-Germanischen Zentralmuseums, Mainz*, i [1954], 237–44, pl. 21), and another of the first half of the eighth century from Hesse (H. Müller-Karpe, *Hessische Funde von der Altsteinzeit bis zum frühen Mittelalter* [Marburg, 1949], 63–65, fig. 29).

Note 5, p. 27. Gessler, op. cit. 43–44, 49, 60. The well-known relief at Hornhausen, showing a rider with shield and heavy spurred spear, has been dated as early as the sixth century. It is, however, probably of the tenth century; cf. C. A. R. Radford, 'The sculptured stones at Hornhausen', *Antiquity*, xvi (1942), 175–7 and pl. IV. The unconscious comedy in which even a great scholar may become involved if he neglects technology is nowhere better illustrated than by A. Goldschmidt, *An Early Manuscript of the Aesop Fables of Avianus* (Princeton, 1947), 25, who, commenting on an eighth–tenth-century drawing of a mounted king, says: 'The characteristic long lance seen on Byzantine imperial coins is likewise given to the rex regum, and by means of a short cross-bar, adjusted to a Christian connotation.'

Note 1, p. 28. The cross-pieces of the new spears were so conspicuous and so easily rendered that artists quickly adopted them; cf. G. Kossina, *Germanische Kultur im 1. Jahrtausend nach Christus*, i (Leipzig, 1932), figs. 347, 352. However, the representation of the lance held at rest made its way very slowly: it lacked the magnificence of gesture of the blow struck with the arm and this latter is found even in the Bayeux Tapestry, from an age when it can seldom have been seen in combat. In the representations it is often difficult to distinguish the heavy lance from the *espieu* or light lance designed to be hurled at arm's length. This latter is still found on the Bayeux Tapestry, but passed out of use in the later twelfth century; cf. U. T. Holmes, jr., *Daily Living in the Twelfth Century*

(Madison, 1952), 171. R. Crozet, 'Nouvelles remarques sur les cavaliers sculptés ou peints dans les églises romanes', *Cahiers de civilisation médiévale*, i (1958), 27–36, emphasizes the complexity and importance of iconographic tradition in such images. The earliest depictions of the lance held at rest occur in the Berne City Library, MS. 264, fols. 31ʳ, 32ʳ, probably of the ninth century (cf. Stettiner, op. cit., pls. 129, 131), and in the great Bible of St. Paul's Outside the Walls (cf. Gessler, op. cit. 55). Tenth-century examples are to be found in Brussels, Bib. Royale, MSS. 9987–91 (cf. Stettiner, op. cit., pl. 68) and Leiden University Library, Cod. Perizoni 17 (cf. Merton, op. cit., pl. LV). Lefebvre des Noëttes's earliest example of the lance at rest (op. cit., fig. 304) he dates *c.* 1120; but Neuss, op. cit. i. 34, ii, fig. 183, places it between 1028 and 1072; cf. also R. S. Loomis, 'Geoffrey of Monmouth and the Modena archivolt', *Speculum*, xiii (1938), 227; M. Schapiro, 'From Mozarabic to Romanesque in Silos', *Art Bulletin*, xxi (1939), 358, narrows it to *c.* 1050–72. M. Avery, *Exultet Rolls* (Princeton, 1936), pl. LXXIV, offers an example from the early eleventh century. The artificiality of many artistic representations, and the persistence of the ancient convention of the gesture of attack, is admirably shown in a frontispiece of 1611 showing a knight in full late-medieval armour carrying his lance in the classic manner, and flanked by Athena and Hercules; cf. A. Gilbert, 'Fr. Lodovico Melo's *Rules for Cavalry*', *Studies in the Renaissance*, i (1954), pl. I. In feudal literature there is a gradual realization of the dramatic elements of shock combat, with growing emphasis upon that swiftness of horse at the charge which was the measure of the violence of the lance's blow, and delineation of the gesture of placing the lance at rest as the horse charges; cf. K. Grundmann, 'Zur Entwicklung der Schilderung des Lanzenkampfes in der höfischen Epik', *Collegii Assistentium Universitatis J. Pilsudski Varsoviensis commentarii annales*, i (1936), 359–66, 374.

Note 1, p. 29. One of the unresolved mysteries of economic history is the sudden change of the Franks, *c.* A.D. 700, from a gold to a silver standard; cf. F. Lot, 'De la circulation de l'or du IVᵉ au VIIᵉ siècle', in his *Nouvelles recherches sur l'impôt foncier et la capitation personnelle sous le bas-empire* (Paris, 1955), 146. Even Italy and Muslim Spain abandoned the minting of gold at that time; cf. C. M. Cipolla, *Money, Prices and Civilization in the Mediterranean World, Fifth to Seventeenth Century* (Cincinnati, 1956), 20, n. 14. A. R. Lewis, 'Le Commerce et la navigation sur les côtes atlantiques de la Gaule du Vᵉ au VIIIᵉ siècle', *Moyen âge*, lx (1953), 278–80, insists that the shift from gold to silver at the end of the seventh century is related to the opening of new silver mines in Gaul and England, and is a sign of commercial activity rather than of economic recession. However, R. Doehaerd, 'Les Réformes monétaires carolingiennes', *Annales: économies, sociétés, civilisations*, vii (1952), 19, shows that the new Carolingian penny was based on a Muslim ratio of coinage, indicating that monetary circulation was more important in the Orient than in the Frankish regions.

Note 5, p. 29. H. Fehr, 'Das Waffenrecht der Bauern im Mittelalter', *Zeitschrift der Savigny-Stiftung für Rechtsgeschichte, Germ. Abt.* xxxv (1914), 116. This orthodox position is brilliantly challenged, but I believe without success, by H. Dannebauer, 'Die Freien im karolingischen Heer', in *Aus Verfassungs- und Landesgeschichte: Festschrift für T. Mayer* (Lindau, 1954), i. 49–64, who maintains that the notion of a general duty of all freemen to military service is the imposition upon the Franks of a nineteenth-century concept: he claims that such service was required only of those settled on royal lands (*centenae*). While, short of total and desperate emergency, logistic considerations alone would have prevented the mustering of the entire free male population to the host, nevertheless in all the Germanic kingdoms there seems to have been enough residual tribalism to equate the free layman with the warrior.

Note 6, p. 29. Nevertheless, the notion that footmen at times presented themselves armed only with clubs seems improbable, despite the *Capit. Aquisgranense* (801–13), § 17: 'Quod nullus in hoste baculum habeat, sed arcum', *MGH, Cap.* i. 172. Mangoldt-Gaudlitz, op. cit. 61, intelligently emends to *jaculum*, in which case the capitulary indicates an effort by Charlemagne to organize his infantry to co-operate efficiently with his cavalry. The javelin brought foes so close together in combat that cavalry could not charge effectively without trampling their own footmen. In Antiquity cavalry had generally guarded the flanks, but in the fully developed medieval battle array the cavalry took position in the rear of the infantry with patrols on the flanks. The footmen opened the battle with a hail of arrows, and then the knights charged the enemy through gaps arranged between units of their own archers; cf. ibid. 83. K. Rübel, 'Frankisches und spätromanisches Kriegswesen', *Bonner Jahrbücher*, cxiv (1906), 138, points out that Frankish arrow-heads are first found in excavations of fortifications of Charlemagne's later years. Increasingly arrows used for battle (as distinct from hunting-arrows) tended to lose their barbs, since the more compact form would better penetrate the constantly heavier armour; cf. *London Museum Medieval Catalogue* (London, 1940), 66–69. Despite their close tactical co-operation with archers, medieval knights spurned missile weapons as the arms of the lower social strata; cf. A. T. Hatto, 'Archery and chivalry: a noble prejudice', *Modern Language Review*, xxxv (1940), 40–54.

Note 1, p. 32. *De procinctu Romanae miliciae*, ed. E. Dümmler, in *Zeitschrift für deutsches Alterthum*, xv (1872), 444 ff. In this section 3, Hrabanus departs notably from his model, Vegetius's *Epitoma rei militaris*, i. 4 (the italics are paraphrases of Vegetius): '*Legebantur autem et assignabantur apud antiquos milites incipiente pubertate*: quod et hodie servatur, ut videlicet pueri et adholescentes in domibus principum nutriantur, quatinus dura et adversa tollerare discant, famesque et frigora caloresque solis sufferre. *Nam si haec aetas absque exercitio et disciplina praeterierit statim corpus pigrescit.* Unde et vulgaricum proverbium ac nostris familiare est quod dicitur: in pube posse fieri equitem, majoris vero aetatis aut vix aut numquam.' Since in his dedication to King Lothar (ibid. 450) Hrabanus states that in condensing Vegetius he has eliminated matters 'quae tempore moderno in usu non sunt', his emphasis (446–7) on Vegetius's discussion (op. cit. i. 11–16) of the use of a post as a dummy opponent in training fighters probably points to the development of the quintain by the ninth century. Although he does not mention stirrups, Hrabanus appends (448) to Vegetius's description (op. cit. i. 18) of the use of wooden horses in training armed men to mount, the note: 'Quod videlicet exercitium saliendi in Francorum populis optime viget.' The increased size of cavalry lances is indicated in the same section; Vegetius speaks of *conti*, Hrabanus of *conti praemagni*. As for the dating of the work: Dümmler's theory (451) that Hrabanus, a man of about 80, composed it in 855–6 during the last four months of his life seems unnecessary, since after Louis's death in 840 Hrabanus had sided with Lothar.

Note 3, p. 32. Strangely little is known about the origins and spread of dubbing; cf. M. Bloch, *La Société féodale: les classes* (Paris, 1949), 49–53, 263; G. Cohen, *Histoire de la chevalerie en France au moyen âge* (Paris, 1949), 183–90. *The Anglo-Saxon Chronicle*, ed. J. Ingram (London, 1823), 290, says that in 1086 King William 'dubbed his son Henry a knight at Westminster at Easter'. Although E. H. Massmann, *Schwertleite und Ritterschlag dargestellt auf Grund der mittelhochdeutschen literarischen Quellen* (Hamburg, 1932), 209, finds dubbing in Germany in the twelfth century, F. Pietzner, *Schwertleite und Ritterschlag* (Bottrop i. W., 1934), 129, insists that there is no evidence of this ceremony in Germany before 1312. That *miles* began to take on strong overtones of religious dedication as early as the fifth century is shown by K. J. Hollyman, op. cit. 132, n. 27; and A. Waas, *Geschichte der Kreuzzüge* (Freiburg, 1956), i. 37, 49, finds one of the roots of the Crusades in a distinctive *Ritterfrömigkeit* which may be as old as the age of Charlemagne. The rituals for dubbing perhaps emerged out of earlier forms for the blessing of a *defensor ecclesiae*. M. Andrieu, *Le Pontifical romain du XIIe siècle* (Vatican City, 1938), 75, 302, describes a liturgy compiled at Mainz about 950 which is ambiguous in its references to *defensor* and *miles*, but which includes the blessing of the knight's banner, lance, sword, and shield.

Andrieu notes that while there is no mention of spurs in this tenth-century liturgy, in an Italian manuscript copy of the thirteenth century a slightly later hand has added a prayer *ad calcaria*. Although spurs had been commonly used in northern Europe since La Tène times (*supra*, p. 1, n. 5), it was not until after the appearance of the stirrup that they were considered worthy of gilding. A gilt spur of the late eighth century comes from Pfahlheim in Würtemberg (L. Lindenschmidt, *Alterthümer*, v [1911], 228, pl. 42, no. 691); we have a magnificent pair of the later ninth century from Mikulčice in Moravia (J. Paulík, 'Some early Christian remains in Southern Moravia', *Antiquity*, xxxii [1958], 165, pl. XIXa), one of the tenth century from Norway (*The Listener*, lxi [1959], 170), and one from Hamburg, *c.* 1000 (R. Schindler, in *Germania*, xxxi [1953], 224–5, pl. 22, no. 1). For the later ornamentation of spurs, see E. M. Jope, 'The tinning of iron spurs: a continuous practice from the tenth to the seventeenth century', *Oxoniensia*, xxi (1956), 35–42. Massmann, op. cit. 156–60, finds no indication in the German vernacular sources that golden spurs had symbolic value before the later thirteenth century. However, *Vita Henrici IV imperatoris*, c. 8, ed. W. Eberhard (Hanover, 1899), 28, which was written shortly after 1106, probably at Mainz or Speyer, indicates that golden spurs were then habitual among German knights, and F. Ganshof, 'Qu'est-ce que la chevalerie?', *Revue générale belge* (1947), 79, believes that spurs, often gilded, were used in dubbing from the twelfth century.

Note 4, p. 33. *The Bayeux Tapestry*, ed. F. Stenton (London, 1957). However, the Farfa Bible, Catalan of the first half of the eleventh century, Vatican Library, MS. lat. 5729, fols. 342r, 352r, shows quite individualized patterns on shields; photographs in Princeton Index of Christian Art; for date and provenance, cf. W. Neuss, *Die katalanische Bibelillustrationen* (Leipzig, 1922), 28. E. Gritzner,

Sphragistik, Heraldik, deutsche Münzgeschichte (Leipzig, 1912), 62, is probably correct in holding that military standards rather than decorated shields are the origin of medieval heraldry. P. Paulsen, 'Feldzeichen der Normannen', *Archiv für Kulturgeschichte*, xxxix (1957), 3–6, notes, without explanation, that while military banners had been common among Romans and barbarians, they do not appear attached to lances until the tenth century. It is said that a vanished mosaic of 796–800 in St. John Lateran showed *vexillum Romanae urbis* as a pennon on a spear (cf. P. E. Schramm, *Herrschaftszeichen und Staatssymbolik* [Stuttgart, 1954], 496, 650), but the surviving sketch may be inaccurate. Beginning with Conrad I (911–18) the German emperor is often shown with a pennoned lance, and the tradition begins in 915 in Italy with Berengar (ibid. 499). The famous Holy Lance of the Imperial Treasure, which appears to be a pre-Carolingian winged lance (ibid., fig. 72; *supra*, p. 147), is first mentioned in 939 in Otto I's possession (ibid. 501). Equipped with a pennon, it quickly became an imperial standard. It should be recognized that the lance-and-pennon standards of tenth-century rulers have origins not only in contemporary military technology, but perhaps also in the ancient Etruscan and Roman use of a spear (without pennon) as a symbol of authority; cf. J. Deér, 'Byzanz und die Herrschaftszeichen des Abendlandes', *Byzantinische Zeitschrift*, l (1957), 427–30; A. Alföldi, 'Hasta—summa imperii: the spear as embodiment of sovereignty in Rome', *American Journal of Archaeology*, lxiii (1959), 1–27.

We have seen (*supra*, p. 8, n. 6) that to prevent too great penetration by the spear, certain Asian nomads attached horse-tails behind the blade. The tails on a chieftain's spear presumably became a military standard, and in 866, replying to questions of the Bulgarian king, Pope Nicholas I says: 'Quando proelium inire soliti eratis, indicatis vos hactenus in signo militari caudam equi portasse'; *MGH, Epp.* vi. 580. However, by that time two-handed lances with cloth pennons were used in Asia (*supra*, p. 8, n. 5, and M. Mavrodinov, 'Le Trésor protobulgare de Nagyszentmiklós', *Archaeologia hungarica*, xxix [1943], 115, fig. 74) and the Balkans (ibid. 126, fig. 79 and pl. IV; also G. László, 'Notes sur le trésor de Nagyszentmiklós', *Folia archaeologica*, ix [1957], 151–2). The Chludoff Psalter (*supra*, p. 25, n. 6), of the late ninth or early tenth century, shows, fol. 97ᵛ, a commander with a pennon on his lance and, fol. 26ᵛ, two soldiers with simple strips of cloth tied below the spear-head. In the tenth century the Volga Bulgars were using pennons on their lances; cf. J. Harmatta, 'Ibn Faḍlān über die Bestattung bei den Wolga-Bulgaren', *Archaeologiai értesítő*, new series, vii–ix (1946–8), 362–81. Since the metal cross-piece of a Carolingian wing-spear may at times have become dangerously entangled in a victim's armour and thus have caused difficulty in retracting a lance, the nomadic pennon had generally displaced it in the West by the later tenth century; e.g. Madrid, Bib. Nacional, MS. B. 31, St. Jerome, *In Danielem*, fol. 269ʳ, datable 975 (photograph in Princeton Index of Christian Art), shows a triangular pennon on a lance, while a miniature of *c.* 1000 shows both cross-piece and pennon on a spear-standard being presented by a saint to a mounted warrior; *Proceedings of the Society of Antiquaries*, xxiv (1911–12), 168, fig. 17. A thousand years later, although its origins in military technology are forgotten, a national flag is still normally attached to a spear.

Note 3, p. 35. The cross-bow was widely used in China from early Han times at least; cf. H. T. Horwitz, 'Die Armbrust in Ostasien', *Zeitschrift für historische Waffenkunde*, vii (1916), 155–83; 'Zur Entwicklungsgeschichte der Armbrust', ibid. viii (1920), 311–17, ix (1921), 73, 114, 139, and 'Über die Konstruktion von Fallen und Selbstschußen', *Beiträge zur Geschichte der Technik*, xiv (1924), 96–100; C. M. Wilbur, 'History of the cross-bow', *Annual Report of the Smithsonian Institution* (1936), 435. The Chinese cross-bow was fitted with a distinctive and efficient trigger, the export of which was forbidden, and the moving parts of which could be reproduced only by a very skilled craftsman; cf. H. H. Dubs, 'A military contact between Chinese and Romans in 36 B.C.', *T'oung pao*, xxxvi (1940), 69–71. Nevertheless, a portion of a Han cross-bow trigger has been found in Taxila as of the first century after Christ; cf. S. van R. Cammann, 'Archaeological evidence for Chinese contacts with India during the Han dynasty', *Sinologica*, v (1956), 10–19. In 36 B.C. Chinese armies were using cross-bows in Sogdiana when they apparently captured over 100 Roman soldiers who had been captured also by the Parthians in 54 B.C.; these the Chinese settled in Kansu province in a new city called by the Chinese word for *Rome*; cf. H. H. Dubs, 'A Roman city in ancient China', *Greece and Rome*, iv (1957), 139–48. Through such channels the idea of the cross-bow, if not the Chinese release, doubtless reached the West. However it was not widely used by the Romans: curiously, the two surviving representations of it, both of the first–second century after Christ, are both at Le Puy, but seem to be authentic; cf. R. Gounot, *Collections lapidaires du Musée Crozatier du Puy-en-Velay* (Le Puy, 1957), 22, 75, 90, pls. XVIII, XXXII. It cannot be traced earlier: Hero's *cheiroballista* is a myth; cf. R. Schneider, 'Herons Cheiroballista', *Mitteilungen des Deutschen Archäologischen Instituts, Rom*, xxi (1906), 142–68. J. Hoops, 'Die Armbrust im Frühmittelalter', *Wörter und Sachen*, iii (1912), 65–68, maintains, by the interpretation of a highly ambiguous Anglo-Saxon riddle, that the cross-bow continued in use during the early Middle Ages. Certainly the wider diffusion of the cross-bow occurred from Europe and not from China: the very simple release of the cross-bows of the Bight of Benin is probably derived from a type until recently used in Norway and presumably introduced to Africa in the late fifteenth or sixteenth centuries not by Portuguese but by Danes, Dutch, or English; cf. H. Balfour, 'The origin of West African crossbows', *Annual Report of the Smithsonian Institution* (1910), 635–50; while the releases of Malabar, Cochin, and Travancore cross-bows are European in type, and in Tamil and Malayālam such weapons are called 'Frankish' (*parangi*, from *feringhi*); cf. J. Hornell, 'South Indian blowguns, boomerangs, and crossbows', *Journal of the Royal Anthropological Institute of Great Britain and Ireland*, liv (1924), 316–46; cf. *supra*, p. 36, n. 2.

Note 3, p. 36. Ibid. 145. J. Oliver Asín, 'Origen árabe de *rebato*, *arrobda* y sus homónimos: Contribución al estudio de la historia medieval de la táctica militar', *Boletín de la Real Academia Española*, xv (1928), 388, cites a variant reading. The exact period of this Frankish influence on Muslim Spain remains to be determined. The tenth-century traveller Ibn Haukal criticizes the appearance of most Andalusian horsemen either because they used no stirrups or else because they dangled their legs free of the stirrups; cf. R. Dozy, *Spanish Islam* (London, 1913), 493. On the conflict between Frankish and North African practices in mounted combat in Spain, see L. Mercier, 'Les Écoles espagnoles dites de la Bride et de la Gineta (ou Jineta)', *Revue de cavalerie*, xxxvii (1927), 301–15: the lance required a long stirrup; bow and javelin, a short stirrup.

Note 4, p. 37. C. Stephenson, 'Feudalism and its antecedents in England', *American Historical Review*, xlviii (1943), 260–5; H. Mitteis, *Der Staat des hohen Mittelalters: Grundlinien einer vergleichenden Verfassungsgeschichte des Lehenzeitalters*, 4th edn. (Weimar, 1953), 211–15. F. Barlow, *Feudal Kingdom of England, 1042–1216* (New York, 1955), 11, believes that there were feudal trends in Anglo-Saxon times, but T. J. Oleson, *The Witenagemot in the Reign of Edward the Confessor* (Toronto, 1955), 96, is closer to the truth when he declares that 'the Anglo-Saxon monarchy and society bore a much closer resemblance to early Merovingian monarchy and society than to those of either eleventh century France or Scandinavia'. Barrow, op. cit. 37–38, 42, correctly states that William had no intention of subverting Anglo-Saxon institutions when he first won England: he did so only when he found that such a social and legal structure could not support the military régime which he considered essential to his power. C. W. Hollister, 'The significance of scutage rates in eleventh- and twelfth-century England', *English Historical Review*, lxxv (1960), 577–89, and in a forthcoming article in the *American Historical Review*, rightly stresses William's preservation of the fyrd and of the Anglo-Saxon tradition of two months' military service in contrast to the forty days' duty which had become customary on the continent.

Note 1, p. 40. The evidence is scattered, but the essential fact seems clear; cf. L. Beck, *Geschichte des Eisens* (Brunswick, 1884), i. 730–7; A. R. Lewis, *The Northern Seas: Shipping and Commerce in Northern Europe, A.D. 300–1100* (Princeton, 1958), 196–7. In the eighth and ninth centuries techniques of mass production of cheap jewellery which had been developed in the seventh century (cf. E. Salin, *La Civilisation mérovingienne*, iii: *Les Techniques* [Paris, 1957], 196, 202) were applied in the Rhineland to the manufacture of great quantities of swords partly for export to the East, where they were greatly valued; ibid. 97, 105–7, 111–12, 196; A. Zeki-Validi, 'Die Schwerter der Germanen nach arabischen Berichten des 9.–11. Jahrhunderts', *Zeitschrift der Deutschen Morgenländischen Gesellschaft*, xc (1936), 19–37. According to H. H. Coghlan, 'A note upon iron as a material for the Celtic sword', *Sibrium*, iii (1956–7), 132: 'upon the evidence available to us at the present time, it would seem that the art of successful tempering belongs to a later time than that of the Roman period.'

Note 5, p. 45. E. Espérandieu, *Recueil général des bas-reliefs, statues, et bustes de la Gaule romaine*, iv (Paris, 1911), no. 3245; R. Lefebvre des Noëttes, *L'Attelage et le cheval de selle à travers les âges* (Paris, 1931), 85. C. Bicknell, *The Prehistoric Rock Engravings in the Italian Maritime Alps* (Bordighera, 1902), shows crude petroglyphs of the Bronze Age which seem to depict plough-teams of 3, 4, 5, and 6 oxen; cf. P. V. Glob, 'Plough carvings in the Val Camonica', *Kuml* (1954), 15–17; E. G. Anati, 'Rock engravings in the Italian Alps', *Archaeology*, xi (1958), 30–39, which distinguishes four periods, the latest proto-Etruscan. F. G. Payne, in *Archaeological Journal*, civ (1947), 84, accepts one of these as representing a six-ox plough; but J. G. D. Clark, *Prehistoric Europe, the Economic Basis* (London, 1952), 101–2, points out that these 3- and 5-ox teams are technically impossible, and believes that the apparent 4- and 6-ox teams merely illustrate two or three 2-ox ploughs working a field close together, as in a Bronze Age Cyprian model; cf. his pl. VI*b*.

Note 2, p. 46. *Atharva-Veda*, vi. 91. 1, tr. M. Bloomfield (Oxford, 1897), 40; cf. H. Zimmer, *Altindisches Leben: die Cultur der vedischen Arier* (Berlin, 1879), 237; J. Bloch, 'La Charrue védique', *Bulletin of the School of Oriental Studies*, viii (1936), 411–12. Haudricourt and Delamarre, op. cit. 171, suspect that the Vedic passages, and 1 Kings xix. 19, refer to successive ploughs in a field rather than to many yokes on one plough. A. K. Y. U. Aiyer, *Agriculture and Allied Arts in Vedic India* (Bangalore, 1949), 14, cites *Yajur Veda*, 189. 20: 'May the sharp-pointed share cleave the soil and push the ploughed earth on both sides of the furrows', thus indicating a scratch-plough. Despite the orthodox Hindu belief that the Vedic texts have been transmitted without alteration from deep Antiquity, it would be rash, in the present state of Indic scholarship, to accept an early Aryan date for any single passage.

Note 3, p. 46. A. Steensberg, op. cit. 253–5; G. Hatt, 'L'Agriculture préhistorique de Danemark', *Revue de synthèse*, xvii (1939), 89; but cf. *History of Technology*, ed. C. Singer, ii (1956), 87, n. 1, fig. 47. There has been an increasing suspicion of the pollenanalytical dating of this plough in the Early Iron Age: it may well have sunk in the bog, or been pushed down, as a sacrifice; cf. Clark, op. cit. 106; Bratanič, op. cit. 52; S. Gasiorowski, 'Some remarks on the wheel plow of Late Antiquity and the Middle Ages', *Kwartalnik historii kulturny materialnej*, ii (1954), 835–6; Haudricourt and Delamarre, op. cit. 351–2. However, G. Mildenberger, 'Der Pflug im vorgeschichtlichen Europa', *Wissenschaftliche Zeitschrift der Universität Leipzig*, v (1951–2), 70–73, still accepts both the wheels and the dating, although pointing out that all the finds of ploughs in Jutland probably represent burials of religious offerings; cf. also B. Brentjes, 'Untersuchungen zur Geschichtes des Pfluges', *Wissenschaftliche Zeitschrift der Universität Halle-Wittenberg*, iii (1952–3), 398.

Note 2, p. 48. H. Mortensen and K. Scharlau, 'Die siedlungskundliche Wert der Kartierung von Wüstungsfluren', *Nachrichten der Akademie der Wissenschaften zu Göttingen, Phil.-hist. Kl.* (1949), 328; H. Jäger, 'Zur Wüstungs- und Kulturlandschaftsforschung', *Erdkunde*, viii (1954), 303; Kerridge, op. cit. 14–36. In a careful local study of fossil fields, W. R. Mead, 'Ridge and furrow in Buckinghamshire', *Geographical Journal*, cxx (1954), 35–38, found that in different places the difference between crest and trough varied from 3 feet to a few inches, and in width the strips varied by 14 yards; yet he could find no correlation between these measurements and the type of soil. R. Aitken, 'Ridge and furrow', ibid. 260, points out that peasants sooner or later reversed their method of ploughing a particular strip to prevent its getting too high and that the measurements in a fossil field give only its scale as it was at the moment of abandonment. Yet there can be little doubt that, just as dry fields were generally left unridged, moist soils were ridged in proportion to the need for drainage; e.g. in some of the Scottish lowlands there was a 3-foot difference of elevation between crest and trough in strips as narrow as 20–30 feet; cf. A. Birnie, 'Ridge cultivation in Scotland', *Scottish Historical Review*, xxiv (1927), 195.

Note 3, p. 48. H. Mortensen, 'Neue Beobachtungen über Wüstungs-Band-fluren und ihre Bedeutung für die mittelalterliche deutsche Kulturlandschaft', *Berichte zur deutschen Landeskunde*, x (1951), 354. Mortensen, 355, indicates that one of the reasons for the late medieval decline in ridge-and-furrow cultivation may have been the development of more satisfactory methods of fertilizing, such as marling, sodding, and more extensive manuring. Virgil had urged peasants to put wood-ashes on their fields; cf. P. Juon, 'Düngung in der Urzeit', *Agrarpolitische revue*, vi (1949–50), 376. Both the two- and three-field systems, by assuring regular pasturing of herds upon the arable, increased manuring; while the increase in legume crops under the latter rotation helped to fix nitrogen in the soil; cf. *supra*, p. 75. There is no adequate history of agricultural fertilizer; cf. R. Grand, *L'Agriculture au moyen âge* (Paris, 1950), 260–9.

Note 3, p. 55. As recent examples of the sort of work which is gradually rectifying the picture of the spread of open fields given by the map contained in the pioneer work of Gray, op. cit., see H. P. R. Finberg, 'The open field in Devon', in W. G. Hoskins and H. P. R. Finberg, *Devonshire Studies* (London, 1952), 265–88; A. H. Slee, 'The open fields of Braunton', *Devonshire Association Report and Transactions*, lxxxiv (1952), 142–9; V. Chapman, 'Open fields in West Cheshire', *Transactions of the Historic Society of Lancashire and Cheshire*, civ (1952), 35–59; D. Sylvester, 'Open fields of Cheshire', ibid. cviii (1956), 1–33; R. R. Rawson, 'The open field in Flintshire, Devonshire and Cornwall', *Economic History Review*, 2nd series, vi (1953), 51–54; G. C. Homans, 'The rural sociology of medieval England', *Past and Present*, iv (1953), 32–43; A. Harris, ' "Land" and ox-gang in the East Riding of Yorkshire', *Yorkshire Archaeological Journal*, xxxviii (1955), 529–35; W. G. Hoskins, *The Midland Peasant* (London, 1957); M. Davis, 'Rhosili open fields and related South Wales field patterns', *Agricultural History Review*, iv (1956), 80–96; D. Sylvester, 'The common fields of the coastlands of Gwent', ibid. vi (1958), 9–26. For Ireland, see recently J. Otway-Ruthven, 'The organization of Anglo-Irish agriculture in the Middle Ages', *Journal of the Royal Society of Antiquaries of Ireland*, lxxxi (1951), 1–13; D. McCourt, 'Infield and outfield in Ireland', *Economic History Review*, 2nd series, vii (1954–5), 369–76.

Note 6, p. 55. To meet the need for cattle fodder the scythe was developed. A. Steensberg, *Ancient Harvesting Implements* (Copenhagen, 1943), 225–49, shows that (perhaps because a worsening of climate made it necessary to keep cattle in barns for a longer period) long scythes began to be used in northern Europe in Roman times, primarily for haymaking: harvesting grain was done with sickles. By the ninth century at least, scythes became more common, and efficiency was increased by adding lateral handles to the haft. A. Timm, 'Zur Geschichte der Erntegeräte', *Zeitschrift für Agrargeschichte und Agrarsoziologie*, iv (1956), 30, correlates the spread of the scythe with early-medieval population pressure, assarting, and increase of barn-feeding of cattle. Charlemagne renamed July *Hewimânoth* or 'Haying Month', (*supra*, p. 56, n. 2) and in an illustrated calendar prior to 830 it is personified with a scythe, whereas August, the 'Harvest Month', carries a sickle; cf. H. Stern, 'Poésies et représentations carolingiennes et byzantines des mois', *Revue archéologique*, xlvi (1955), 143, fig. 1; 146. In view of the ambiguity of the Roman evidence for the scythe, its absence from the Byzantine area, and the total lack of Merovingian testimony for it, J. Le Gall, 'Les "falces" et la "faux" ', *Études d'archéologie classique*, ii: *Annales de l'Est*, no. 22 (1959), 55–72, questions whether it was known (south of Scandinavia) before the ninth century.

Note 3, p. 57. *Dictionnaire d'archéologie chrétienne et de liturgie*, vi (1924), 2056. G. Carnot, *Le Fer à cheval à travers l'histoire et l'archéologie* (Paris, 1951), reviews the earlier literature and is convinced by nothing before the ninth–tenth century. Since then M. Hell, 'Weitere keltische Hufeisen aus Salzburg und Umgebung', *Archaeologia austriaca*, xii (1953), 44–49, and H. E. Mandera, 'Sind die Hufeisen der Saalburg römisch?', *Saalburg-Jahrbuch*, xv (1956), 29–37, defend early datings, whereas L. Armand-Caillat, 'Les Origines de la ferrure à clous', *Revue archéologique de l'Est et du Centre-Est*, iii (1952), 32–36; P. Lebel, 'La Ferrure à clous des chevaux', ibid. 178–81; F. Franz, 'Kannten die Römer Hufeisen?', *Der Schlern*, xxvii (1955), 425, and M. U. Kasparek, 'Stand der Forschung über den Hufbeschlag des Pferdes', *Zeitschrift für Agrargeschichte und Agrarsoziologie*, vi (1958), 38–43, agree upon the ninth–tenth century.

Note 1, p. 60. *L'Attelage et le cheval de selle à travers les âges* (Paris, 1931), 159, shows that a team of horses or mules which would be expected to pull 1,980 to 2,480 kgm. today could pull only about 492 kgm. in ancient harness. A. P. Usher, *History of Mechanical Inventions*, 2nd edn. (Cambridge, Mass., 1954), 157, concludes, on the basis of late nineteenth-century tables of work normally expected from horses, that 'the net effectiveness of ancient draft animals in harness was not more than one-third of the modern expectation'. He adds, however, that 'the figures in the modern table are distinctly low', and that the assertion 'that animals in antiquity achieved only one-third of the modern expectation is really a moderate statement, under- rather than overstated'. We may therefore accept Lefebvre des Noëttes's estimates as being close to the truth. A. Burford, 'Heavy transport in classical Antiquity', *Economic History Review*, 2nd series, xiii (1960), 1–18, emphasizes the inadequacy of ancient horse harness but properly underscores the fact that, despite this relative inefficiency, the ancients achieved great results using oxen.

Note 2, p. 60. H. Schäfer, 'Altaegyptische Pflüge, Joche und andere landwirtschaftliche Geräte', *Annual of the British School at Athens*, x (1903–4), 133, fig. 8, shows a relief of the time of Amenophis IV with a plough drawn by two onagers, and 135, n. 1, cites a tale of the New Kingdom which speaks of horses at the plough. P. V. Glob, 'Plough carvings in the Val Camonica', *Kuml* (1954), 7–8, 16, figs. 1, 2, shows a crude but distinct petroglyph of two mules or horses drawing a scratch-plough, perhaps 1000 B.C.; cf. E. Anati, 'Prehistoric art in the Alps', *Scientific American*, ccii (1960), 54. The rarity of these exceptions underscores the fact that the use of horses for farm labour was a medieval innovation. A. K. Y. U. Aiyer, *Agriculture and Allied Arts in Vedic India* (Bangalore, 1949), 15, believes that horses were used for ploughing in ancient India on the basis of *Rig Veda*, x. 9. 2. 3, 5. 7: 'Set up the cattle trough, bind the straps to it, let us bail out water from the well which is not easily exhausted. Satisfy the horses, accomplish the good work of ploughing.' This is, however, no more than an enumeration of tasks.

NOTES 157

Note 1, p. 6. A. G. Haudricourt, 'Lumières sur l'attelage moderne', *Annales d'histoire sociale*, vii (1945), 117–18, corrects his view expressed in 'De l'origine de l'attelage moderne', *Annales d'histoire économique et sociale*, viii (1936), 515–22, that *hames* and *Kommut* are of Mongol origin, and declares them to be Turkic *qom, qomit*. But W. Jacobeit, 'Zur Geschichte der Pferdespannung', *Zeitschrift für Agrargeschichte und Agrarsoziologie*, ii (1954), 24, derives these words from an Indo-European root. The claim of J. Needham, 'An archaeological study-tour in China, 1958', *Antiquity*, xxxiii (1959), 117, and, with Lu Gwei-Djen, 'Efficient equine harness; the Chinese inventions', *Physis*, ii (1960), 143, fig. 14, that a painting of *c.* A.D. 477–99 in the Thousand Buddha Caves near Tunhuang in Kansu implies the modern harness, is inadequately supported: the horse is equipped with a withers yoke or strap between shafts, and with a strap high around its neck which has no evident connexion with traction. Indeed, this harness is much less 'modern' than that in the Ostia mosaic cited *supra*, p. 60, n. 6. Unambiguous evidence for the modern harness in China has not emerged earlier than A.D. 851; cf. ibid. 138–41, figs. 11–13.

Note 5, p. 61. H. Stolpe and T. J. Arne, *La Nécropole de Vendel* (Stockholm, 1927), 25, 59, pl. XV, fig. 1; D. Selling, *Wikingerzeitliche und frühmittelalterliche Keramik in Schweden* (Stockholm, 1955), 127, n. 31. For similar remains of the tenth century, cf. Stolpe and Årne, pl. XVIII, fig. 1; XXIII, fig. 1; XXIV, fig. 1; pp. 34, 59; P. Poulsen, 'Der Stand der Forschung über die Kultur der Wikingerzeit', *Bericht der Römisch-Germanischen Kommission*, xxii (1932), 230; J. Brøndsted in *Acta archaeologica* (Copenhagen), vii (1936), 144; H. F. Blunck, *Die nordische Welt* (Berlin, 1937), 143; P. Poulsen, *Der Goldschatz von Hiddensee* (Leipzig, 1936), pl. X. 1. No comparable remains have been found outside Scandinavia. The objects from Lombard graves in Italy identified as horse-collar mountings by N. F. Åberg, *Die Gothen und Langobarden in Italien* (Uppsala, 1923), 123, fig. 261, are more probably ornaments for the cantles of saddles.

Note 4, p. 63. Ordericus Vitalis, *Historia ecclesiastica*, ix. 3, ed. A. Le Prevost (Paris, 1845), iii. 471. Unfortunately, C. Parain in *Cambridge Economic History*, i. 132, has wrought havoc among the facts, and has already led astray N. E. Lee, *Travel and Transport through the Ages* (Cambridge, 1956), 117, and R. Trow-Smith, *History of British Livestock Husbandry to 1700* (London, 1957), 56. Parain states that in the *Lex salica* horses pull ploughs, overlooking the meaning of *carruca* in that text, as noted *supra*, p. 50, n. 5. He then asserts that since in the second half of the eleventh century 'Jean de Garlande' mentions horse-collars (*epiphia equina*), 'probably the horse was already being used on the land in the Paris region'. Probably it was, but not on this evidence: he has confused a Burgundian abacist of the later eleventh century with the famous English lexicographer of the early thirteenth; cf. G. Sarton, *Introduction to the History of Science*, i. 758; ii. 696.

Note 2, p. 67. F. Steinbach, 'Gewanndorf und Einzelhof', *Historische Aufsätze Aloys Schulte gewidmet* (Düsseldorf, 1927), 57–59; K. Fröhlich, 'Rechtsgeschichte und Wüstungskunde', *Zeitschrift der Savigny-Stiftung für Rechtsgeschichte, Germ. Abt.* lxiv (1944), 299–301; H. Mortensen, 'Zur deutschen Wüstungsforschung', *Göttingische gelehrte Anzeigen*, ccvi (1944), 199–200; W. Müller-Wille, 'Zur Genese der Dörfer in der Göttinger Leinetalsenke', *Nachrichten der Akademie der Wissenschaften in Göttingen, Phil.-hist. Kl.* (1948), 13–14; F. Trautz, *Das untere Neckarland im früheren Mittelalter* (Heidelberg, 1953), 40–43; A. Timm, *Studien zur Siedlungs- und Agrargeschichte Mitteldeutschlands* (Cologne, 1956), 137; H. Jäger, 'Entwicklungsperioden agrarer Siledungsgebiete im mittleren Westdeutschland seit·dem frühen 13. Jahrhundert', *Würzburger geographische Arbeiten*, vi (1958), 19.

Note 3, p. 73. Cf. G. C. Homans, *English Villagers in the Thirteenth Century* (Cambridge, Mass., 1941), 56–57. P. de Saint-Jacob, 'L'Assolement en Bourgogne au XVIIIᵉ siècle', *Études rhodaniennes*, xi (1935), 209–19, cites Burgundian two-field villages in the eighteenth century which wished to switch rotational systems because the monoculture of wheat and rye was subject to ruin in bad years and the peasant was unoccupied for long months. P. Féral, 'L'Introduction de l'assolement triennal en Gascogne lectouroise', *Annales du Midi*, lxii (1950), 249–58, shows the great economic benefit of the spread of a modified three-year rotation to Gascony in recent times. On the other hand, L. Musset, 'Observations sur l'ancien assolement biennal du Roumois et du Lieuvin', *Annales de Normandie*, ii (1952), 150, notes a Norman community which was on the three-year plan in 1291 but in 1836 was on the two-year. E. Juillard, 'L'Assolement biennal dans l'agriculture septentrionale: le cas particulier de la Basse-Alsace', *Annales de géographie*, lxi (1952), 40, believes that such 'reversals' may have occurred when, in the later Middle Ages or modern times, a village near a great city market wished to increase wheat production for that market and to harvest less barley, oats, and the like. Yet again, G. Schröder-Lembke, 'Entstehung und Verbreitung der Mehrfelderwirtschaft in Nordostdeutschland', *Zeitschrift für Agrargeschichte und Agrarsoziologie*, ii (1954), 131, points to communities which in the thirteenth century were on the triennial plan but which by the early fourteenth century had developed a four-year crop rotation, presumably in an effort to increase production of summer crops; for further complexities, cf. her 'Wesen und Verbreitung der Zweifelderwirtschaft im Rheingebiet', ibid. vii (1959), 14–31.

Note 2, p. 74. W. Müller-Wille, 'Das Rheinische Schiefergebirge und seine kulturgeographische Struktur und Stellung', *Deutsches Archiv für Landes- und Volksforschung*, vi (1943), 561, publishes a map of the three-field area of Europe. It should be noted that the plan never penetrated Flanders, the Netherlands, or the North Sea coast of Germany. Here there was no system of rotation: the individual peasant elaborately manured his fields with turf or peat, and the moist climate provided such lush pasturage that fallow was not needed for browsing; cf. p. 538. However, Müller-Wille's reasoning is faulty when he maintains (561) that the triennial rotation must have been invented by the Franks to secure pasture for their cattle when they spread into the 'continental' climate of the interior which provided less grazing and where likewise the pastoral economy was in greater competition with an agriculture of cereals. They had no need to invent a triennial rotation for such a purpose, since a biennial rotation likewise gives pasture on the fallow.

Note 6, p. 76. Careful study should be made of other new sources of protein in this period, and of new methods of preserving and transporting meat, fish, and cheese. The great expansion of water-mills, and consequently of mill-ponds, certainly increased the supply of fresh fish available at all seasons, as is shown by the frequency with which the rent of mills was paid in fish and eels; cf. R. Grand, *L'Agriculture au moyen âge* (Paris, 1950), 535–46. An Armenian manuscript of the thirteenth century shows a fishing reel; the same device appears in China in the first half of the fourteenth century; but as yet it has not been found in Europe before 1651; cf. Sarton, *Introduction*, iii (1947), 237. While white fish such as cod contain relatively little fat, and can therefore be smoked or salted easily, the very oily herring contains an unsaturated fat which easily becomes rancid by combination with the oxygen of the air, thus rendering both storage and transportation difficult—a matter particularly unfortunate since herring, in contrast to most white fish, run seasonally in great schools. The technique of salting herrings in barrels, in such a way as to exclude air and thus permit distant transport and storage for years, appears first in 1359; cf. C. L. Cutting, *Fish Saving: A History of Fish Processing* (London, 1955), 57. E. M. Veale, 'The rabbit in England', *Agricultural History Review*, v (1957), 85–90, shows that the rabbit reached England in 1176 and became common in the thirteenth century. In 1341 at Milan, Flamma notes, after remarking on the selective breeding of destriers and 'Alan' dogs: 'et cuniculis castra et civitatem repleverunt'; cf. *supra*, p. 62, n. 1.

Note 7, p. 76. The great vitality of Italy, Provence, and Spain in this period cannot be explained in terms of agricultural technology. G. Luzzatto, 'Mutamenti nell' economia agraria italiana dalla caduta dei carolingi al principio del secolo XI', in *Settimane di Studio del Centro Italiano di Studi dell' Alto Medio Evo*, ii (1955), 604, is correct in saying that the treatises of Cato, Varro, and Columella seem almost to describe an Italian estate of the year 1800. However, D. Herlihy, 'Treasure hoards in the Italian economy, 906–1139', *Economic History Review*, x (1957), 1–14, and 'The agrarian revolution in Southern France and Italy, 801–1150', *Speculum*, xxxiii (1958), 21–41, presents not a technological but an agrarian-managerial revolution contemporary with the technological upheaval occurring north of the Loire and the Alps. Because of inheritance, land holding had become fractioned in the south to the point of complete agricultural inefficiency. From *c.* 960, and culminating *c.* 1070, jewellery and other hoarded possessions were increasingly turned into cash which was invested in consolidating fragments of farm land into effective production units. The efforts of the Gregorian Reform to re-establish looted ecclesiastical endowments had the same result. In northern Europe the widespread replacement of independently farmed scattered strips by open fields, communally controlled and operated as a unit, was a revolution in management which undoubtedly contributed to the high productivity of the new northern agricultural technology. In the Mediterranean lands the new skills of management were applied to the old Roman agrarian technology which was admirably suited to the regional conditions, and the results were excellent. Despite Herlihy's conclusion that some of the vitality left this managerial movement in the twelfth century, Italian merchants invested heavily in land improvement in the thirteenth century, somewhat less in the fourteenth, but more than ever in the fifteenth; cf. C. M. Cipolla, 'Trends in Italian history in the later Middle Ages', *Economic History Review*, ii (1949), 182–3. Indeed, in the fifteenth century, when most of Europe was in a population decline, northern

and central Italy seem to have been growing; cf. K. Helleiner, 'Europas Bevölkerung und Wirtschaft im späteren Mittelalter', *Mitteilungen des Instituts für
Österreichische Geschichtsforschung*, lxii (1954), 262, n. 21. It would be interesting
to discover whether the development of 'castelli', fortified villages of free peasants,
in Italy from the tenth century onward is a phenomenon related to, or different
from, the balling of peasant population into large villages which one sees in
Germany; cf. G. Luzzato, 'L'Inurbamento delle populazioni rurali in Italia
nei secoli XII e XIII', *Studi in onore di Enrico Besta* (Milan, 1938), ii. 183–203.
My suggestion, *supra*, pp. 67–68, that the transition from ox to horse in agriculture may have assisted the northern balling, is irrelevant to the growth of
castelli, since the ox remained predominant in the peninsula.

Note 2, p. 79. F. M. Feldhaus, *Die Technik der Antike und des Mittelalters*
(Potsdam, 1931), 277, asserts that the word 'engineer' first appears in Johannes
Codagnellus, *Annales placentini*, ed. O. Holder-Egger (Hannover, 1901), 23,
which, although written in the early thirteenth century, refers, as of 1196, to
an 'Alamannus de Guitelmo, enccignerius communis Mediolani'. Feldhaus holds
that it is derived from *incingere*, 'to fortify'. However, in 1190–2 Ambroise,
L'Estoire de la guerre sainte, ed. G. Paris (Paris, 1897), v. 2274, explicitly connects
engineers with engines: 'engineors qui savaient d'engins plusors.' I cannot find
the word earlier than 1170, when 'Ricardus ingeniator, vir artificiosus . . . et
prudens architectus' appears at Durham; cf. V. Pevsner, 'The term "architect"
in the Middle Ages', *Speculum*, xvii (1942), 555; but 'Ailnoth ingeniator' flourished
1157–90; cf. J. Harvey, *English Mediaeval Architects* (London, 1954), 17. For
engineers from the early thirteenth century onward, cf. H. Charnier, 'Notes
sur les origines du génie, du moyen âge à l'organisation de l'an VII', *Revue du
génie militaire*, lxxxvii (1954), 17–44.

Note 1, p. 81. A. Steensberg, *Farms and Mills in Denmark during Two Thousand
Years* (Copenhagen, 1952), 294–7. Such mills are very widely distributed in
both time and space; cf. E. C. Curwen, 'The problem of early water mills',
Antiquity, xviii (1944), 130–46, and 'A vertical water mill near Salonika', ibid.
xix (1945), 211–12. Presumably because their Indian workers were unfamiliar
with gearing, Franciscan missionaries in the early nineteenth century built such
a mill at San Antonio de Padua in California, which I have seen. E. Eude,
Histoire documentaire de la mécanique française (Paris, 1902), 11, shows that the
modern water turbine is directly descended from primitive horizontal water-
wheels which were often fitted with spoon-blades and encased; cf. F. M.
Feldhaus, 'Beiträge zur älteren Geschichte der Turbinen', *Zeitschrift für das
gesamte Turbinenwesen*, v (1908), 569–71. The ascription to the third or fourth
century of a sophisticated turbine-like water-wheel preserved in the Conservatoire
des Arts et Métiers in Paris is unwarranted: nothing is known of its provenance;
cf. *Power*, lxxiv (1931), 502.

Note 3, p. 82. In the Naples Museum a water-wheel reconstructed from
cavities in the ash of Pompeii is so small that F. M. Feldhaus, 'Ahnen des
Wasserrades', *Die Umschau*, xl (1936), 472, believes that it may have run not
a mill but some sort of automaton; but of this last there are no remains. R. J.
Forbes, *Studies in Ancient Technology*, ii (Leiden, 1955), 96, and in Singer,

History of Technology, ii (1956), 601, asserts that Vespasian (A.D. 69–79) refused to erect a water-driven hoist lest it cause unemployment. Since no other hoists operated by water-wheels are known before one in the Tyrol in 1515, pictured in E. Kurzel-Runtscheiner, 'Das Unterinntal, eine technikgeschichtliche Landschaft', *Blätter für Technikgeschichte*, xiii (1951), 39, fig. 8 (cf. also G. Agricola, *De re metallica* [Basel, 1556], tr. H. C. and L. H. Hoover, 2nd edn. [New York, 1950], 199, and the *Schwazer Bergbuch* of 1556, in F. Kirnbauer, 'Das "Schwazer Bergbuch", eine Bilderhandschrift des österreichischen Bergbaues aus dem Jahre 1556', *Blätter für Technikgeschichte*, xviii [1956], 85, pl. 7), this would be a matter of importance. However, Forbes's source, Suetonius, *Vespasian*, ch. 18, implies no such apparatus: 'Mechanico quoque grandis columnas exigua impensa perducturum in Capitolinum pollicenti praemium pro commento non mediocre optulit, operam remisit, praefatus sineret se plebiculam pascere.'

Note 5, p. 82. Villard de Honnecourt: Kritische Gesamtausgabe des Bauhüttenbuches MS fr. 19093, der Pariser Nationalbibliothek, ed. H. R. Hahnloser (Vienna, 1935), pl. 44; for date, cf. 229, 232. Dr. P. J. Alexander of the University of Michigan, who is preparing a new edition of Gregory of Nyssa's sermons on *Ecclesiastes*, suggests that a passage in Hom. III (*Patrologia graeca*, xliv [Paris, 1863], 656A),'πόσα τὰ μηχανήματα των μὲν ὕδατι καὶ σιδήρῳ διαπριόντων τὰς ὕλας', used in reference to the sawing of marble, indicates water-powered saws in fourth-century Anatolia. However, the cutting of marble with 'water and iron' more probably means that water was used to cool the horizontal iron saw and carry the abrasive down the crack to the saw; cf. *supra*, p. 82, n. 7. Eleven centuries later, Bessarion viewed water-powered saws as a novelty; cf. *infra*, p. 129, n. 2.

Note 8, p. 86. The assertion of Ibn ʿAbd al-Mun ʿim al-Ḥimyarī, *La Péninsule ibérique au moyen âge*, ed. E. Lévi-Provençal (Leiden, 1938), 153, that 'one of the curiosities of Tarragona consists of the mills built by the ancients: they turn when the wind blows and stop with it', cannot safely be applied to the Caliphal period. Lévi-Provençal, p. xv, points out that our version of this work was finished in A.D. 1461, although it may be based on a book of the late thirteenth century. On the basis of a morphological classification of Hispano-Portuguese windmills, F. Krüger, 'Notas etnográfico-lingüísticas da Povoa de Varzim', *Boletim de filologia*, iv (1936), 156–77, suggests that while the La Mancha mills are of northern derivation, others in the Iberian Peninsula, the Mediterranean islands, and the Canaries may be descended from a more primitive Hispano-Moorish variety. J. C. Baroja, 'Le Moulin à vent en Espagne', *Laos*, ii (1952), 40, leans in this direction because *c.* 1330 Juan Ruiz, Archpriest of Hita, says 'Ffazen con much viento andar las atahonas': the modern word *tahona*, 'mule mill', comes from the Arabic *tahūna* which al-Maqqadasī used for 'windmill'. However, the Arabic term does not specifically indicate 'windmill' but rather any mill operated by a means other than water: the late-thirteenth-century *Vocabulista in arabico* glosses the Arabic *raha* as 'molendinum', i.e. a mill powered by water, but defines *tahūna* as 'molendinum bestie, sine aqua'; cf. J. Oliver Asin, 'El híspano-arabe *al-farnāt* "los molinos harineros" en la toponimia peninsular', *Al-Andalus*, xxiii (1958), 458. In judging the question of the diffusion of windmills, it is significant that all Mediterranean and Iberian windmills rotated on horizontal axles until towards the middle of the fifteenth century; cf. *supra*, p. 86, n. 9.

Note 1, p. 87. Attention has recently been called to Henry II's confirmation of Swineshead's properties by R. E. Latham, 'Suggestions for a British–Latin dictionary', *Archivum latinitatis medii aevi*, xxvii (1957), 199, and by M. W. Beresford and J. K. S. St. Joseph, *Medieval England, an Aerial Survey* (Cambridge, 1958), 64, n. 2, both of which cite the *Calendar of the Charter Rolls*, iii (London, 1908), 319, where the relevant passage identifies certain lands 'ubi molendinum ad ventum situm fuerit': a curious form of the verb. W. Dugdale, *Monasticon anglicanum*, 2nd edn. (London, 1682), i. 773, had read it simply 'situm fuerat'. The recent writers date it not later than 1181, presumably because it was witnessed by Roger, Archbishop of York, who died on 21 Nov. 1181; but it is also witnessed by Richard de Luci who retired completely from public affairs in April 1179 and died on 14 July of the same year. R. W. Eyton, *Court, Household and Itinerary of King Henry II* (London, 1878), 136, believes, on the basis of the list of witnesses and their simultaneous presence at Windsor, that the charter was given about 5 Apr. 1170. The text survives only as incorporated in a much larger confirmation of Swineshead's properties given by Edward II on 20 Sept. 1316. Since no windmills are known between 1170 and 1185, although they appear frequently thereafter, it is probable that the clause mentioning the windmill is a marginal gloss of the thirteenth or early fourteenth century which was intended to identify the location of a bit of land inadequately described in Henry II's confirmation, and that this gloss crept into Edward II's version.

Note 6, p. 92. The first steam-pumps were patented in 1630 and 1661; cf. C. Matschoss, *Entwicklung der Dampfmaschine* (Berlin, 1908), i. 284. However, something of the sort was perhaps developing earlier in the mines of Central Europe. J. C. Poggendorff, *Geschichte der Physik* (Leipzig, 1879), 529, cites the famous Lutheran pastor of Joachimsthal in Bohemia, J. Mathesius, *Sarepta oder Bergpostilla* (Nuremberg, 1562), as exhorting his flock: 'Ihr Bergleute sollet auch in euren Bergreyen rühmen den guten Mann, der Berg (Gestein) und Wasser mit dem Wind auf den Platten anrichten zu heben, wie man jetzt auch, doch am Tage, Wasser mit Feuer heben soll!' Moreover, the Czech J. J. V. Dobrzensky, *Nova, et amaenior de admirando fontium genio, philosophia* (Ferrara, 1657 or 1659), 65–67, 77, 104–7, describes machines using heat to raise water in some ways similar to that of R. D'Acres, *The Art of Water Drawing* (London, 1659), ed. R. Jenkins (Cambridge, 1930), viii–ix, 6–7, and of Edward Somerset, Marquis of Worcester, *A Century . . . of Inventions* (London, 1663), ed. H. Dircks (London, 1865), 551. Dircks, 540–4, emphasizes the *sufflator* as the chief ancestor of the steam-engine.

Note 1, p. 93. R. Hennig, 'Beiträge zur Frühgeschichte der Aeronautik', *Beiträge zur Geschichte der Technik und Industrie*, viii (1918), 105–8, 110–14, and J. Duhem, 'Les Aérostats du moyen-âge d'après les miniatures de cinq manuscrits allemands', *Thalès*, ii (1935), 106–14, find forerunners of the hot-air balloon of early modern times in fifteenth-century aerial dragons sustained by lamps placed in the head. They neglect, however, the most spectacular evidence:

such a dragon, on the end of a rope held by three soldiers, flying over a besieged city and dropping fire-bombs on it; cf. Walter de Milimete's *De nobilitatibus... regum* of 1327, ed. M. R. James (Oxford, 1913), pl. 154. D. Schwenter, *Deliciae physico-mathematicae* (Nuremberg, 1636), i. 472, illustrates a similar dragon-aerostat governed by a cord on a reel. According to P. Huard, 'Sciences et techniques de l'Eurasie', *Bulletin de la Société des études indochinoises*, 2nd series, xxv (1950), 137, in 1812 the Russian army was still using fiery dragons as psychological warfare against Napoleon's army.

Note 5, p. 96. T. L. Davis and J. R. Ware, 'Early Chinese military pyrotechnics', *Journal of Chemical Education*, xxiv (1947), 522–37; T. L. Davis, 'Early Chinese rockets', *Technology Review*, li (1948), 101; Wang Ling, op. cit. 172; L. C. Goodrich and Fêng Chia-shêng, 'The early development of firearms in China', *Isis*, xxxvi (1946), 117. The bamboo tubes carried by two soldiers and filled with an explosive powder in 1132 (ibid. 116) were doubtless also Roman candles rather than bazookas. In 1259 a tube shooting not only some form of Greek fire but also a projectile, perhaps a fire-ball, seems to have been used in China, but since the tube was still of bamboo, it cannot have involved much explosion; ibid. 117. The evaluation of the Chinese records is made difficult by the frequent use of the same word both for the projectiles and for the machines throwing them; and, understandably, no line is drawn between incendiary materials and explosives. But by 1231 metal bombs or grenades filled with an explosive powder, often hurled by the man-powered proto-trebuchet, were being used in East Asia, ibid. 117; Wang Ling, op. cit. 170.

Note 3, p. 99. Christ Church, Oxford, MS. of Walter of Milimete's *De officiis regum*, fol. 70ᵛ. The copying of the manuscript began in 1326, but since it was dedicated 'ad honorem illustris domini Edwardi dei gracia Regis anglie incipientis regnare', and given to the king, and the picture of the gun is on the last page, this latter cannot be earlier than the end of 1327 when the boy Edward III began to reign; cf. *The Treatise of Walter de Milimete De nobilitatibus, sapientiis et prudentiis regum, reproduced in facsimile*, ed. M. R. James (Oxford, 1913), pl. 140; O. Guttmann, *Monumenta pulveris pyrii* (London, 1906), pl. 69; F. M. Feldhaus, 'Die älteste Darstellung eines Pulvergeschützes', *Zeitschrift für historische Waffenkunde*, v (1909–11), 92. B. Rathgen, *Das Aufkommen der Pulverwaffe* (Munich, 1925), 65, holds that the illuminations of this manuscript 'sind mindestens 75 Jahre jünger als die Handschrift selber'; but does one give unfinished manuscripts to a king? Diels, op. cit. 110, n. 2, believes that this picture represents not a cannon with gunpowder but the final development of a device for projecting Greek fire together with an arrow. In view of the considerable evidence for cannon immediately thereafter, the hypothesis seems strained.

Note 6, p. 99. L. Lacabane, 'De la poudre à canon et de son introduction en France', *Bibliothèque de l'École des Chartes*, vi (1844), 36. The numerous claims for earlier appearances of guns are screened by Rathgen, op. cit.; Allouche, 'Un texte relatif aux premiers canons', *Hespéris*, xxxii (1945), 81–84, claims the first evidence of such artillery in the Muslim siege of Huescar in 1324, when a red-hot missile was thrown by a machine functioning with the use of *naft*. Rathgen, 11, following primarily Romocki, op. cit. 80–82, shows that similar claims from the

Magrib for the early fourteenth century all refer to the throwing of Greek fire; cf. D. Ayalon, *Gunpowder and Firearms in the Mamluk Kingdom: A Challenge to a Mediaeval Society* (London, 1956), 7, n. 7. Since Greek fire often produced a thunderous noise when discharged, the appearance of a Johannes Donerschutte de Osterike at Soest in 1330 and 1331 is not in itself evidence of cannon; cf. H. Rothert, 'Wan und wo ist die Pulverwaffe erfunden?', *Blätter für deutsche Landesgeschichte*, lxxxix (1952), 84–86.

Note 4, p. 100. Ibid. 3–4. A more exact dating is desirable for the picture, from an Arabic manuscript credited to the early fourteenth century, of a hand-gun at the end of a stick; cf. O. Baarmann, 'Die Entwicklung des Geschützlafette bis zum Beginn des 16. Jahrhunderts und ihre Beziehungen zu der des Gewehr-schaftes', *Festschrift M. Thierbach* (Dresden, 1905), 55, fig. 1. It may represent a tube for shooting Greek fire. Syed Abu Zafar Nadvi, 'The use of cannon in Muslim India', *Islamic Culture*, xii (1938), 405, believes that the 'Western stones (*sang-i-maghribī*)' used at the siege of Ranthambar in A.D. 1299–1300 were cannon-balls. However, the 'Western engines (*manjaniqhā-i-magribī*)' used in India, as in Islam after *c.* 1220, were a kind of trebuchet; cf. M. A. Makhdoomee, 'Mechanical artillery in medieval India', *Journal of Indian History*, xv (1936), 193; C. Cahen, 'Un traité d'armurerie composé pour Saladin', *Bulletin d'études orientales de l'Institut Français de Damas*, xii (1948), 158, n. 6.

Note 3, p. 101. In England the first person of note to be killed by a hand-gun was the Earl of Shrewsbury in 1453; cf. Clephan, op. cit. 52. A mechanical device intimately related to the efficiency of the hand-gun, but as yet inadequately studied, is rifling. The ancients knew that a javelin thrown twirling was more accurate than one without a twist; cf. R. F. Crook, 'Did the ancient Greeks and Romans understand the importance of the effect produced by rifling in modern guns?', *Classical Review*, xxx (1916), 46–48. Mr. Stephen Grancsay, Curator of Arms and Armour of the Metropolitan Museum of Art, has shown me spirally-fletched Turkish arrows of uncertain date, and such fletching is con-sidered normal by R. Ascham, *Toxophilus, the Schole of Shooting* (London, 1545), in *English Works*, ed. W. A. Wright (Cambridge, 1904), 91: 'Youre fether muste stande almooste streyght on, but yet after that sort that it maye turne rounde in flyinge . . . the shafte in flyenge must turne rounde.' It is reported, but with inadequate dating, that certain late-medieval cross-bows projected their bolts through spirally-grooved barrels; cf. M. Bennett, *The Story of the Rifle* (London, 1944), 8; C. H. B. Pridham, *Superiority of Fire* (London, 1945), 9. L. A. Muratori, *Antiquitates Italiae medii aevi* (Milan, 1739), ii. 518–19, discusses rotating cross-bow quarrels, *gerectoni, werrestones, veretoni*, a word of German origin. According to M. Thierbach, *Geschichte der Handfeuerwaffen* (Leipzig, 1899), 169, rifled hand-guns were used at a shooting match at Leipzig in 1498 and thereafter became common in central Europe for hunting. Perhaps because of the expense of rifles, only smooth-bored guns were used by European infantry until the middle of the nineteenth century. Immigrants from Switzerland and the Palatinate introduced the rifle to Pennsylvania, where it developed a longer barrel, a smaller and more economical bore, and became the typical weapon of the American frontiersman; cf. F. Reichmann, 'The Pennsylvania rifle: a social interpretation of changing military techniques', *Pennsylvania Magazine of*

History and Biography, lxix (1945), 8–9. Speed of loading was greatly increased, and wear was reduced, by the adoption of a 'patch' of greased buckskin, greased patches of felt having first been mentioned in 1644 by the Spaniard Alonzo Martines de Espinar; cf. W. M. Cline, *The Muzzle-loading Rifle* (Huntington, 1942), 9. The superiority of the Pennsylvania rifle over British arms is thought by some to be one of the reasons for the success of the American Revolution.

Note 1, p. 102. Goodrich and Fêng Chia-shêng, op. cit. 114; Wang Ling, op. cit. 168. The earliest Chinese pictures of this artillery are much later; cf. Goodrich and Fêng, figs. 1 and 2; Wang Ling, 171; W. Gohlke, 'Das Geschützwesen des Altertums und des Mittelalters, III: Das mittelalterliche Wurfzeug', *Zeitschrift für historische Waffenkunde*, v (1909–11), 379, fig. 26; K. Huuri, *Zur Geschichte des mittelalterlichen Geschützwesens aus orientalischen Quellen* (Helsinki, 1941), 215, figs. 13, 14. The opinion of Huuri that the man-powered proto-trebuchet was diffused westward *c*. A.D. 700 lacks adequate evidence, as does that of F. Lot, *L'Art militaire et les armées au moyen âge* (Paris, 1946), i. 222, that the 'nova et exquisita machinamentorum genera' used by Charles the Bald in 873 against Angers (Regino of Prüm, *Chronicon*, ed. F. Kurze [Hannover, 1890], 106) or the machines used by the defenders of Paris in 886 (Abbo, *De bello parisiaco*, ed. G. H. Pertz [Hannover, 1871], ll. 156–7, 213–14, 360–6) were counterweight trebuchets.

Note 3, p. 102. *De expugnatione Lyxbonensi*, ed. C. W. David (New York, 1936), 143, where it was operated by shifts of 100 men, and was called a Balearic sling. This name probably does not indicate diffusion through the still Muslim Balearic Isles, but is rather a reference to the ancient prowess of the inhabitants of the Balearics as slingers; cf. E. Hübner, 'Baliares', in Pauly–Wissowa, *Real-Encyclopädie der classischen Altertumswissenschaft*, ii (1896), 2824. For other pictures of this transitional device, see the plates of Pietro de Eboli, *Liber ad honorem Augusti*, ed. G. B. Siragusa (Rome, 1905); this manuscript may be dated 1196–7; for another picture dated 1182, cf. *Annales januenses*, ed. G. H. Pertz, *MGH*, *Scriptores*, xviii (1863), pl. III; cf. also W. Erben, 'Beiträge zum Geschützwesen im Mittelalter', *Zeitschrift für historische Waffenkunde*, vii (1916), 85–102, 117, 129.

Note 1, p. 103. H. Yule, *The Book of Ser Marco Polo*, 3rd edn. (London, 1929), ii. 159–60, 168. Chinese records, on the contrary, credit this new engine, called *hui-hui-p'ao*, to Muslim technicians; cf. L. C. Goodrich and Fêng Chia-shêng, op. cit. 118, esp. n. 15. This valuable article unfortunately does not consider Chinese artillery in the context of Muslim and Frankish developments, and therefore misconstrues the *hui-hui-p'ao* as a cannon with a barrel which can be raised or lowered in angle so as to regulate the range of the projectile; cf. p. 119. But on the basis of the texts which the authors adduce, it is the *magribī* or 'Western' trebuchet with a swinging counterweight container which can be adjusted in relation to the pivot of the sling-beam so that by change of leverage the trajectory is modified. On the general problem of the discrepancies between Marco Polo's account of this episode and the Chinese records, cf. L. Olschki, *Marco Polo's Asia* (Berkeley, 1960), 342–4.

Note 4, p. 103. B. R. Motzo, *Il compasso da navigare* (Cagliari, 1947), p. xlii, cites a poem of Francesco da Barberino, written 1306–13, which says that the navigator depends on compass, chart, and 'arlogio', presumably a sand-glass. In 1345, in England, payment is recorded 'pro xii orlogiis vitreis', purchased in Flanders for navigation; cf. N. H. Nicolas, *History of the Royal Navy* (London, 1847), ii. 476. In 1374 a clock for a ship is mentioned at Cologne; cf. E. Zinner, 'Aus der Frühzeit der Räderuhr', *Deutsches Museum: Abhandlungen und Berichte*, XXII. iii (1954), 17. G. P. B. Naish, 'The dyall and the bearing-dial', *Journal of the Institute of Navigation*, vii (1954), 205, cites a Spanish poem, *El Vitorial* of 1404, showing that sand-glasses were then used to help ascertain direction and speed; in 1410–12 such glasses, called 'dyalls', appear in English ship inventories; loc. cit. Representations of sand-glasses first appear in 1442 in a painting by Petrus Christus now in the Detroit Institute of Art, and 1440–50 in one in Nuremberg; cf. E. Zinner, 'Die Sanduhr', *Die Uhr*, ix, no. 24 (1955), 38–39, figs. 2, 3. Not until towards the end of the fifteenth century does the sand-glass appear as an attribute of Father Time; cf. E. Panofsky, *Studies in Iconology* (New York, 1939), 80, 82, n. 50, fig. 55.

Note 5, p. 103. The learned literature contains only two studies of the crank: H. T. Horwitz, 'Die Drehbewegung in ihrer Bedeutung für die Entwicklung der materialen Kultur', *Anthropos*, xxviii (1933), 721–57; xxix (1934), 99–125; B. Gille, 'La Naissance du système bielle-manivelle', *Techniques et civilisations*, ii (1952), 42–46.

No conclusive data for the history of the crank emerge from its etymologies. The Romanic words *manivelle*, *manovella*, &c., come from the Latin *manubriolum* meaning any small handle. The German *Kurbel* probably is derived from the hypothetical Latin *curvulum*, a 'small crooked thing', rather than from the related French *courbe*. The *Oxford New English Dictionary* notes Anglo-Saxon *crancstæf* or 'crank shaft' from the *Gerefa* of the early eleventh century, and derives it from an old root meaning 'crooked' or 'bent', surviving metaphorically in the German *krank*. (E. von Erhardt-Siebold, 'The Old English loom riddles', in *Philologia: the Malone Anniversary Studies*, ed. T. A. Kirby and H. B. Woolf [Baltimore, 1949], 17, n. 10, describes how the *crancstæf* worked as a weaving implement in shedding, and adds that 'attaching a guided rope to the crank and to a treadle is the obvious next step', cf. *supra*, p. 107, n. 4.) However, a curious development in Spanish suggests the possibility of an alternative origin related to *crane* rather than to *crone*. A synonym for *manivella de máquina* is *cigüeñol*, which J. Corominas, *Diccionario crítico etimológico de la lengua castellana*, i (Berne, 1954), 800, derives from *cigüeña* or *cigoña* ('stork' or 'crane') meaning a pole pivoted on a vertical forked post to draw water from a well, and which looks and moves like a crane. This device, the ancient shadoof or well-swipe, is mentioned by Isidore of Seville, *Etymologiarum sive originum libri XX*, ed. W. M. Lindsay (Oxford, 1911), Bk. XX, xv. 3, as *ciconia*, although the customary Latin word was *tolleno*. It may be that, as in Spain so in England (where *crane* was used at least by 1375 to indicate a hoisting machine; cf. *OED*, s.v.), the replacement of the traditional well-swipe by a cranked pole resting on *two* forked posts did not demand a new word, and that by semantic change the old word eventually focused on the most novel element in the new device, the crank handle. (Possibly the assimilation of *crane* to the older *cranc* was aided by the introductiou, in the latter part of the Hundred Years War, of the cranked ratchet for spanning cross-bows [*supra*, p. 111, n. 3] called *crannequin*, a word which É. Littré, *Dictionnaire de la langue française* [Paris, 1883], derives from the Low German *Kraeneke* 'crane', so called because of its shape.) However, I cannot date the origin of the common cranked well-hoist satisfactorily. The Princeton Index of Christian Art, which is nearly complete for Christian iconography down to 1400, contains no such device: all well-hoists with horizontal axles are equipped with X-like handles. The first cranked device of this sort appears in a miniature of *c.* 1425 in the *Hausbuch* of the Mendel Foundation in Nuremberg; cf. *Deutches Handwerk im Mittelalter* (Leipzig, 1935), pl. 13.

Note 1, p. 105. M. A. de la Chausse, *Le Gemme antiche figurate* (Rome, 1700), tab. 99, reproduced a line drawing of an engraved gem showing Cupid sharpening his arrows on a rotary grindstone equipped with treadle and crank, and mounted on a push-cart. It has not since been seen. De la Chausse, 37, notes, 'È da osservarsi questa machina per arrotare i ferri simile a quella che si adopera oggi da' nostri rotatori', and it has long been considered suspect; cf. Neuburger, op. cit. 54, fig. 65. We shall see that both rotary grindstones (*infra*, p. 169) and treadles (*supra*, p. 117) are medieval rather than ancient. A. Schroeder, *Die Entwicklung des Schleiftechniks* (Haya-Weser, 1931), 31, fig. 8, holds that the first authentic rotary grindstone fitted with treadle and crank appears *c.* 1480 in a copper engraving by Israhel von Meckemen, while (60, fig. 58) the earliest mounted on a push-cart is found in a Cologne engraving of 1589.

Note 3, p. 105. W. Treue, *Kulturgeschichte der Schraube* (Munich, 1955), 22–28. Vitruvius, *De arch.* x. 6; Singer, *History of Technology*, ii (1956), 676–7; F. M. Feldhaus, 'Ahnen des Wasserrades', *Die Umschau*, xl (1936), 473 and *Die Machine im Leben der Völker* (Basel, 1954), 138, fig. 99; C. N. Bromehead in *Antiquity*, xvi (1942), 196; T. A. Rickard, 'The mining of the Romans in Spain', *Journal of Roman Studies*, xviii (1928), 131, pl. 12; L. Jacono in *Notizie degli scavi* (1927), 84–89, pl. IX: O. Davies, 'Roman and medieval mining techniques', *Bulletin of the Institute of Mining and Metallurgy*, no. 348 (1933), 9, 19; C. C. Edgar, 'A terra cotta representation of the screw of Archimedes', *Bulletin de la Société Archéologique d'Alexandrie*, new series, i (1904–5), 44–45, fig. 13. E. Treptow, 'Der älteste Bergbau und seiner Hilfsmittel', *Beiträge zur Geschichte der Technik und Industrie*, viii (1918), 180–1, states that in 1906 a mining engineer named Pütz informed him that, in the exploitation of an old mine near Alcaracejos in the province of Cordoba, an Archimedes screw of wood was discovered with an iron bottom pivot and an iron crank. Treptow did not see this object, but assumed it to be Roman. It was not subject to archaeological control, nor has it been published. There is every reason to believe that mining continued in Spain under the Visigothic and Muslim régimes, as well as after the Reconquista: Isidore of Seville, *Etymologiarum sive originum libri XX*, Lib. XVI, cap. 22, ed. W. M. Lindsay (Oxford, 1911), seems particularly aware of lead mining in his day; under the Caliphs iron was extracted at Castillo del Hierro, mercury at Almaden, tin in Algarve, lead near Cabra, and silver near Murcia; cf. A. R. Lewis, *Naval Power and Trade in the Mediterranean, A.D. 500–1100* (Princeton, 1951), 169. The Saracens also worked the mines of Aljustrel in Portugal; cf. W. G. Nash, *The Rio Tinto Mine* (London, 1904), 43, also 44-45, 87; and it was probably the Portuguese who introduced the cranked Archimedes screw to Japan by 1637; cf. Treptow, op. cit. 181, fig. 48; C. N. Bromehead, 'Ancient mining processes as illustrated by a Japanese scroll', *Antiquity*, xvi (1942), 194, 196, 207. I know of no cranked Archimedes screw before *c.* 1405; cf. *supra*, p. 111, n. 4. The next is in R. Valturio, *De re militari* (Verona, 1472), fol. 169ᵛ.

Note 4, p. 105. W. Springer, *Historische Baggermaschinen: ein techno-historischer Beitrag* (Berlin, 1938), 19, is incorrect in asserting that the first chain of buckets appears in J. Besson, *Theatrum instrumentorum et machinarum* (Lyons, 1578), pl. 39 (he overlooks another in pl. 44). Although H. Chatley in *Engineering*, clxiii (1947), 196, is probably correct in maintaining, against H. P. Vowles, ibid. 41–42, 244, that a chain of pots was not used to irrigate the hanging gardens of Babylon in the sixth century B.C., in the third or second century B.C. Philo of Byzantium, ed. B. Carra de Vaux (Paris, 1902), 224–5, describes such a device for wells. A chain of bailers was discovered in a well in Pompeii (i.e. before A.D. 79); cf. R. Pemp, 'Wasserhebewerke in Pompeji', *Technik Geschichte*, xxviii (1939), 159–60. A chain of buckets operated by a water-wheel appears in a late-medieval Arabic treatise; cf. H. Schmeller, 'Beitrag zur Geschichte der Technik in der Antike und bei den Arabern', *Abhandlungen zur Geschichte der Naturwissenschaften und der Medizin*, vi (1922), 10–13.

Note 3, p. 106. What is the probable date of the Nemi pump and chain of bailers? It seems unlikely to be in the first Christian century. The two ships were well constructed, with hulls protected by a layer of impregnated cloth and then by lead-sheeting. They stayed above water long enough for a fungus to rot some of the beams and for repairs to be made; cf. ibid. 293. As the ships aged, their custodians would be troubled by leaks and would doubtless install new apparatus for handling bilge-water. The shrine of Diana Nemorensis, with which the ships seem to have had some connexion, long remained famous. G. B. Rubin de Cervin, 'Mysteries and nemesis of the Nemi ships', *Mariner's Mirror*, xli (1955), 39–41, points out that coins as late as *c.* A.D. 164 were excavated with the ships. One suspects that they foundered during the anarchy of the third century.

Note 3, p. 108. R. J. Forbes, in Singer, *History of Technology*, ii (1956), 111, in asserting that 'the first certain literary reference to a rotary hand-mill in the Roman countryside is given by Virgil (70–19 B.C.)', overlooks the fact that the *Moretum* (in *Appendix Vergiliana*, ed. O. Ribbeck [Leipzig, 1868], 138, l. 126) was not written by Virgil, that its dating is most uncertain, and that it was first included in a Virgilian list in the library catalogue of the Abbey of Murbach of the ninth–tenth century; cf. T. Birt, *Jugendverse und Heimatpoesie Vergils* (Leipzig, 1910), 4. F. L. Douglas, *A Study of the Moretum* (Syracuse, N.Y., 1929), 78–99, attempts to show that Columella's *De cultu hortorum* is partly based on *Moretum*, as it explicitly is based on the *Georgics* and *Eclogues*. But if any relationship is established, which is questionable, it is equally possible that the *Moretum*'s author found inspiration in Columella. And if Columella knew that *Moretum* was from Virgil's pen, it is curious that Servius knew nothing of it.

Note 5, p. 108. F. Hörter, F. X. Michels, and J. Röder, 'Die Geschichte der Basaltlavaindustrie von Mayen und Niedermendig, I: Vor- und Frühgeschichte', *Jahrbuch für Geschichte und Kultur des Mittelrheins*, ii–iii (1950–1), 9; Abb. 2, fig. 4; Abb. 6 b. The authors associate this type of quern with the entire

NOTES 169

La Tène period. P. Orsi, 'Gli scavi intorno al Athenaion di Siracusa', *Monumenti antichi*, xxv (1918), 567–8, fig. 159, claims to have found such a specimen in a stratum between the Siculan III and the Archaic Greek. V. G. Childe, 'Rotary querns on the Continent and in the Mediterranean basin', *Antiquity*, xvii (1943), 22–23, wrongly assumes a vertical handle-socket in this quern, which therefore 'would in Britain be classed as Romano-British at earliest'; Moritz, op. cit. 55, is sceptical of its stratification. S. P. O'Riordain, 'Excavations at Cush, Co. Limerick', *Proceedings of the Royal Irish Academy*, xlv, Sect. C (1940), pl. xxxvi, fig. 389, seems to show such a rope-loop perforation in Ireland not later than *c.* A.D. 100; cf. 177–80.

Note 2, p. 109. On the basis of finds at Numantia and in Aragon, Childe, op. cit. 19–21, concludes that 'there existed in Spain by II B.C. a group of querns, quite distinct from the Celtic and Hellenistic beehives, being both flatter and fitted with vertical handles'. But A. Schulten, *Numantia*, iv (Munich, 1929), 227, pl. 50, shows the 'best preserved' fragments of querns found in the Roman camp. Only one has a vertical hole in the upper stone, and since no more than a quarter of the stone survives, it may well have had a second hole on the opposite edge. Ibid. iii (1927), pl. 29. 3, shows a pen drawing of a confusingly reconstructed quern with one vertical peg-hole but likewise with a horizontal peg-hole. Clearly no conclusion may be based on it. As for Curwen's other source, R. Bosch Gimpera, 'Les Investigacions de la cultura ibèrica al Baix Aragó', *Institut d'Estudis Catalans, Secció historico-arqueològica: Anuari*, vi (1915–20), 653, fig. 490, provides the basic cut for Curwen's fig. 1; however, in his fig. 492, Bosch Gimpera reconstructs the vanished wooden parts of this quern not with vertical handles but with a horizontal handle-bar attached to the rider by means of pegs in slots on opposite sides of the stone. It is thus improbable that vertical-handled querns were used in Spain by the second century B.C.

Note 1, p. 110. I first pointed to this in 'Technology and invention in the Middle Ages', *Speculum*, xv (1940), 153; cf. *The Utrecht Psalter*, ed. E. DeWald (Princeton, 1932), pl. 58; R. J. Forbes, *Man the Maker* (New York, 1950), 113, pl. 2. Although the illuminator was basing his work, either directly or at second hand, on a now vanished psalter possibly of the early fifth century, we must not ascribe this detail to his prototype; cf. D. Panofsky, 'The textual basis of the Utrecht Psalter illustrations', *Art Bulletin*, xxv (1943), 50–58; E. A. Lowe, 'The uncial Gospel leaves attached to the Utrecht Psalter', ibid. xxxiv (1952), 237–8; F. Wormald, *The Utrecht Psalter* (Utrecht, 1953), 8. For a middle-twelfth-century rotary grindstone directly inspired by that in the Utrecht Psalter, see M. R. James, *Canterbury Psalter* (London, 1935), fol. 108ᵛ. L. F. Salzman, *Building in England down to 1540* (Oxford, 1952), 337, finds rotary grindstones in 1253, 1278, 1324, and 1339.

Note 7, p. 110. Herrade de Landsberg, *Hortus deliciarum* (Strassburg, 1901), pl. xi *bis*. This manuscript, usually ascribed to the later twelfth century, must be dated *c.* 1205; cf. F. Zschokke, *Die romanischen Glasgemälde des Strassburger Münsters* (Basel, 1942), 59–60; O. Demus, *Mosaics of Norman Sicily* (London, 1949), 446–8, 455. For other *organistra* cf. E. Millar, op. cit., pl. 80 (*b*), for a specimen of *c.* 1250, and his *Library of A. Chester Beatty, the Western Manuscripts* (Oxford, 1927), i, pl. XCI (*a*), for one of *c.* 1240. Mr. Geoffrey Ashburner has kindly sent me the photograph of a specimen in the Robert de Lindseye Psalter, fol. 38ᵛ, an English manuscript of 1220-2 now in the library of the Society of Antiquaries, London. The fact that all but the earliest of these four hurdy-gurdies are English and that the English specimens date from the first half of the century, may mean that by *c.* 1200 the *organistrum* was going out of fashion on the continent but remained popular a bit longer across the Channel.

Note 6, p. 111. E. Wiedemann and F. Hauser, 'Über Vorrichtungen zum Heben von Wasser in der islamischen Welt', *Beiträge zur Geschichte der Technik und Industrie*, viii (1918), 144, figs. 20-21. However, that al-Jazarī did not entirely grasp the meaning of the crank for joining reciprocating with rotary motion is shown by his extraordinarily complex pump (ibid. 145-6, figs. 22-24; A. K. Coomaraswamy, *The Treatise of al-Jazarī on Automata* [Boston, 1924], 17, pl. VII) powered through a cog-wheel mounted eccentrically on its axle. The axle turns in a socket at one end but in an open ring at the other end. Since the axle does not pass through the centre of the cog-wheel, the axle itself makes a cone-shaped orbit as the cog turns. This movement of the axle is transformed into reciprocating motion by means of a vertical rod, pivoted at the bottom but slit at the top, which embraces the axle and sways to-and-fro with it. By means of lateral connexions this swaying rod operates the pumps. After al-Jazarī I have found no Islamic cranks until a drawing in an early-fifteenth-century manuscript of the late-ninth-century Arabic translation of Hero's *Mechanics*, cf. B. Carra de Vaux, 'Les Mécaniques ou l'Élévateur de Héron d'Alexandrie sur la version arabe de Qostā ibn Lūqā', *Journal asiatique*, 9th series, ii (1893), 462, fig. 40. Ibid. i (1893), 461, fig. 1, shows a simple lever-handle which Carra de Vaux wrongly calls a crank.

C. Daremberg and E. Saglio, *Dictionnaire des antiquités grecques et romaines*, i (Paris, 1887), 1110, fig. 1405, show a single-crank borer for surgical trepanation 'des manuscrits d'Albucasis', the great Spanish Muslim surgeon who died *c.* A.D. 1013. This instrument is not to be found in the extraordinarily uniform tradition of published illustrations from Abū'l-Kāsim's works as represented by *Albucasis chirurgicorum ... libri tres* (Strassburg, 1532); H. von Gersdorff, *Feldtbüch der Wund Artzney sampt vilen Instrumenten der Chirurgen uss den Albucasi contrafayt* (Strassburg, 1540); Albucasis, *Methodus medendi* (Basle, 1641); J. Channing, tr., *Albucasis de chirurgia arabice et latine* (Oxford, 1778); L. Leclerc, tr., *La Chirurgie d'Abulcasis* (Paris, 1861); E. Gurlt, *Geschichte der Chirurgie* (Berlin, 1898), i, pl. IV, V; or K. Sudhoff, 'Die Instrumenten-Abbildungen der lateinischen Abulquasim-Handschriften des Mittelalters', *Studien zur Geschichte der Medizin*, xi (1918), 16-86.

For a general brief survey of Islamic machine design, cf. H. J. J. Webster, 'Muslim mechanics and mechanical appliances', *Endeavour*, xv (1956), 25-28. There is no analytical study of the development of applied mechanics in the Saracenic world, but new elements, and more intricate uses of old elements, are observable in the later treatises. The best introductions are E. Wiedemann, 'Zur Mechanik und Technik bei den Arabern', *Sitzungsberichte der Physikalisch-medizinischen Sozietät zu Erlangen*, xxxviii (1906), 1-56, 307-57, and H. Schmeller, 'Beiträge zur Geschichte der Technik in der Antike und bei den Arabern', *Abhandlungen zur Geschichte der Naturwissenschaften und der Medizin*, vi (1922), 1–47. The treatises of the Banū Mūsā (c. A.D. 850), *Kitab al ḥiyal*, ed. M. Curtze in *Nova acta Academiae Germanicae Naturae Curiosorum*, xlix (1885), 105–67 (cf. F. Hauser in *Abh. z. Gesch. d. Naturwiss.* i [1922], 1–188), and of al-Khāzinī (c. A.D. 1121), *Book of the Balance of Wisdom*, tr. N. Khanikoff in *Journal of the American Oriental Society*, vi (1860), 1–128, both seem less mechanically sophisticated than those of the Hellenistic period. Al-Jazarī's treatise on automata (A.D. 1206) is considerably more advanced, but has not been properly edited; cf. B. Carra de Vaux, 'Note sur les mécaniques de Bédi ez-Zamān el Djazarī, et sur un appareil hydraulique attribué à Appolonius de Perge', *Annales internationales d'histoire, Congrés de Paris, 1900: 5ᵉ section, Histoire des sciences* (Paris, 1901), 112–20; A. K. Coomaraswamy, *The Treatise of al-Jazarī* (Boston, 1924); R. M. Riefstahl, 'The date and provenance of the automata miniatures', *Art Bulletin*, xi (1929), 206–15; M. Aga Oglu, 'On a manuscript of al-Jazarī', *Parnassus*, III. vii (1931), 27–28; P. Wittek, 'Datum und Herkunft der Automaten-Miniaturen', *Der Islam*, xix (1931), 177–8; L. Mayer, 'Zum Titelblatt der Automata-Miniaturen', *Orientalistische Literaturzeitung*, iii (1932), 165–6; I. Stchoukine, 'Un manuscrit du traité d'al-Jazarī sur les automates', *Gazette des beaux-arts*, xi (1934), 134–40; H. W. Glidden, 'A note on the automata of al-Djazarī', *Ars islamica*, iii (1936), 115–16; E. Schroeder, *Persian Miniatures in the Fogg Museum of Art* (Cambridge, Mass., 1942), 21–27.

For aspects of Islamic technology, cf. B. Carra de Vaux, 'Notice sur deux manuscrits arabes', *Journal asiatique*, 8th series, xvii (1891), 287–322; 'Notice sur un manuscrit arabe traitant de machines attribuées à Héron, Philon et Archimède', *Bibliotheca mathematica*, 3rd series, i (1900), 28–38; 'Le livre des appareils pneumatiques et des machines hydrauliques par Philon de Byzance édité d'après les versions arabes', *Notices et extraits des manuscrits de la Bibliothèque Nationale*, xxxviii (1903), 27–235; *Les Penseurs d'Islam* (Paris, 1921), ii. 168–94. E. Wiedemann devoted a lifetime to the subject. His contributions are listed in J. D. Pearson, *Index islamicus, 1906–1955* (Cambridge, 1958), *sub nom.*

Note 7, p. 112. L. F. Salzman, *Building in England down to 1540* (Oxford, 1952), pl. 13; Singer, op. cit., pl. 30a. According to the British Museum *Catalogue of Additional Manuscripts*, the Add. MS. 18,850 was executed for John, Duke of Bedford and Regent of France, and for his wife Anne, daughter of John, Duke of Burgundy, who were married in 1430. It was then presented to Henry VI of England by Anne on Christmas Eve, 1430.

The fourth known brace is in a French miniature of c. 1460; cf. J. van den Gheyn, *Cronicques et conquestes de Charlemaine, reproduction des 105 miniatures de Jean de Tavernier d'Audenarde (1460)* (Brussels, 1909), pl. 95; Salzman, op. cit., 336, pl. 19. The fifth is in a Flemish rubbed block print of St. Joseph's carpenter's shop, done 1480–1500; cf. *Einblattdrucke des fünfzehnten Jahrhunderts*, ed. P. Heitz, XIV: *Formschnitte des fünfzehnten Jahrhunderts aus der Sammlung Schreiber* (Strassburg, 1908), no. 4, and pp. 7–8; cf. W. L. Schreiber, *Manuel de l'amateur de la gravure sur bois et sur métal au XVᵉ siècle*, i (Berlin, 1891), 180, no. 638. F. M. Feldhaus, *Technik der Vorzeit* (Leipzig, 1914), 114, fig. 79, pictures this brace out of context and with defective references.

Note 1, p. 115. B. Gille, 'Machines', in Singer, op. cit. ii (1956), 654, states that the crank and connecting-rod combination was very slow of adoption: 'Even in the seventeenth and eighteenth centuries, the crank and connecting-rod were seldom combined'; cf. also his 'Bielle-manivelle', 46. His judgement may have been influenced by a crowning absurdity in the history of the crank which occurred in Aug. 1780, when James Pickard of Birmingham was able to patent the crank and rod which he had applied to the steam-engine, thus making steam-power available for rotary motions and transport; cf. F. W. Brewer, 'Notes on the history of the engine crank and its application to locomotives', *Locomotive, Railway Carriage and Wagon Review*, xxxviii (1932), 373–5. (R. Jenkins, *Collected Papers* [Cambridge, 1936], 98–106, erroneously assigns the patent to Matthew Wasbrough.) Gille considers Leonardo precocious in his interest in the combination of crank and connecting-rod. It was, however, common in his day: in addition to the eight European examples already cited, see Francesco di Giorgio's relief of a sawmill (1474) at Urbino (F. M. Feldhaus, *Die Maschine im Leben der Völker* [Basel, 1954], fig. 167), his drawing for a similar project (A, Uccelli, *Storia della tecnica*, fig. 200), and his manuscript of 1482–1501 (*supra*, p. 114, n. 3), fol. 96^r (fig. 8), and, north of the Alps, *c.* 1480, the *Mittelalterliches Hausbuch*, ed. H. T. Bossert and W. F. Storck (Leipzig, 1912), pl. 32. Complete examination of the technological literature of the sixteenth and seventeenth centuries would discover many other examples of cranks with connecting-rods; however, the following instances will serve to disprove Gille's view that it was neglected: a drawing by Giulio Campagnola, dating from before 1514, in Singer, op. cit. ii (1956), pl. 8; V. Biringuccio, *Pirotechnia* (Venice, 1540), tr. C. S. Smith and M. T. Gnudi (New York, 1942), title-page, fols. 140^v, 142^r; G. Agricola, *De re metallica* of 1556, tr. H. C. and L. H. Hoover (New York, 1950), 180, 185, 187, 189, 305; C. Piccolpasso, *Li tre libri dell' arte del vasaio* (written 1556–9), ed. B. Rockham and A. Van de Put (London, 1934), pls. 39, 40, 42; J. Besson, *Theatrum instrumentorum et machinarum* (Lyons, 1578), pl. 13; A. Ramelli, *Le Diverse et Artificiose Machine* (Paris, 1588), eighteen examples; M. F. Pisek, 'Un manuscrit en langue tchèque provenant de la seconde moitié du XVIe siècle sur l'art de la fonderie', *Techniques et civilisations*, ii (1951), 16–17, figs. 13, 14; V. Zonca, *Novo teatro di machine* (Padua, 1607), 103, 107, 110; Vatican Library, Barbarini lat. 4353, an anonymous engineer's notebook of the late sixteenth or early seventeenth century which I used at the Vatican Film Library, St. Louis, fols. 46^r, 52^r, 61^r, 62^r, 64^r; B. Lorini, *Delle fortificationi*, 4th edn. (Venice, 1609), 231, 239, 241; H. Zeising, *Theatrum machinarum* (Leipzig, 1612–14), ten examples; F. Veranzio, *Machinae novae* (Venice, [1615–16]), pl. 22; G. Branca, *Le Machine* (Rome, 1629), figs. 1, 27, 33, 43, 51, 52, 53, 67; J. Wilkins, *Mathematicall Magick* (London, 1648), 42; E. E. Löhneijss, *Bericht vom Bergwerk* (Hamburg, 1660), pl. 10, 12; G. A. Böckler, *Theatrum machinarum novum* (Nuremberg, 1661) has forty-five examples in 154 plates.

Note 1, p. 117. Cf. MS. B, fol. 54^r, ed. C. Ravaisson-Mollien (Paris, 1883), for a pendulum operating a reciprocating pump. Although F. M. Feldhaus, 'Das Pendel bei Leonardo da Vinci', *Deutsche Uhrmacher-Zeitung*, xxxiv (1910), 23–24, is probably correct in identifying Leonardo's sketch in *Codice atlantico*, fol. 257^r*a* (*c.* 1497–1500; cf. Pedretti, op. cit. 277) as a pendulum escapement for clockwork, the idea had no horological application until the 1650's; cf. also his 'Das Pendel im Maschinenbau vor Erfindung der Pendeluhr', ibid. xxxii (1908), 160. S. A. Bedini, *Johann Philipp Treffler, Clockmaker of Augsburg* (Ridgefield, Conn., 1957), 5–12, shows that Treffler anticipated Huygens in the invention of the pendulum clock. A remarkable precursor of the pendulum clock is found in the cross-beat escapement of Justus Bürgi who died at Cassel in 1632; cf. Tycho Brahe, *Opera omnia*, ed. J. L. E. Dreyer, vi (Copenhagen, 1919), 347; Singer, *History of Technology*, iii (1957), 660, fig. 400.

Note 4, p. 117. E. Chavannes, *Mission archéologique dans la Chine septentrionale* (Paris, 1909), pl. 75, shows a loom with two clear pedals; for the date, cf. W. Fairbank, 'The offering shrines of "Wu Liang Tz'u" ', *Harvard Journal of Asiatic Studies*, vi (1941), 1. H. E. Winlock, *The Monastery of Epiphanius at Thebes* (New York, 1926), i. 69–71, maintains that in this seventh-century site at Thebes there is indication of loom pedals, but the interpretation of the evidence is doubtful; cf. R. J. Forbes, *Studies in Ancient Technology*, iv (Leiden, 1956), 215. E. von Erhardt-Siebold, 'The Old English loom riddles', in *Philologica: the Malone Anniversary Studies*, ed. T. A. Kirby and H. B. Woolf (Baltimore, 1949), 12, denies evidence of the use by Greeks or Romans of treadles to control the leashes of looms. The 'classical' vertical loom with four treadles, designed to weave seamless garments, reproduced by H. L. Roth, *Studies in Primitive Looms* (Halifax, 1934), 122, fig. 192, from a seventeenth-century source, is unrelated to any ancient evidence.

Note 1, p. 119. F. Keutgen, *Urkunden zur städtischen Verfassungsgeschichte* (Berlin, 1901), 373, no. 278, § 16: 'Item cum rota filari potest, sed fila quae filantur in rota nullo modo in aliquo panno apponi debet zetil; sed zetil totaliter filari debet cum manu et fusa.' For a similar Speyer regulation of 1298, cf. F. J. Mone, 'Zunftordnungen einzelner Handwerker', *Zeitschrift für Geschichte des Oberrheins*, xv (1863), 281; F. M. Feldhaus, 'Spinnräder', *Daheim*, XLII. i (1905–6), no. 10, p. 22; and his 'Zur Geschichte des Spinnrades', *Melliand Textilberichte*, vii (1926), 93–94. The wheels pictured in Delaporte, op. cit. ii, pl. CXXIX, and iii, pl. CCLXXI, in windows at Chartres somewhat earlier than 1280, may be quilling wheels, devices for winding yarn on bobbins for the shuttle (cf. Singer, *History of Technology*, ii [1956], fig. 183, for an example of *c.* 1310), out of which the spinning-wheel probably developed.

Note 1, p. 122. C. Frémont, 'Un échappement d'horloge au treizième siècle', *Comptes rendus de l'Académie des Sciences*, clxi (1915), 690–2, found a mechanical escapement *c.* 1235 in the notebook of Villard de Honnecourt, ed. H. R. Hahnloser (Vienna, 1935), 134–5, pl. 44, showing devices for keeping an angel's finger pointed towards the sun and for turning the head of an eagle on a lectern; cf. Usher, op. cit. 193–4. That eventually some such apparatus was perfected is shown by the mention of a turning angel at St. Paul's in London in 1344; cf. G. Baillie, *Watches* (London, 1929), 38, citing Cottonian charter, xxi. 24; and until the fire of 1826 such an angel surmounted the chevet at Chartres; cf. E. Mâle, *Religious Art in France in the Thirteenth Century* (New York, 1913), 22, no. 3. But these devices sketched by Villard are unworkable as automatic mechanisms and may be adduced only to show his ambitions rather than his achievements in utilizing gravitational force; cf. F. M. Biebel, 'The "Angelot" of Jean Barbet', *Art Bulletin*, xxxii (1950), 340, n. 28.

Note 2, p. 125. For medieval pleasure in automata other than those in clocks, cf. J. W. Spargo, *Virgil the necromancer* (Cambridge, Mass., 1934), 117–35; M. Sherwood, 'Magic and mechanics in mediaeval fiction', *Studies in Philology*, xliv (1947), 567–92. At least as early as 1299 an extraordinary 'fun house' filled with mechanical practical jokes, distorting mirrors, &c., was built at Hesdin in Artois and was still being maintained by the dukes of Burgundy in the later fifteenth century; cf. J. M. Richard, *Une petite-nièce de Saint Louis: Mahaut, comtesse d'Artois et de Bourgogne (1302–1329)* (Paris, 1887), 308, 333–42. For Montaigne's interest in similar machines for practical jokes in the gardens of the grand dukes of Tuscany, cf. his *Journal de voyage*, ed. L. Lautrey (Paris, 1909), 187, 195–6, also J. Plattard, 'Les Jardins français à l'époque de la Renaissance', *Revue du XVIe siècle*, ii (1914), 252–3.

Note 3, p. 125. Cf. M. Clagett, *Giovanni Marliani and late medieval physics* (New York, 1941), 125, n. 1, for the earlier literature; more recently A. Maier, *Die Vorläufer Galileis im 14. Jahrhundert* (Rome, 1949), 132–54, *Zwei Grundprobleme der scholastischen Naturphilosophie: das Problem der intensiven Grösse; die Impetustheorie*, 2nd edn. (Rome, 1951), 113–314, and *Zwischen Philosophie und Mechanik* (Rome, 1958), 343–73; E. J. Dijksterhuis, *Die Mechanisierung des Weltbildes* (Berlin, 1956), 201–8. The new theory was first explicitly formulated in the Parisian lectures of Franciscus de Marchia in 1319–20; cf. *Grundprobleme*, 165, n. 11. However, in his *De ratione ponderis*, Jordanus de Nemore (d. 1237) anticipates the later theory of impetus, probably on the basis of observation of the action of large and irregular objects, such as dead horses, being thrown by the new counterweight artillery; cf. E. A. Moody and M. Clagett, *The Medieval Science of Weights* (Madison, 1952), 226, 412.

Note 5, p. 125. Cf. L. Thorndike, *History of Magic and Experimental Science*, iii (1934), 405; iv (1934), 169. The expression 'machina mundi' appears in Lucretius, but Arnobius Afer heaps sarcasm both on Lucretius ('rerum ipsa quae dicitur appellaturque natura') and upon his mechanical concept: 'Numquid machinae huius et molis, quae universi tegimur et continemur inclusi, parte est in aliqua relaxata aut dissoluta constructio?' (*Adversus nationes*, i. 2, ed. A. Reifferscheid [Vienna, 1875], 4, ll. 6–7, 9–11). Nevertheless, Dionysius the Areopagite, in a passage which I have not traced to its context, says, in commenting on the Crucifixion: 'Aut deus nature patitur, aut machina mundi dissolvetur.' In his *Tractatus de sphera*, probably written before 1220, John of Sacrobosco cites these words of Dionysius in his last sentence; cf. ed. L. Thorndike (Chicago, 1949), 117: clearly they fuse his cosmology and his faith, for 'machina mundi' likewise appears in his first chapter; ed. cit. 78. Robert Grosseteste's *De sphera*, probably written shortly before 1224, uses 'machina mundi' three times in his first thirteen lines; cf. L. Baur, *Die philosophische Werke des Robert Grosseteste* (Münster, 1912), 11. A century later, Jean Buridan, in *Quaestiones super Libris quatuor de caelo et mundo*, ed. E. A. Moody (Cambridge, Mass., 1942), 180, impressed by the fact that a rotary grindstone, once set in motion, is stopped only by friction (*resistentia*), suggests that angelic intelligences may not be needed to move the celestial spheres, which perhaps rotate by an initial impetus: 'Posset enim dici quod quando deus creavit sphaeras coelestes, ipse incepit movere unamquamque earum sicut voluit; et tunc ab impetu quam dedit eis, moventur adhuc, quia ille impetus non corrumpitur nec diminuitur, cum non habent resistentiam.' The path for Oresmus's clockmaker God was thus made straight.

Note 2, p. 127. E. von Bassermann-Jordan, *Die Standuhr Philipps des Guten von Burgund* (Leipzig, 1927). The authenticity of this clock has most recently been challenged by A. Leiter, 'Fälschung oder echt? Eine Betrachtung über die Standuhr "Philipps des Guten von Burgund" ', *Die Uhr*, xii, no. 21 (1958), 39–40, who claims that the case is a reliquary of *c.* 1400 into which clockwork was put *c.* 1550. But it seems most improbable that in a later, presumably Protestant, reworking of a reliquary the arms of Burgundy would have been permitted to remain. Moreover, H. A. Lloyd, *Some Outstanding Clocks over Seven Hundred Years, 1250–1950* (London, 1958), 31, pl. 26, produces a spring-clock of *c.* 1440–50 in a Burgundian portrait. Since the principle of the fusee was known by 1405 (*supra*, p. 128, n. 4), and was certainly applied to clocks by 1477 (*supra*, p. 128, n. 3), a clock of *c.* 1430 cannot be rejected simply because it has a fusee. To challenge its authenticity because of its metal holding-screws is likewise rash, since such screws appear *c.* 1405 in Kyeser's *Bellifortis*, fols. 125^r, 129^v, and are found in fine metalwork by the 1480's; cf. W. Treue, *Kulturgeschichte der Schraube* (Munich, 1955), 156.

Note 1, p. 129. In late medieval Europe there were few qualms about techno-logical progress, despite St. Augustine's reservations, *De civitate Dei*, xxii, cap. 24, ed. E. Hoffmann in *Corpus script. eccles. lat.* XL. ii (1900), 645: 'The human genius has invented and put into practical use many and great arts ... and human industry has made wonderful and stupefying advances', [yet] 'for the injury of men, how many kinds of poison, how many weapons and machines of destruction have been invented!' It is curious that the less materially advanced Indians of Peru and Mexico anticipated the retributive concept of technology long before Mary Wollstonecraft Shelley's *Frankenstein* (London, 1818). The 'Revolt of the Artifacts' in their art shows arms and implements combating and defeating human beings; cf. W. Krickeberg, 'Mexikanisch–Peruanische Paral-lelen', in *Festschrift P. W. Schmidt*, ed. W. Koppers (Vienna, 1928), 386–8; E. Seller, *Gesammelte Abhandlungen*, v (Berlin, 1915), 132, fig. 4.

Note 1, p. 130. The general histories of perpetual motion are inadequate for the earlier developments; cf. H. Dircks, *Perpetuum mobile* (London, 1861), and the expanded version under the name P. Verance (Chicago, 1916); F. M. Feldhaus, *Rühmesblätter der Technik* (Leipzig, 1910), 217–30, and *Technik der Vorzeit* (Leipzig, 1914), 784–5; F. Ichak, *Das Perpetuum Mobile* (Leipzig, 1914); J. Michel, *Mouvements perpétuels, leur histoire et leurs particularités* (Paris, 1927). M. Tramer, *Technisches Schaffen Geisteskranker* (Munich, 1926), depends entirely on Feldhaus and Ichak. For sixteenth-century theoretical discussion, cf. P. Duhem, *Origines de la statique* (Paris, 1905), i. 52–60. Experiments with *perpetua mobilia* were undoubtedly one of the reasons for the rapid rise of interest in friction and in methods of reducing it; cf. F. M. Feldhaus, *Geschichte der Kugel-, Walzen- und Rolleranlagen* (Schweinfurt a. M., 1914); H. T. Horwitz, *Entwick-lungsgeschichte der Traglager* (Berlin, 1914).

Note 2, p. 132. Lib. II, cap. 98, ed. T. Wright (London, 1863), 183; also in Neckham's *De utensilibus*, in *A Volume of Vocabularies*, ed. T. Wright (London,

1857), 114. W. E. May, 'Alexander Neckham and the pivoted compass needle', *Journal of the Institute of Navigation*, viii (1955), 283–4, points out that Neckham does not speak of a *pivoted* compass. May, 'Hugues de Berze and the mariner's compass', *Mariners' Mirror*, xxxix (1953), 103–5, ascertains that no one has located the original statement credited in the seventeenth century to Hugues, *c.* 1204, regarding the compass. The supposed letter of Brunetto Latini telling how Roger Bacon showed him a compass is a forgery of 1802; cf. May and H. L. Hitchins, *From Lodestone to Gyrocompass* (New York, 1953), 21–22. For general discussion of early European sources of the history of the compass, see A. Schück, *Der Kompass*, ii (Hamburg, 1915), 26–30; H. Balmer, *Beiträge zur Geschichte der Erkenntniss des Erdmagnetismus* (Aarau, 1956), 52.

Note 6, p. 133. Pars I, cap. 10, ed. Hellmann, 8: 'Per hoc autem instrumentum excusaberis ab omni horologio; nam per ipsum scire poteris ascensus in quacumque hora volueris, et omnes alias celi dispositiones quas querunt astrologi.' Peter's automatically rotating magnetic sphere was to have a great destiny. Cardinal Nicholas of Cusa (d. 1464) knew it only through Bacon's writings; cf. Balmer, op. cit. 249. Nevertheless, to judge by the number of extant manuscripts, the *Epistola* continued to be fairly widely read (cf. T. Bertelli, 'Intorno a due codici Vaticani della *Epistola de magnete* di Pietro Peregrino di Maricourt', *Bullettino di bibliografia e di storia delle scienze matematiche e fisiche*, iv [1871], 4–9), and even before Peter's treatise was printed in Rome, before 1520, under the title *De virtute magnetis* and falsely credited to Raymond Lull (cf. G. Sarton, 'The first edition of Petrus Peregrinus "De magnete," before 1520', *Isis*, xxxvii [1947], 178–9), the Dominican (and later Calvinist) Amadeus Meygret, *Questiones . . . in libros de celo et mundo Aristotelis* (Paris, 1514), fol. 12$^{r, v}$, writes in high excitement about Peter's rotating sphere: 'Si magnes fiat spherice figure, et ponatur in medio axis, et situetur secundum situm celi, pars videlicet que est septemtrionalis versus polum articum, et meridionalis versus antarticum: non enim est eiusdem dispositionis in omnibus partibus: immo experimento probatur quod quemadmodum polus articus est oppositus antartico, ita etiam in magnete. Si enim acus fricetur ab ea parte que subiacet septemtrioni, et appropietur parti opposite non attrahet eam, sed repellet et e converso, si acus fricetur a parte que subiacet meridiei. Talis inquam magnes circulariter moveretur, et non per ascensum et descensum, quia tunc talis motus esset violentus; motus autem magnetis, si magnes imperpetuum duraret esset perpetuus, ergo non esset violentus. Forte ad hoc quis negaret quod moveretur, sed hoc esset subterfugere: immo est quidam tractatus de compositione talis magnetis; ideo concedatur ille motus. Et si dicas quod erit perpetuus si duraret magnes in tali dispositione, concedatur et nego consequentiam, quia illa perpetuitas provenieret ex eo quod virtus movens semper applicaretur unde si virtus motiva figuli semper applicaretur rote, rota semper moveretur. Similiter si duo homines perpetuo percuterent pilam, ipsa semper moveretur. Et quia tunc a sola virtute celesti movetur et ipsa est perpetua perpetuo applicata, non est inconveniens quod perpetuo duret.' (I am grateful to Dr. Bern Dibner of Norwalk, Connecticut, for having supplied me with a photograph of the relevant passage in the Burndy Library's copy of this very rare book.) Presumably in his edition of Alchabitius, *Praeclarum opus ad scrutanda stellarum magisteria isagogicum* (Venice, 1521), which I have not seen (cf. Thorndike, op. cit. vi [1941], 471, n. 21), Antonio de Fantis describes the rotating magnetic sphere; and this in turn is cited by G. Cardano in his *De rerum varietate* of 1557; cf. Balmer, op. cit. 249. In 1558 a second edition of Peter's work entitled *De magnete seu rota perpetui motus*, ed. A. P. Gasser, appeared at Augsburg. Four years later J. Taisnier, *Opusculum perpetua memoria dignissimum, de natura magnetis et eius effectibus* (Cologne, 1562), 8–9, not only described such an automatic armillary but provided an elaborate diagram of it; indeed, he was so proud of it that he placed a picture of it conspicuously in his own portrait at the beginning of the work. G. B. della Porta, *Magia naturalis*, Lib. VII, cap. 37 (Naples, 1589), facsimile of the English tr. of London, 1658, ed. D. J. Price (New York, 1957), 207, likewise discussed the automatically turning magnetic sphere. Clearly by that time this idea was in the public domain.

In his *De magnete* (London, 1600), William Gilbert was more indebted to Peter of Maricourt than to any other author; cf. E. Zilsel, 'The origins of William Gilbert's scientific method', *Journal of the History of Ideas*, ii (1941), 11–12. Although Gilbert repudiated the idea of perpetual motion machines and was dubious that the magnetic sphere would actually rotate (cf. Bk. VI, ch. 4, ed. D. J. Price [New York, 1958], 223), nevertheless Zilsel, op. cit. 5, is correct in perceiving that he 'would like to accept the statement of Peter of Maricourt that a spherical magnet rotates continuously by itself', because from it he had conceived by analogy the idea that Earth itself is a vast magnet which rotates because it is such; cf. ed. cit., Bk. I, ch. 17, 39–44; Bk. VI, ch. 1, 211–12; ch. 3, 214–20; also P. F. Mottelay, *Bibliographical History of Electricity and Magnet sm* (London, 1922), 47, n. 1. Although Gilbert's hypothesis of the magnetic diurnal rotation of the Earth's globe could not be conclusively demonstrated, the prior spread of Peter of Maricourt's notion of a rotating *terrella* made the idea seem so plausible that, even with inadequate proof, it quickly abolished one of the major physical objections to the Copernican system; cf. F. R. Johnson, *Astronomical Thought in Renaissance England* (Baltimore, 1937), 215–19. For an analysis of how Gilbert was led from the supposed phenomenon of the *terrella* to the conclusion that our planet is a rotating magnetic sphere, cf. A. Wolf, *History of Science, Technology and Philosophy in the 16th and 17th Centuries*, 2nd edn. (London, 1950), 294–6.

Index

Aachen, regulations (807), 6; stirrups shown on ivories on pulpit at, 20, 143.

Åberg, N., and archaeological finds in East Prussia, 22.

Abu-Dāwūd (d. A.D. 888), with reference to stirrups, 18.

Abū'l-Kāsim (d. c. 1013), Spanish Muslim surgeon, 170.

Aeolian heads, see Blowers.

Aeolipyle, see Blowers.

Aerial dragons, 162–3.

Afghanistan, conquered by the Sassanids, 17; with reference to stirrup, 15; to windmills, 86.

Agricola, Georgius (1494–1555), De re metallica, with reference to crank with connecting-rod, 172.

Agriculture: agricultural revolution of Middle Ages, 40, 57, 159; arable land, extension of, 41, measurement, 64, 68; assarting, 72 f., co-operation in medieval village, 41, 47; drainage 43–44, 48 f., 55; fertilizing, 56, 155, 158; fields, 'Celtic', 43, S-shape, 55, square, 42, 44, 46–47, strips, 43 f., 46–48, 51, 54; grain-stripper, 60 n. 6; harrowing, 60, 62 ff; harvest, 69–70, 72; land divided among heirs and strip cultivation 47, 51; open-field system, 44, 46 ff., 54 ff. and n. 1, 78, 155, 159, and cattle, 55, fallow, 55, 69, 71 f., 158, three-field and two-field rotation, 69–75, 78, 155, 158; pasture, 51, 155; subsistence farming, 56; winnowing fan, 104. See also Animal-power, Crops, Horses, Oxen, Ploughs, Tools.

Al-Battānī (d. 926), and geared astrolabe, 123.

Albert the Great, see Albertus Magnus.

Albertus Magnus (? 1193–1280), and brazen head, 91; De animalibus, with reference to eels in search of peas, 76 and n. 1; De meteoris, origin of earthquakes, 90 n. 5, steam, 92; steam-pressure and blower, 90.

Al-Biruni (d. 1048), and geared machine showing lunar phases, 123.

Alemans, and horse-burials, 24; and lance, 139.

Alexander VI, Pope (1492–1503), and chemical warfare, 96 n. 2.

Alexandria, gunpowder artillery, 100.

Alfonso X, king of Castile (1252–84), clock, 120–2.

Alfred the Great, English king (871–901), and laws of Ine, 51; and plough horses in Norway, 61.

Al-Ḥasan al-Rammāh (c. 1280–95), and rockets, 97 and n. 2, 98.

Al-Herewi (d. 1211), with reference to Frankish tactics, 35.

'Ali (d. 661), and stirrups, 18.

Al-Jāḥiz (d. 868), and contempt of Persians for Arabs, 18; and stirrups, 18 f.

Al-Jazari (c. 1206), with reference to cranks, 111, 170; treatise on automata, 171.

Al-Makkari (d. 1632), with reference to first Umaiyad Caliph of Spain, 12 n. 6.

Al-Mubarrad (d. 898), quoted on stirrups, 18 f.

Al-Muhallab (c. 694), general, with reference to stirrups, and cropping tails of horses, 18 and n. 5.

Alsace, horse equipment from grave in, 24.

Altai mountains, central Asia, rock-scratching of stirrup, 17; stirrups in Turkish tombs, 16.

Al-Tirmidhi (d. c. 883–93), with reference to stirrups, 18.

Ambroise, L'Estoire de la guerre sainte, with reference to windmill, 87.

Andelfingen, Württemberg, stirrups found at, 23.

Anglo-Saxons: agriculture, 51 n. 4, 64, open fields, 51 and n. 7, 'oxgang', 52, ploughs, 43, 50, 52; Chronicle, dubbing of knight, 150; crancstæf, 107 n. 4, 110 n. 3, 166; feudalism, 36, 153; 'hide', 52 f.; invasion of Britain, 50; weapons and fighting methods at Hastings, 37 and n. 2.

1. Kushan engraved gem, c. A.D. 100, probably showing rigid hook-stirrups. See p. 15, n. 1.

2. Magi going to Bethlehem, equipped with the second Christian representation of stirrups. Illumination in a Syriac homilary of *c.* A.D. 800, probably from Northern Mesopotamia. See p. 25, n. 2. For the first Christian picture of stirrups, cf. p. 143.

3. The earliest European picture of modern harness, *c.* A.D. 800. See p. 61, n. 4.

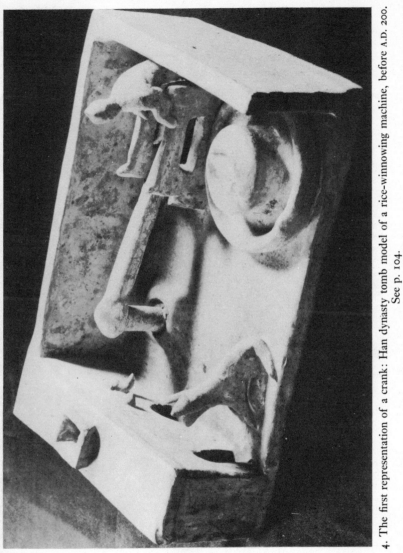

4. The first representation of a crank: Han dynasty tomb model of a rice-winnowing machine, before A.D. 200. See p. 104.

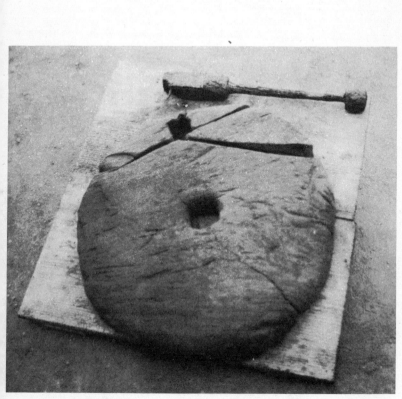

5. Wooden disk and eccentric peg from the second Nemi ship. See p. 106.

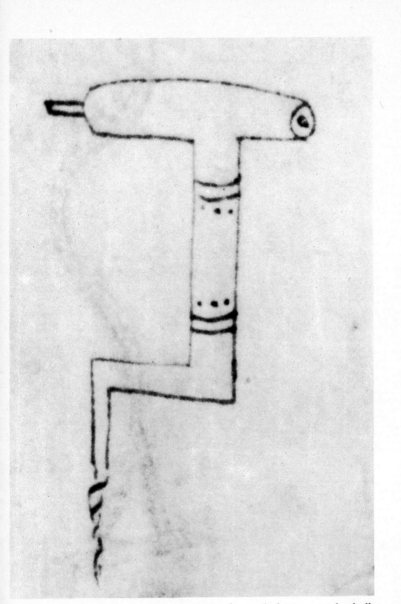

6. Giovanni da Fontana's sketch, *c.* 1420–49, of a cranked auger, mechanically misunderstood. See p. 113, n. 1.

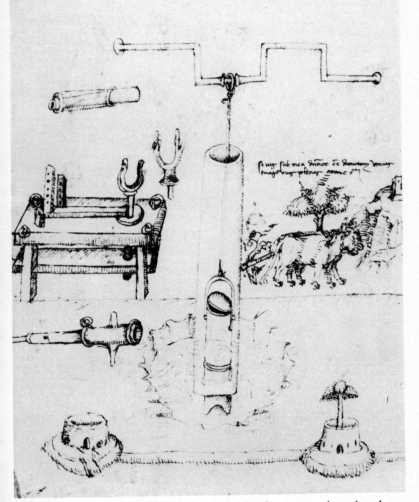

7. Mariano di Jacopo Taccola's drawing, 1441–58, of a compound crank and connecting rod, mechanically misunderstood. See p. 113, n. 5.

8. Francesco di Giorgio's drawing, 1482–1501, of parallel crankshafts with connecting rod for transferring continuous rotary motion to a parallel plane. See p. 114, n. 4.

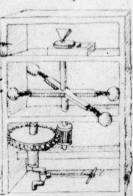

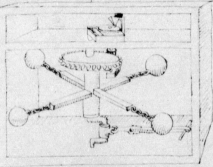

9. Francesco di Giorgio's drawing, 1482–1501, of ball-and-chain governors in relation to compound cranks and connecting rods. See p. 116, n. 8.

10. Illumination of a water clock, *c.* 1250, presumably at the court of St. Louis at Paris. See p. 120, n. 3.

REPRINTED LITHOGRAPHICALLY IN GREAT BRITAIN
AT THE UNIVERSITY PRESS, OXFORD
BY VIVIAN RIDLER
PRINTER TO THE UNIVERSITY